T3-BRL-683

The Unshattered Rock

by

FRANCIS A. McLAUGHLIN, F.D.D.S.K.

A STUDY OF THE INVALIDITY OF
ANGLICAN AND PROTESTANT EPISCOPAL ORDERS,
AND RELATED SUBJECTS.

ALSO

PRESENTATION OF RITUAL CEREMONIES USED
IN THE VARIOUS ORIENTAL CHURCHES
NOT IN COMMUNION WITH
THE SEE OF PETER,
YET POSSESSING VALID ORDERS.

Comet Press Books New York

Library of Congress Catalogue Card Number: 56-9420

Manufactured in the United States of America

65

Contents

Bibliography

Consumation of the marriage of Prince Arthur and Catherine of Aragon (Letters and papers of Henry VIII, Vol. VI, pages 273, 311, 317, 491).

Petition of Henry VIII to Rome for annulment of his marriage to Catherine of Aragon, (Letters and Papers, Vol. 14, page 527, public records office).

Pope Clement ordered Henry VIII to leave Ann Boleyn, and take Catherine back again (Legrand III, page 536. For verification of all particulars in this case, see Dean Hook in the *Lives of the Archbishops of Canterbury,* Vol. II, pp 88, 456, 461).

Decision of Clement VII declaring marriage between Henry VIII and Catherine of Aragon to be valid was issued March 23, 1534, and will be found in Dodd (ed. 1737, Vol. I, page 294).

The History and Antiquities of Anglo-Saxon Churches, containing Wolsey's Works, and death, by John Lingard, 1806-16. *Grant of Supreme Head and sole Protector of the Church of England by Convocation* by Samuel Lawson Gardiner, English historiographer, in his "Letters and papers," (*Reign of Henry VIII,* Vols. 5-16. Also Wilkin's *History of England,* Vol. III, page 746).

Letters and papers, Henry VIII, Vol. 8, preface 20.

Will of Henry VIII, Peter Heylyn's *History of England,* and Heylyn's *Edward's in London,* (1661) also Fuller, *Church History,* Editor Brewer, Vol. III, pages 214-219.

Burial obsequities of Henry VIII, with Latin Mass, John Strype's *Memorials,* Vol. IV-290.

Reformation in England, French and English, George Constant, 1934.

"Perils of Idolatry" from the "Book of Homilies" by Dr. F. G. Lee in *Edward VI,* 2nd Vol. page 74.

Book of Common Prayer, accepted by Parliament, November 1534. Dixon's *History of the Church of England,* Vol. IV, page 37 (concerning Cranmer's denunciation of the Latin Mass).

Oaths taken by Cranmer at his consecration as Archbishop of Canterbury (Strype's *Memorials of Cranmer,* ed. 1848, page 331).

Supreme Head of the church incorporated by Letters Patent, January 15, 1535 (Rymer, historian, Vol. XIV, p. 549) also *Letters and Papers of Henry VIII,* Vol. VIII, p. 52).

Archbishop Warham protests to the granting of Supreme Head of the Church to Henry VIII (Wilkin's *History,* Vol. 111, p. 746).

Divorce of Catherine of Aragon (Freidman's *Ann Boleyn,* Vol. II, p. 323, also, Pollard, *Thomas N. Cranmer,* page 60, note I).

Brown and Hilsey, Augustine and Dominican Friars (*Letters and Papers, Henry VIII,* XIII, pages 756, 751, 761, 911).

Surrender of 150 religious houses (Burnet's *History,* Vol. I, p. 232-59) J. Gairdner, about Bishop Fisher, in *Lollardy and the Reformation,* Vol. I, p. 437 to 504.

History of the Church of England, from the abolition of Roman Catholic jurisdiction, 1878-1902, by Richard Watson, 1883-1902, Vol. I, p. 158.

Ordination and Consecration of Reginald Poleas, priest, bishop and Archbishop, March 1556 (Wriothesly's *Chronicles,* Vol. 2, page 134).

Appointment of William Barlow as bishop in the Church of England (John Strype's *Memorials* Vol. I, page 347).

Thomas Rymer, English histiographer (1641-1713) on various Sees occupied by Barlow: also Stubbs Registrum Sacrum, pages 77-78.

W. Maguire Brady, Vol. 8, page 20, in article "The Anglican" on the restoration of Catholic Allegiance.

Burnet's *History of the Reformation,* Vol. I, page 184 record.

Strype's *Memorials,* Vol. I page 184.

Rev. Dr. Bailey, "The Defense of Holy Orders in the Church of England," pages 45, 46, Vol. I.

Consecration of Matthew Parker as Archbishop of Canterbury, by William Kennedy, English Historian.

John Charles Ryle, (1816-1990) in his work "Principles of a Churchman" (1884), also in *Liverpool Guardian,* Nov. 4, 1896, also statement of Rev. Dr. Taylor, Archdeacon, in London *Tablet,* Nov. 6, 1896.

Foreword

For almost two thousand years the Church of Christ has withstood the vicious assaults of the satellites of Satan. From Diocletian in the year A.D. 305 to Tito and Stalin in the year A.D. 1950, and continuing, the road has been a most tortuous one. The full waves of Nestorianism, Photianism, Lutheranism, Anglicanism, heresies of gigantic proportions, were mediocre in comparison with the reign of terror now rampant in European Catholic countries which are under the heel of Russian atheistic communism. These powers of darkness have determined to drive out of the heavens the Lord God Who created them; they have lashed continuously but unsuccessfully at the foundation of His church; they have imprisoned Cardinals, Bishops, Priests, Nuns; every form of persecution has been employed to destroy the Papacy—even the person of the Holy Father, Pius XII, is not immune from threats of violence. Amidst all the carnage of two world wars, the Church of Christ and His Vice-regent, the Pope of Rome, persisted in their efforts to bring peace to the world; but the world would not listen. Holy Mother Church, the Light of the world, stands impregnable; the same yesterday, today, tomorrow—the imperishable—"The Unshattered Rock."

FRANCIS A. MCLAUGHLIN

October 15, 1954

Author's Preface

What is the purpose of this work and who will profit from reading it, and secondly, why should a layman write a volume of this character, dealing with matters ordinarily reserved to clerical authorities?

The ordinary layman finds it difficult to grasp the meaning of scriptural references and encyclical letters so far removed from his ordinary subjects of conversation. As a matter of fact, if he had the disposition to do so, he has neither the time nor the facilities of research requisite for clear understanding. If the subjects were set forth in simple language, the layman's trouble would be solved. He also would be better equipped to combat the insidious assaults being waged against Holy Mother Church, and the Pope of Rome, Christ's Vicar on earth.

One of the most insistent challenges leveled at the Catholic Church is fostered by the Anglican Church of England. For the past four centuries the hierarchy of this church have contended with the See of Peter over the question of holy orders, claiming that they never lost the Apostolic succession—that their bishops are direct descendants of the Apostles, and that they possess true priests, valid sacraments, and true bishops. Their claims are invalid. Four Pontiffs have declared them to be "null and void from the beginning." The latest decision was handed down by

Pope Leo XIII in March, 1896, in an encyclical letter *Apostolicae Curae* wherein he supports the positions of his predecessors. This decision of Pope Leo XIII is the basis of this study of the invalidity of Anglican and Protestant Episcopal Orders.

The purpose of this study is twofold: first, it is intended to inform Catholic and non-catholic alike relative to the misinformation extensively spread against the Catholic Church by those who separated from obedience to the Vicar of Christ, charged that the Holy Father desired to destroy all Christians not in communion with the See of Peter; second, to prove that Rome has no designs against any group of people, whether in communion, or not. The See of Peter recognizes many churches as having valid sacraments, true priests and bishops, and rather than condemn them makes every effort to bring them back into unity with the Church of Christ. The author takes particular delight in presenting proof of this statement.

In preparing this work many estimable persons were of great assistance. Among them two splendid priests of God gave generously of their time and advice. Reverend Frederick Minigan of St. Joseph's Church, Roxbury, Grand Chaplain of the Order of Alhambra was graciously cooperative in furnishing the ritual of ordination of priests and consecration of bishops in the Catholic Church. When the work got tiresome, he was there with kindly assistance and encouragement. The author is particularly indebted to Right Reverend Monsignor Robert H. Lord, formerly professor of history at Harvard University. He is now pastor of St. Paul's Catholic Church at Wellesley, Mass. A convert from Anglicanism to Catholicism he has a profound knowledge of both sides of the controversy, and was never too busy to advise and discuss the author's efforts. His criticism of the study was always sound; he was very generous in his laudations at the conclusion of the study, as is evidenced by his letter of commendation which appears in the early pages of this work; the author expresses his deep appreciation to this brilliant prelate of Holy Mother Church.

To Thomas J. McInerney and Thomas H. Murray, Past Grand Knights of Brighton Council 121, Knights of Columbus, sincere thanks for their invaluable assistance is also extended. Many of the authorities quoted was due to their unlimited efforts in research.

This study has many facets which may appear rough or unpolished, but all are based on reliable authorities both Catholic and Protestant. In a work of this character it is always possible to plagiarize, though every effort has been made to give proper recognition to authorities quoted. If, inadvertently mistakes have been made along this line, the author offers sincere apology.

It is customary, and proper for an author to submit his educational background for the work he undertakes to present to the public. In this regard the author is conscious of his limited erudition, but makes no apology for it. His formal education terminated with his graduation in 1895 from the Sacred Heart School in East Boston, Massachusetts. This was an elementary school, staffed by the Sisters of Notre Dame, and he graduated therefrom at the age of thirteen years. He entered the marts of trade laboring assiduously for the past fifty-nine years. Unmindful of lack of higher education he applied himself to the task of writing this study with the tools at hand, namely: research in libraries, seminaries, information centers, conversations with clergy of varying shades of belief. Pamphlets of every description, Catholic, Protestant, Greek, were studied relentlessly, with many hours "burning the midnight oil." The work has been absorbing, intensely interesting, ofttimes intriguing and always worthwhile. If it proves informative to others the labor and sacrifice of other fraternal activities is of secondary importance.

In his many addresses to the various Catholic societies, the Most Reverend Richard J. Cushing, D.D., Archbishop of Boston continuously stressed the importance of knowing the essential truths of our Holy religion. He urged repeatedly that we study the history of the Church, learn its dogma and doctrines, be familiar with the glorious record of struggle and conquest over the powerful forces who are ever assailing it. He exhorts his people to be able to explain the truths of the Catholic Faith to the countless numbers of non-catholics who sincerely desire the assurance of possessing the true Faith. In a word, be militant Catholics carrying the banner of Christ, in the Church triumphant.

This study of Anglican Orders and related subjects, is the author's answer to the plea of the Archbishop "to know your religion."

With deep reverence, I dedicate this work to the memory of those valiant "defenders of the Faith" who gave their lives that the Church of Christ would endure until eternity.

FRANCIS A. MCLAUGHLIN

May 22, 1955

Introduction

Since 1532, the Church of England has maintained it is one of the three branches of the holy Catholic Church, declaring that the other two branches, the Greek and the Roman Catholic, while possessing valid orders and sacraments, have lost the primitive faith.

The Church of England, or Anglo-catholic Church, as their clergy prefer to call it, graciously grant that it is of course true that the Roman and Greek Orthodox Churches have a true priesthood and hierarchy, but have become separated from the primitive apostolic Church by virtue of error and schism, with the result that the Anglican Church is the sole preserver of the apostolic doctrine and tradition. This claim is ludicrous. Any student of history, without entering into discussion of the theological questions involved, could establish its falsity.

The termination of the American Revolution meant the evacuation of the Anglican hierarchy in America, and the Protestant Episcopal Church came into being. The first bishop of the Protestant Episcopal Church in America was the Reverend Samuel Seabury. He was elected bishop by the clergy of Connecticut, but his choice was not recognized in England and as consecration was denied him in England he was later consecrated by the non-juror bishops in Aberdeen, Scotland, on the 14th day of November 1784. Other bishops followed, being consecrated in America.

Reverend James Madison of Virginia was consecrated on September 19, 1790.

A general convention of laymen, clergy, and bishops of the Episcopal Church was held in Virginia in 1784 and again in 1789 for the purpose of uniting the discordant elements in the Church. The convention expressly defined and accepted the liturgy of the Church of England, definitely affirmed the two sacraments of Baptism and the Lord's Supper as instituted by Christ; they recognized the three orders of deacons, priests, and bishops as necessary for Apostolic Succession; insisted that canon law be made by a more representative body of clergymen and laity conjointly; they set forth their independence of all foreign authority and government of the church in America. A constitution and canons were eventually adopted and the "Book of Common Prayer" was set forth as the accepted ritual. The Protestant Episcopal Church in America was formed, free from dominion of the mother church—the Anglican communion of England. The word Protestant is repugnant to "high churchmen" in the church of England, and is usually used by them in identifying churches outside the Roman, Greek, or Anglican groups.

The Anglican and Episcopal churches while essentially alike in their doctrine and ritualistic ceremonials, differ in the selection or election of the hierarchy. In the Anglican church, the King appoints the Archbishop of Canterbury, Primate of all England who confirms and consecrates or designates who shall officiate. In the Protestant Episcopal church however, a bishop is elected by the diocese, and must be confirmed by a majority of the bishops and standing committees of the different dioceses.

Up until 1910 the senior bishop was presiding bishop, but by adoption of an amendment to the constitution this rule was abrogated and the presiding bishop is now chosen by the General Convention. This form of government of the church obtains in the Episcopal church of Scotland and other countries where the Episcopal church is organized.

The Protestant Episcopal church of the present day is divided into three distinct sections, namely, "High Church," "Low Church," and "Broad Church" differing from each other in their tenets of faith, yet all claiming the true Catholic faith—or as they prefer to call it—the primitive faith. A short statement of each section will suffice to show the variance in creeds and the difficulties they must experience in supporting their pretensions of being Catholic.

The "High Church," so called, represents those who desire to be known as having definite leanings toward Roman ceremonials in their exterior characteristics and liturgy; their churches may have three altars, tabernacle, stations of the cross, confessions, baptismal fonts, chapels of our Blessed Lady, rosaries in her honor, sodalities dedicated to her, processions, first Friday services, novenas to saints, and lastly, the sacrifice of the Mass. The clergy of this section prefer to be known as Anglo Catholics, or American Catholics. They resent being designated as Protestant Episcopalians.

The so-called "Low Church" section of the Anglican and Episcopal churches do not consider possession of the apostolic succession essential to constitute a valid ministry, regarding the sacraments and sacramental rites as mere signs or symbols rather than as true causes of grace, and oppose ornate ritual or "sacerdotalism." In 1561, Bishop Ridley ordered the destruction of altars and substituted the communion table. With rare exceptions, notably, Trinity church, and St. Paul's Cathedral in Boston, this ruling of Ridley has been adhered to. The "Low Church" sympathize with and have inter-communion with most all non-episcopal denominations; of course they have no communion with the Greek Orthodox or Roman Catholic churches.

The remaining section termed "Broad Church" is made up of

those who demand the utmost liberty in doctrinal beliefs and practices. They care nothing for Apostolic succession, reject transubstantiation (as do all other branches) and have free communication with all "Free Evangelical Churches." In fact, Calvinism and Presbyterianism are equally efficacious spiritually, in their judgment, to either Anglican or Episcopalian doctrines and traditions. The Episcopal Church is further divided by various branches of Methodist-Episcopalians who make no pretensions of possessing Apostolic succession or valid sacrament or orders, and therefore do not come within the scope of this study of Anglican orders.

This thesis will consist of a presentation of the age-old question of the validity of Anglican Orders, their rites of ordination of priests and consecration of bishops. A comparison of the ancient liturgies for ordination of priests and consecration of bishops will also be shown. Finally the rites of ordaining and consecration of bishops according to the ritual of the Roman Catholic Church will be elucidated.

It is imperative that these comparisons be made. The statement of Archbishop Thomas N. Cranmer, Primate of the Anglican church, "Rome was solely interested in destroying the churches which would not accept the yoke of anti-christ—the Pope of Rome," must be shown to be absolutely false, and was uttered with malice predicated on a desire to destroy the Roman Church throughout the kingdom of England. A careful study of the various Rites of the churches not in communion with Rome, yet recognized by Rome as having valid sacraments, true priests and true bishops, will easily prove the deliberate malice of Cranmer.

In the study of Anglican orders extreme caution has been taken to avoid all account of political intrigue, whether civil or ecclesiastical, and both were rampant. There is no doubt that political animosities were many times responsible for the cruelties that were perpetrated on those who would not accept the dictates of unscrupulous men who temporarily possessed great power. Every effort has been made to weigh and analyze every phase of this delicate question, and the results are presented without rancor; but no attempt has been made to gloss over the deliberate acts of ambitious men to bring about the destruction of the Roman Catholic Church in England, and throughout Europe.

In order that a complete picture of the Anglican Church might be presented, it is necessary that attention be given the individuals directly responsible for the establishment of it. This necessitates a brief summation of the lives and works of the king Henry VIII, his Primate, Thomas N. Cranmer, Archbishop of Canterbury, his ecclesiastical advisor and Chancellor, the Lord Cardinal Wolsey, and Matthew Parker, the first Elizabethan Archbishop of Canterbury.

Unfortunately for the record there is not much known about the consecrators of Matthew Parker, namely, bishops William Barlow, John Scory, Miles Coverdale, and John Hodgkins. There is, however, sufficient proof that none of the co-consecrators, except John Hodgkins, had ever been a consecrated bishop in the Catholic Church, and therefore they possessed no powers to transmit valid Orders to others. In continuity then, from King Henry to William Barlow, Consecrator, this study will be presented.

Chapter One

Henry VIII, King of England and Ireland, and the dominions over the seas, was born at Greenwich, the third child and second son of Henry VII and Princess Elizabeth of York, daughter of Edward IV of England. Henry's eldest son Prince Arthur had been proposed in infancy as a husband to Catherine, daughter to Ferdinand of Aragon. They were married on November 14, 1501, at St. Paul's church. Since Arthur was 15 years old the co-habiting of the young couple was wisely delayed. He died the following April 12, definitely establishing that the marriage between them had not been consummated, thus permitting the marriage of Catherine to the young brother Prince Henry on April 22, 1509, the day his father, Henry VII had died and he succeeded to the throne. Henry was 18 years of age and his queen was eight years his senior. English historians insist it was a "marriage of state" and Henry registered a protest against marrying his brother's widow. The laws of England and the Church also forbade a marriage between a man and the widow of his brother, if that marriage had been consummated. But evidence had been presented which satisfied the Pope that while Catherine of Aragon had been a bride she had never been a wife—therefore the marriage had not been consummated. And Pope Julius II had in 1504 granted the necessary dispensation permitting the marriage.

During the first ten years of their marriage six children were born to Henry and Catherine; five of them died in infancy, the one daughter, Mary Tudor, later succeeded her half-brother Edward on the throne of England. Henry and Catherine ruled as king and queen of England for more than twenty years previous to the divorce decree being issued against her by Archbishop Cranmer.

As early as 1514 there were indications that all was not serene in the matrimonial affairs of the king and queen. There was much dissatisfaction because the queen did not produce a male heir to the throne of England. There had never been a female sovereign in England and Henry used this fact as an excuse for his amorous shortcomings. For years Eleanor Blount, daughter of Lord Mountjoy's sister had been his mistress and as a consequence of this illicit attachment a son was born to them and upon him the king conferred the title of "Duke of Richmond," designating him as his heir to the throne. The boy died in his ninth year, and the king and his mistress soon parted. Later on his attention centered on Mary Bolyn and she became his mistress, but he soon tired of his amorous relations with her and she was cast aside.

The interest of Henry in the affairs of the Boleyn family did not cease with the termination of his clandestine relations with Mary. In 1514 Mary Tudor accompanied by Ann Boleyn was sent to France by King Henry to represent England at the marriage of Louis XII. Shortly after the festivities she returned to England, but Ann Boleyn remained as a lady in waiting to Queen Claude. She remained but a short time returning to England to become a lady in waiting to Queen Catherine. It was then that she came under the notice of King Henry and infatuation was soon manifest. The king granted many favors to the father of Ann Boleyn; he created him Earl of Wiltshire; he became one of the king's closest advisors, heading a committee sent to Rome by the king to facilitate his contemplated divorce from Queen Catherine.

Ann Boleyn was of different fibre from her unfortunate sister Mary. She was determined to be Henry's queen, and left no stone unturned until her ambitions were realized. She went to France with Henry in October 1532, and upon their return to England she was found to be pregnant. In consequence of this she was secretly married to Henry on January 25, 1533, but the marriage was not made public till the following Easter. On the 23rd of May following Cranmer declared her marriage to Henry to be valid, and that of Henry and Catherine to be invalid . . . "null and void from the beginning."

It is more than passing strange that Ann Boleyn should suffer the same disappointment experienced by Queen Catherine of Aragon. Instead of a son—a daughter was born—Elizabeth, afterwards Queen of England. Historians assert this birth caused Henry to lose affection for his Ann. The following year Queen Ann suffered a miscarriage, and on January 29, 1536, she gave birth, a miscarriage again, a dead male child. It was on this day that Queen Catherine passed to her eternal reward, an outraged queen, but in the minds of the English people, a genuinely beloved sovereign, and time has done naught to erase this affection. On the second of May 1536, by order of the king, Queen Ann Boleyn was committed to the "Towers," charged with adultery with six of the young bloods of the court, and with incest with her own brother, Lord Rochford. All were found guilty and were executed on the 17th day of May 1536, and two days later Queen Ann Boleyn was beheaded on Tower Green. Shortly after, Henry married Jane Seymour. She died in 1537 after presenting a son to Henry who became the boy king, Edward VI, in 1547.

No further reference need be made to the marital escapades of King Henry as they had no bearing upon the establishment of the Anglican church. It is necessary that the marriages of Ann Boleyn and Jane Seymour be recorded as both queens were responsible for future spiritual heads of the Anglican church, as sovereigns of England, namely, Edward VI and Queen Elizabeth.

There is no denying that for years there had been strained relations between the crown of England and the Vatican. The papal insistence upon ecclesiastical appointments to benifices in England and the payment of first fruits to the Pope of Rome had gradually forced a showdown between the crown and Rome. Some time previous (1521) Henry had been honored by the pope with the title of "Defender of the Faith" for his treatise on the seven sacraments, written against Luther. Henry was personally averse to an open break with Rome; he never was partial to Protestantism, and even after his severance from obedience to papal authority he would not permit the slightest deviation from catholic practices, and would summarily punish any who attempted it.

Despite this tenacity to the tenets of the catholic faith Henry was determined to effect an annulment of his marriage to Catherine of Aragon. His infatuation for Ann Boleyn outweighed all other problems. He sent various emissaries to Rome to procure annulment. Among them were the Pope's Legatine, Lord Cardinal Wolsey, the Earl of Wiltshire, Thomas N. Cranmer, then an ordinary priest; all to no avail. Pope Clement VII would not grant an annulment. The king was undaunted by these reverses. He desired the divorce but he wanted it by papal authority. According to documents in possession of the Public Records Office, a letter from his agent and Henry's answer, thoroughly demonstrate his desire to have Rome support his petition. He stated: "The king is loth to recur to any remedy except the authority of the See Apostolic, if he can find there favor answering to its merits." (Letters and papers, foreign and domestic of the reign of Henry VIII—vol. 14—page 527)

In August 1529 England was stricken with a plague known as the "swetting sickness," and thousands of the people suffered death. In the Cambridge area, it was exceedingly severe. Those who could get away did so, and among them was Thomas N. Cranmer, priest, staying with relatives at Waltham, Essex. The king accompanied by Gardiner, his Secretary of State, later bishop of Winchester, and Edward Fox, Lord High Almoner, afterwards bishop of Hereford, were also visiting in the neighborhood with the Cressy family, relatives of Cranmer. During the visit, the question of Henry's meditated divorce came up and Cranmer volunteered the opinion that if the canonists and universities should decide that marriage with a brother's widow was illegal, which it certainly would be if consummated, and if it could be substantiated that Prince Arthur's marriage came into that category, then her marriage was in violation of God's law, and the Archdiocesan Courts could declare the marriage was null and void, and an appeal to Rome was unnecessary. When Gardiner and Fox reported Cranmer's opinion to the king, he observed, "send this man to me, I trow he has the sow by the right ear."

When Cranmer appeared before the king and made known his reasons for his opinion he was commanded to drop all work and prepare the cause for submission to the universities and canonists. He was to live at the palace of the Earl of Wiltshire, the father of Ann Boleyn, and remain there until he completed his work on the appeal to the canonists and universities. He was joined by Gardiner and Fox in the presentation before the universities. History records that both Oxford and Cambridge accepted his arguments and unanimously voted in 1530 to support the king in his suit for annulment.

Upon completion of his work Cranmer was sent to Rome as a member of a committee to place the matter before the Pope. The Holy Father received them courteously and was much impressed with the apparent sincerity of Cranmer. Cranmer was a brilliant orator, and the impression he made upon the Holy Father resulted in his appointment as "Grand Penitentiary of England." But, as for obtaining an annulment, it was wasted effort. The Holy Father declared the marriage and Henry and Catherine lawful and binding, and forbade Henry setting his queen aside to marry Ann Boleyn.

Cranmer returned to England in September 1530 and was received with marked favor by King Henry, who, shrewdly recognizing that the Pope was favorably disposed towards Cranmer, made plans to use this young priest in his own interests. Accordingly, he appointed him *Consiliarius Regius et a Caesarum Orator,"* and sent him as his ambassador to the Emperor of Germany. While there Cranmer married the niece of one Ossiander, one of the leaders of the Lutheran movement at Nuremburg. This marriage was a violation of his vow of celibacy, and had it been known would have definitely disqualified him from subsequent honors in the service of the Catholic Church.

In August 1532, William Warham, Archbishop of Canterbury, died and King Henry immediately appointed Thomas N. Cranmer to the See of Canterbury. The papal bulls of confirmation arrived from Rome in February of 1533, and on March 30, 1533, he was enthroned as Archbishop of Canterbury.

The stage was now set; the actors in one of the greatest dramas of all time had been selected and assigned. The petitioner was the king of England; he appointed the judge, and the witness was himself, and none appeared in defense of the respondent, Queen Catherine of England. This infamous trial had its origin in the fertile mind of the newly enthroned Archbishop Cranmer. Unctuously protesting his concern for the future welfare of the realm he petitioned the king for permission to try the case of the annulment in the Archdiocesan Matrimonial Court. Permission being granted, the Qoeen Catherine was ordered to appear at the priory of Dunstable. The queen refused to recognize their demands and did not appear. Because of her refusal to obey the summons she was adjudged contumacious, and on the 23rd of May 1533, Archbishop Cranmer declared the marriage of Henry and Princess Catherine of Aragon, widow of Prince Arthur, was null from the beginning, thus leaving Henry free to marry again. That this decision had been previously agreed upon by the king and archbishop is proven by the fact that the Parliament had already enacted the "Act of Appeals" which prohibited any appeal from decisions rendered by the court of the archbishop. Less than a week after this atrocious act against the queen had been committed Archbishop Cranmer was compelled to pronounce as valid the marriage of Henry and Ann Boleyn which had been secretly celebrated on January 25, 1533. On the first of June following (1533) he crowned Ann Boleyn as Queen of England. And to complete the act Cranmer stood as godfather to the illegitimate Elizabeth, the future queen of England.

In recording these momentous episodes in the turbulent life of King Henry VIII English historians with rare exceptions (whether civil or ecclesiastical) are prone to relegate Henry's concupiscence as having little bearing upon the rupture with the Apostolic See. They agree he had many mistresses, but will also solemnly aver that he was solely interested in having a male heir to succeed him as King of England.

In the light of the history of this era it is difficult to account for the conduct of Archbishop Warham and Cardinal Wolsey. It was the seasoned opinion of both these prelates that the Holy Father, Clement VII, might be prevailed upon to annul the marriage, and so certain was Wolsey that Rome would ratify his action he invited Cardinal Campeggio of Rome (sent by the Holy Father to study the facts) to sit with him in his "Legatine Court." But the court adjourned as Clement had issued his decree forbidding Henry to set aside his lawful wife, for in the sight of Almighty God no earthly power could annul it.

During this period Cardinal Wolsey was the most powerful figure in England. In 1511, thirteen years after his ordination as priest, he became a privy counsellor, and a most domineering force in the government of England. He served as bishop of Lincoln and Tournai, the archbishopric of York, and in 1515 was elevated to the Cardinalate, and upon the expressed wish of King Henry was appointed "Legate de Latere" by the Pope, superseding Archbishop Warham of Canterbury, thus gaining supreme control of the government of the church in England.

The meteoric rise of Wolsey, not only in the church, but the king's favor as well, naturally generated a strong anti-Wolsey feeling, and his enemies among the clergy and the nobility soon set plans on foot to destroy him. The conspiracies leveled against Wolsey eventually bore fruit. Charges of violation of the "Statute of Praemunire" by acting as *Legate de Latere* of the Pope of Rome were lodged against him with the approval of Thomas Cromwell, lay vicar-general. The fact that he was acting upon the personal request of the king, was of no consequence; his enemies were determined to destroy him, and fair play was the last thing in their minds.

The "Statute of Praemunire" was first passed in 1353, imposing outlawry, forfeiture, and imprisonment on those who should sue in foreign courts for matters cognizable in England, and thereafter not appear when summoned to answer for their contempt. In 1392, a second statute was enacted, designed to check the power of the Pope in England, by punishing those who procured from the papal authority any process against the king or his crown or realm. (Richard II, 16c.)

Cardinal Wolsey did not underestimate his enemies, whether civil or religious. He knew his clerical enemies were angered by his suppression of the monasteries, and his absolute monopoly of ecclesiastical power. Strangely, the only support he had was from the king, but his enemies persisted with their pressure and eventually the king weakened, and his enemies accomplished their wish to undermine him.

The Cardinal also had his supporters, but the hostility of parliament was gradually enlisted and the inevitable ensued. Despite the entreaties of his friends, Wolsey pleaded guilty to the charges preferred against him, and threw himself upon the mercy of the king. He relinquished all his wealth, his palaces, his gold plate, vast realty holdings, contenting himself only with the archbishopric of York, and he retired to that See until called to London to defend himself against a charge of treason.

Thomas, Cardinal Wolsey, brilliant scholar, magnificently equipped statesman, administrative genius, stern disciplinarian, died humbly at Leiscester Abby where he was taken ill on November 30, 1530. His ending will always be of interest to historians, as his death-bed dialogue with constable and captain of the guard of the Tower of London, Sir William Kingston, shows the futility of attempting to serve two masters—God and mammon. As the cardinal lay dying, Kingston demanded payment of 1500 pounds in gold which he alleged Wolsey owed the king. Wolsey denied the debt, insisting he had paid all to his sovereign, admitting he had distributed the meagre balance of his possessions to his servants. The captain accused the dying cardinal of being unfaithful to his king. The cardinal's reply will live while language is spoken: "Master Kingston, I see the matter how it is framed against me; but if I had been as diligent in my service to my God as I have to the king, He would not have given me over in my gray hairs" and turning his face to the wall, he passed to the great beyond. Henry VIII had been frustrated; the King of Kings had taken over.

The death of Cardinal Wolsey was hailed with satisfaction by those intent on taking over control of the affairs of the church of England. The wily Cromwell, aided by the subservient and vacillating Warham, Archbishop of Canterbury, had prepared the way for the seizure of all ecclesiastical power by the king. Cromwell, knowing the vanity of his king, and desirous of safeguarding his own preferment submitted a daring proposal to Henry. He stated: "Your Majesty, at present England is a monster with two heads, but if the king would take the power now usurped by the foreign bishop, the Pope of Rome, into his own hands everything would be well and the clergy finding that their lives and possessions were at the king's mercy, would be ready to do his bidding." (Lingard—Vol. 16-3.)

This statement was based upon the fact that "inasmuch as the episcopacy and clergy obeyed Wolsey as Pope's Legate and had submitted to his authority, they had participated in and were partakers of his crimes and were therefore subject to the same penalties prescribed for violation of the 'Statute of Praemunire,' namely, imprisonment at the king's pleasure, and the forfeiture of all their possessions. The revenues of their churches, cathedrals, all monies collected for church purposes, all reverted to and accrued to the crown."

The king quickly acquiesced to the plan. The attorneys-general were ordered to draw up the indictments against the entire clergy in the court of "King's Bench." The clergy thus indicted were in a sad and sorry plight. They knew the injustice of the charges alleged against them, but there was no available remedy at hand that could be operative in their defence.

The king's action was not motivated for financial gains only. He desired the wealth of the church under his sole control, but the real purpose was to set up a new ecclesiastical regime with himself as the "Supreme Head of the Church of England." He was formulating a ruthless, daring, and unscrupulous plan to vest both civil and ecclesiastical power in his own hands.

On February 7, 1531, the convocation of Canterbury assembled and voted to offer the king a gratuity of one hundred thousand pounds if he would pardon them from the charge of violation of the "statute of Praemunire" alleged against them. The king refused to accept the gift unless it carried with it an acknowledgment of him as "the Sole protector and Supreme Head of the Church of England."

The convocation turned down the king's demand. A committee was appointed to carry on negotiations between the king, Cromwell, and convocation. Thomas Boleyn acted for the king and Cromwell, as liaison to the bishops of the church of England.

Shortly after making demands the king ordered archbishop Warham of Canterbury to summon the bishops before him. To them he made solemn promises "upon the word of a king" that if convocation would acknowledge him as Supreme Head of the Church of England he would never violate that grant by assuming himself more power, jurisdiction, or authority over them than other kings before him had done; nor would he take upon himself to make or promulgate any spiritual law, or exercise any spiritual jurisdiction, nor yet by any means intermeddle with them in altering or judging of any spiritual business."

The next day in convocation, Thomas Boleyn and other Lords representing the king told the assembly what the king had promised the bishops and thundered that "anyone who should now oppose the king's designation as 'Supreme Head of the Church of England' would be guilty of questioning the honesty and honor of his king, after the king had made so solemn an oath."

To use a modern vernacular, the clergy "were on the spot," no matter how they acted. The majority of the bishops and clergy agreed to grant the king's request. The most outstanding opponent to this demand of the king was John Fisher, Bishop of Rochester. In solemn words he stated to the assembly:

"My Lord Bishops:

"Beware that you leap not out of Peter's ship to be drowned

in the waves of all heresies, sects, schisms, and divisions. Take heed to yourselves and to the whole flock wherein the Holy Ghost placed upon bishops to rule the church of God was not said to kings but to bishops. We cannot grant this unto the king without renouncing our unity with the 'See of Peter.' In doing this we should forsake the first four general councils. We should thereby renounce all canonical and ecclesiastical laws of the church of Christ. We renounce thereby the unity of the Christian world.

"The first general council acknowledged the authority of Sylvester Bishop of Rome, by sending their decrees to be ratified by him. The Council of Constantinople did also acknowledge Pope Damasus to be their chief, by admitting him to give judgment against the heretics Macedonius and Sabellius. The Council of Ephesus admitted Pope Celestine to be their chief judge by accepting his condemnation of the heretic Nestorius. The Council of Chalcedon admitted Pope Leo to be their head; and all general councils of the world admitted the Pope of Rome to be the Supreme Head of the Church of Christ.

"And now, Fathers, shall we acknowledge another head—or one to be in England—and another in Rome? By this argument Herod must have been the head of the Jews, Nero must have been the Head of the Church of Christ. The king's highness is not susceptible of this distinction."

The absurdity of this tremendous grant to a layman as bishop Fisher pointed out was a dangerous precedent to establish, and if it was to be granted over his objections he would insist that a clause be inserted to read "quantum per legem Dei licet" (as far as God's law allows).

The king realizing he could not get this grant of power as "Supreme Head of the Church" without accepting this clause, acquiesced to it. He knew he had no intention of respecting it once the power was in his hands. He then pardoned the clergy of their alleged violation of the "statute of Praemunire" and accepted their offer of one hundred thousand pounds (gold) as a gift. Dr. Lingard observes: "It is plain that the introduction of the clause (as far as the law allows) served to invalidate the whole recognition; since the bishops who might reject the king's supremacy could maintain it was not allowed by the laws of God."

During the entire session of Convocation not one word was uttered by either side relative to any contemplated rejection of spiritual allegiance to Christ's vicar at Rome. The master-minds of the pending so-called "Reformation" kept all reference to Rome out of their discussions. The bishops and clergy objected to the title of "Supreme Head." It was too vague—something new—portentous—and uneasiness was manifest. The more conservative bishops like Fisher and Tunstall began to be concerned and fearful that the liberty, powers, and privileges of the "bishops bench" might be infringed upon, if not completely curtailed by the king. They were somewhat heartened by the fact that convocation, by vote, at this session had not issued a decree setting forth the king's status as "Supreme Head of the Church in England." Their joy was short-lived. At a convocation held three months later, Archbishop Warham of Canterbury advised convocation to vote the one hundred thousand pounds (gold), and the title of "Supreme Head of the Church in England." The only voices raised against the usurpation of the rights of the Pope of Rome were bishops Fisher and Tunstall. Gairdner, English historian, in his articles, in "letters and papers" reign of Henry VIII, Vol. I-5-160 states:

"The act granting the king the title of 'Supreme Head of the Church,' and the payment of one hundred thousand pounds was repented of almost as soon as made, for however theoretically defensible the title to which they had agreed, and whatever plans they might make against misconstruction, the clergy could not but feel the disadvantage at which they stood by having yielded; yet they were altogether helpless."

Under the "statute of Praemunire" the entire clergy were at the king's mercy. While the Episcopacy were quiescent and permitted in large measure the emoluments of their office, the inferior clergy were ground to the last extremity. In their desperate circumstances they petitioned the bishops to request Parliament to retract the acknowledgment of the king's supremacy granted in convocation. A protest against any infringement of, or encroachment upon the liberty of the church, or against the authority of the Holy See signed by a great number of the clergy of both provinces was presented to the king; and a few months later Archbishop Warham of Canterbury, regretting the part he had played in the granting of the title to the king, drew up a solemn protest against all enactments passed in that Parliament derogatory to the Pope and his authority, and the independence of the clergy. (Wilkins History)

Despite solemn promises made to the English bishops by the king "that he would not meddle with the affairs of the church" he directed the Parliament in January 1534 "that no canon or decree should be made by convocation without consent of the king; appeals might be made from the bishops to the 'court of chancery,' but not to the Pope; that bishops should be made and consecrated without the consent or approval of the Pope; that dispensations usually granted by the Pope should be obtained from the Archbishop of Canterbury; and that all payments made to Rome as first fruits, should cease."

The king further required that all clergy, bishops as well as priests both secular and regular, take the oath of succession, at the same time making the declaration that the "Bishop of Rome" had no more jurisdiction, or authority in England, than any other foreign bishop; and that the king was the "Supreme Head of the Church of England"; the saving clause (as far as the laws of God allows) being omitted. To refuse this oath was admission of treason, punishable by perpetual imprisonment and forfeiture of all property.

The clergy in general subscribed to the oath, and a formal declaration renouncing the authority of the pope was obtained from both convocation and the universities of Oxford and Cambridge, as well as all other lesser institutions. Later in 1534 Parliament enacted an additional law that the king and his heirs should be recognized as the lawful "Heads on earth of the church of England," and any such denial of the law or title was made high treason punishable by death. (Letters and papers, Henry VIII, vol. 8, page 20.)

The enactment of these outrageous laws was particularly pleasing to Thomas Cromwell. He enforced them with bloodthirsty vehemence. A reign of terror, organized with consummate skill and absolute merciless action, held England panic-stricken.

In fairness it must be stated that during these turbulent times of persecution, neither convocation nor parliament initiated any antagonistic outbursts against Rome or the Catholic faith; all measures of persecution emanated from King Henry, abetted by Cromwell and Cranmer, successor to Warham as Archbishop of Canterbury.

King Henry VIII, defender of the faith, king of England, Ireland, and dominions over the seas, was indeed an enigmatic character. Persecuting the hierarchy of the church, yet he would not countenance any deviation from the Catholic faith—he insisted on the celebration of the Latin Mass; the people were free to attend the sacraments and conduct themselves in the Catholic tradition with the sole exception—he would not allow any semblance of obedience to papal authority, by clergy or people.

In Heylin's history of England, published in London, 1661, is found this final clause of the will of Henry VIII.

["We do instantly require and desire the Blessed Virgin, His Mother, with all the company of heaven, continually to pray for us and that there be provided, ordained, and set and apparelled with manner of things necessary for daily Mass, there to be offered perpetually while the world endures."] In his will he also ordered that his body be interred in the choir of St. George's Chapel at Windsor, and "as for my body which when the soul is departed shall remain as a dead carcass and so return to the vile matter that it was made of; we would be content to have it buried in any place accustomed for Christian people, were it never so vile, for it is but ashes and to ashes it shall return again. Nevertheless, because we would be loathe in the reputation of the people to do any injury to the dignity we are unworthily called into, we are content, also by the presents do ordain our body be buried and entered in the choir of our chapel in the college at Winchester." This will is dated December 12, 1546, and published by Fuller. (Church history edition, Brewer III, 214-19.)

King Henry VIII died on Friday January 28, 1547, and four days later was interred with Jane Seymour, his third wife, the Queen and mother of Edward VI, king of England. Three masses were sung, the third being offered by Gardiner, the bishop of Winchester, who preached the sermon and pronounced the final absolution.

Despite statements to the contrary, King Henry was buried with a Latin Catholic Mass, according to the Roman Pontifical, by validly consecrated Catholic bishops, possessing full sacerdotal powers; schismatical, yes, but in matter of papal jurisdiction only; heretical in matters of Catholic Faith—no. It is also fact that Francis I, King of France, ordered a solemn Pontifical Requiem Mass to be sung for King Henry in Notre Dame Cathedral, the celebrant of which was the Reverend Father DeRohan, brother of the French ambassador to the Holy See, assisted by their Eminences, Cardinals Givey, Sanguin and D'Armagnac, and a number of bishops, and no disciplinary action was taken against them. (Strypes memorials, and the "Reformation in England" by G. Constant, French and English, 1934.)

While it is historically true that the Church of England separated from spiritual communion with the See of Peter by direct action of Henry VIII, it is also true the Church of England during Henry's life retained the Catholic faith, valid priesthood, bishops, and sacraments, similar to the Greek Orthodox Church.

Chapter Two

The first Archbishop of the so-called "Reformation" upon whom it might be said the whole structure of the Anglican Church depended was Thomas Cranmer, Archbishop of Canterbury, successor of William Warham in the See.

Thomas N. Cranmer was born at Ashlocton in Nottinghamshire, England, on July 2, 1489, the second son of Thomas Cranmer and Ann Hatfield. His father died in 1501—when Thomas was fourteen years of age, and his mother sent him to Jesus College for his education. In 1510 he was elected a fellow of Jesus College, which he was soon to vacate, as he had married. His wife dying in child birth (the child also) during the year, he, being within the year of grace, was allowed to become reinstated to his fellowship. He continued his study for the priesthood and in 1523 was ordained to the priesthood.

Due to Cranmer's solution to the king's marital difficulties he early found favor with his king, and new honors were showered on him. He was sent as special ambassador to the Emperor of Germany in 1532 and while there he contracted a second marriage with the niece of one Osiander, a disciple of Martin Luther. This was Cranmer's second marriage; the first was legal, he was not in Holy Orders; the second marriage was definitely illegal, he was an ordained priest in the Catholic Church; and he knew his was guilty of grievous sin . . . he also knew he was living in concubinage, in violation of his vows of celibacy and chastity. While dallying at the home of his bride he received word to return to England. Archbishop Warham of Canterbury had died and the king had nominated Cranmer as his successor in that See. Cranmer was in a difficulty; he knew if it was known he was married, it would disqualify him from promotion to the Hierarchy, and result in his expulsion from his priesthood also. He sent his wife back to England where she remained in seclusion, and never made public appearance until the overthrow of the Catholic authority had been effected, and parliament removed the clause affecting the clergy in the Church of England, permitting them to marry.

In its acceptance of Cranmer's nomination to the See of Canterbury Rome proved it had no knowledge of Cranmer's marriage. The appointment was confirmed in February 1533, and the consecration took place on March 30, 1533.

The elevation of Cranmer to the primacy of England did not find favor among the older bishops, many of whom had served long years in the Episcopacy, and rightfully believed promotion to the Primacy should be from among their own group. Cranmer was a priest of ten years service, and a married man to boot (but unknown to them). His elevation was a deliberate and studied affront to the English hierarchy. The king knew his appointee, and the appointee knew his king.

The hierarchy of the ancient English church were intimately interwoven with the affairs of the realm; tradition required that upon the consecration of an Archbishop of Canterbury, the consecrand take two oaths: one of episcopal allegiance to the Pope, the other in recognition of the Royal Supremacy. The oath of allegiance to the Royal Supremacy was couched in such language that it actually superseded the episcopal allegiance to the Pope. In other words, if the consecrand was called upon to make a choice between the allegiances, the Royal Supremacy must take precedence. Cranmer, Archbishop-elect of Canterbury, was fully aware of this situation, and was not satisfied with its provisions. He recalled the ending of Cardinal Wolsey, and was determined to protect himself against such callous treatment. He had a special protest recorded in which he swore allegiance to the king first and always, the oath of allegiance to the pope was secondary. The taking of these two incompatible oaths caused no burden on his conscience.

A study of each will clearly show their incompatibility; they are translated from the Latin as written by Cranmer in his register at Lambeth Palace. The following oath is that to the Pope.

"In the name of God, amen; I, Thomas, elect of Canterbury from this hour forward shall be faithful and obedient to St. Peter and to the holy church of Rome, and to my Lord, the Pope Clement VII, and his successors canonically entering. I shall not be of counsel nor consent that they lose either life or member, or shall be taken, or suffer any violence, or any wrong by any means. Their counsel to me accredited by them, their messengers or letters I shall not willingly discover to any person. The papacy of Rome, the rules of the Holy Father, and the regality of St. Peter I shall help and maintain, and defend against all men (saving my order). The Legate of the See Apostolic going and coming I shall honorably entreat and assist in his necessities (in suis necessitalibus). The rights, honors, privileges, authorities of the church of Rome and of our Pope and his successors I shall cause to be conserved, defended, augmented and promoted. I shall not be in council, treaty, or any act, in which anything shall be against him, or the church of Rome, their rights, seats, honors, or powers. And if I know any such to be moved or compassed, I shall resist it to my power and as soon as I can, I shall advise him or such as may give him knowledge. The rules of the Holy See, the decrees, ordinances, sentences, dispositions, reservations, provisions, and commandments apostolic to my power I shall keep and cause to be kept by others. Hereafter, heretics, schismatics, and rebels to our Holy Father and his successors I shall resist and prosecute to my power. I shall come to the Synod when I am called, except to be letted by a canonical impediment. The threshold of the Apostles I shall visit yearly, personally or by my deputy. I shall not alienate or sell the possessions of the Archbishop without the consent of the Pope's counsel, so help me God, and the holy Evangelists."

This oath of allegiance to the Pope was taken on the day of his consecration as Archbishop of Canterbury, March 30, 1534. Immediately after pledging his allegiance to the Pope, he took the following oath to the king for his temporalities.

"I, Thomas Cranmer, renounce and forsake all such claims, words, sentences, and grants which I have received of the Pope's Holiness in his 'Bulla' of the Archbishop of Canterbury, that in any way, manner, wise, is or may be hurtful or prejudicial to your Highness, your heirs, successors, estate or dignity royal, knowing myself and acknowledging myself to take and hold the said Archbishopric, immediately and only of your Highness and of none other."

This oath was taken before four witnesses and notary summoned by Cranmer, both before consecration and after receiving the pallium. (Canon Dixon, Anglican, in "History of the Church of England," vol. 1, page 158.)

As Primate of all England, Cranmer exercised tremendous authority both spiritual and temporal. It was true that the breach between Rome and England had been well under way before Cranmer's elevation, but the movement required the impetus furnished by the new Primate. More than any other ecclesiastic in England he was responsible for the definite demarcation between Anglican faith and the primitive Catholic doctrines.

When King Henry lay dying, Cranmer was at his bedside. He gave Henry his solemn promise he would protect the interests of his daughter, Mary Tudor in the matter of the succession to the throne of England. Henry had decreed that his son Edward, born of Jane Seymour, his third queen, should succeed, and in the event of Edward's death without issue Mary would come to the throne. He administered the last rites of the church, and pontificated at the Solemn High Requiem Mass for the king on January 28, 1547.

In his last will and testament Henry set forth that a "regency council" of sixteen members including Archbishop Cranmer, and Edward, Earl of Hertford, a brother of Jane Seymour, should govern England until the maturity of Edward. The Earl of Hertford was chosen as "Lord Protector" to the boy king. Letters patent were issued March 13, 1547. Each of the "Regency Council" were elevated to the peerage by voting such elevation to each other, with all the revenues, perquisites, and emoluments attached thereto, and dear old "merrie England" paid the piper.

The coronation of the boy king was held in Westminster Abbey on February 20, 1547, and all the ancient solemnities were publicly observed. The king was crowned by Archbishop Cranmer. On this occasion the Archbishop really distinguished himself, and demonstrated to the world his abject servility to the king and his "regency council." In the course of his address to the king, couched in the language of the "Anglican Homilies," he incorporated this angelic admonition.

"Your Highness, as God's Vice-regent on earth, within your dominions, is bound to see that those committed to your governess, God be truly worshipped, idolatry destroyed, images removed, and the tyranny of the Roman bishops overthrown." (Heylin's History of England, London, 1611.)

Conforming to Henry VIII's direction Cranmer had ever maintained that "all jurisdiction, both spiritual and temporal was vested in and came from the king alone." It was set forth by act of parliament at the insistence of Cranmer, that "henceforth, the deans and chapters could not elect their bishops, but that all bishops would be appointed like the judges and other civil magistrates, by 'letters Patent' subject to removal at the monarch's pleasure." (Act I—Edward VI.)

This act of parliament further decreed that all citations and legal processes previously issued in the names of the various bishops should be sent out thereafter in the name of the king, and be sealed with the royal arms of the boy-king, "Supreme Head of the Church" though the bishops were required to countersign them. The "pallium," the true symbol of the spiritual jurisdiction, which for centuries appeared in the armorial bearings of the "See of York," was discarded, and the royal crown and crossed keys were submitted; they still remain the official court coat of arms borne by the Primate of England.

In May 1547, mandates in the king's name were issued by the "regency council" suspending all bishops from exercising any jurisdiction whatsoever. The parish clergy were forbidden to preach unless by license granted by "commissioners," invariably laymen, appointed by the "regency council."

Even the exalted position of Cranmer as Primate of England, and the moving spirit in the promulgating of the new rules regarding "letters patent" was not exempt. He took out a new "patent" for himself. His act of perfidy on the day of his consecration in no sense was a protection. The regency council was in the saddle, and he made certain that his position under this ruthless group would be as secure as human chicanery could make it. He knew the boy-king was in the hands of the "lord protector," and the day was not too distant when he would be no more.

One of the striking innovations in the new order was the publishing of the "Book of Homilies," the major portion of which was the work of Cranmer. In his preamble he states: "they were intended to bring to the people the principles of the true religion." Inasmuch as the clergy had been expressly forbidden by the king's regency council to preach their own sermons, they were ordered to read these ridiculous compositions to their congregations, many of which were in no wise satisfied with the sentiments expressed. They were particularly offensive to the Catholic and conservative nobility, but this resentment was the purpose of their creation.

A paragraph taken from the third part of the sermon against "perils of idolatry" (published in "Homilies" at Oxford in 1816 —page 222) recorded in Dr. F. G. Lee's volume on Edward the VI, second volume, page 74, will suffice to show the venom spread throughout the kingdom. It states: "True religion then, and pleasing of God, standeth not in making, setting up, painting, gilding, clothing and decking up of dead and dumb images (which be but great puppets and babies for old folks and fools in dotage, and wicked idolatry, to dally and play with) nor in kissing of them, incensing of them, setting up of candles, hanging up of legs, arms, or whole bodies of wax before them, of praying or asking of them, or of saints, things belonging only to God to give. But all these be vain and abominable, and most damnable before God." This seraphic outburst is hardly proof of the assertion contained in the "39 Articles of Religion" that the book of Homilies "contain a goodly and wholesome doctrine necessary for the times."

Inasmuch as preaching by priests without licence from lay commissioners was enforced, and the reading of the Book of Homilies was also mandatory, the ecclesiastical authorities deemed further innovations were required to efface all resemblances of Popish formularies and so ordered that a "Book of Common Prayer" be instituted. Accordingly, on the 4th of November 1548, the new book of common prayer was sanctioned by parliament in special session (incidentally, it was the only sanction it ever received). It was accepted by the hierarchy and clergy individually.

When parliament approved its use as mandatory in the Church of England, the same enactment abolished the "statutes of Six Articles" which were ordered by Henry VIII and approved by Cranmer. The particular innovation most acceptable to Archbishop Cranmer was that which permitted the clergy to marry, so there was no further need of him visiting his wife clandestinely, so she moved into Lambeth Palace with him, and "they lived happily ever after."

The same parliament ordered the celebration of Holy Communion under both forms of bread and wine to be administered to the people, changing its designation from Holy Eucharist, to the "supper of the Lord," but denying the Real Presence.

The advent of the new book of common prayer was pleasing to the innovators. It destroyed every vestige of the ancient faith, but in so doing it created spiritual chaos. Because of the confusion and indecision it had to be revised in 1552 within less than two years of its publication. As it was the child of parliament, no other authority could change it, and accordingly acting under the advice of the king's "privy council" parliament revamped the book. Again with the approval of Archbishop Cranmer it was ordered to be used in the churches.

The boy-king died on July 6, 1553. Ironically it was the same day of the month that his father, Henry VIII ordered the cruel murder of his brilliant Lord Chancellor, Sir Thomas More. The king Edward VI was buried from Westminister Abbey, the Protestant services being conducted by Archbishop Cranmer.

The boy-king Edward had become bitterly anti-Catholic, and one of his last acts as king (he was now 15 years old) was the signing of "devices" so called, which automatically excluded his half-sisters Mary and Elizabeth from succeeding him on the throne. He directed that Lady Grey, a granddaughter of his father's sister Mary, should succeed him on the throne. Cranmer, Lord Somerset, the two Lords Dudley and Lady Grey's husband were all in the plot and agreed to place her on the throne of England. She lasted just nine days on the throne. The people all over the land rebelled and Mary Tudor, daughter of Henry VIII and Queen Catherine of Aragon, was crowned Queen of England.

The conduct of all participating in the plot to deprive England of a Catholic queen (with the exception of Cranmer) might be excused upon the grounds of personal aggrandisement. Not so however with Cranmer. He was father confessor to King Henry VIII. He made solemn promise to his king, on his death-bed, that he would safeguard his daughter's succession, and yet he deliberately entered into this despicable plot to depirve Mary of her throne as Queen of England. Anglican historians attempt to color the venality of Cranmer's act by asserting pressure was exerted by the Privy Council to protect themselves in the plundering of the church revenues and property, but an altogether different interpretation can be arrived at by recalling the leading part Cranmer had played in ruining the life of Mary's mother, Catharine of Aragon. Cranmer was no fool, whatever else he may be termed. He was an opportunist, yet he knew his race was run with the accession of Mary to the throne.

Cranmer's star had set. The failure to keep Lady Jane Grey upon the throne had wrecked the fortunes of all concerned in the plot. The return of Catholicism under Queen Mary naturally foretold the exit of those prelates who had proven false to the principles of the Catholic faith and traitors to the Holy See. Cranmer retired to Lambeth Palace and had he remained quiescently aloof from church affairs he would in all probability have been permitted to remain there without participating in any ecclesiastical function.

The Latin Mass had been restored in the kingdom, and when publicly celebrated in the Cathedral of Canterbury and other Anglican churches, it was pointedly rumored that Cranmer, to gain favor with Queen Mary, had suggested the celebration of the Latin Mass and had actually pontificated at the Cathedral. Concerning these rumors, Dixon (Anglican historian) in his "History of England" volume IV, page 37, states: "Cranmer, having learned that he was charged with offering to celebrate the Latin Mass in the Cathedral became so enraged, he threw discretion to the winds, and issued his celebrated venomous tirade against the Mass, a renunciation so complete that it should settle for all time the question whether the Church of England teaches or believes in the sacrifice of the Mass or a sacrificing priesthood." From the renunciation of Cranmer, this is taken:

"As the devil, Christ's ancient adversary is a liar, and the father of all lies, even so hath it stirred up his servants and members to persecute Christ, and His true word and religion, which he ceaseth not to do most earnestly at this present. For whereas the most noble prince of famous memory, King Henry VIII the Vice-regent of God, seeing the great abuses of the Latin Masses, reformed something therein, in this time; and also our late Sovereign Lord, Edward VI, took the same whole away, for the manifold errors and abuses thereof, and restored in the place thereof the Lord's Holy Supper, according to Christ's own institution, and as the Apostles in the primitive church used the same in the beginning, the devil goeth about by lying, to overthrow the church, and the Lord's Holy Supper, and to restore the Latin satisfactory Masses, a thing of his own invention and devise. And to bring the same more easily to pass, some have abused the name of me, Thomas, Archbishop of Canterbury, and that I offered to say Mass before the 'Queen's Highness' and at St. Paul's Church and I wot not where. I have been well exercised these twenty years to suffer and bear evil reports and lies and have not been much aggrieved thereat, and have borne all things quietly. Yet, when untrue reports and lies turn to the hindrance of God's truth they be in no wise to be tolerated and suffered.

"Wherefore, these be to signify to the world, that it was not I that did set up the Mass at Canterbury; but it was a false, flattering, lying and dissembling monk which caused the Mass to be set up there without my consent and counsel. And as for offering myself to say Mass before the 'Queen's Highness,' or in any other place I never did, as Her Grace knoweth well. . . . But if Her Grace will give me leave, I shall be ready to prove against all who say the contrary, that the Communion Book, set forth by the most innocent and godly Prince, Edward VI in his high court of Parliament, is conformable to the order which our Saviour Christ did both observe and command to be observed, and which His disciples, and Apostles, and primitive church used many years.

"Whereas the Mass in many things not only hath no foundation of Christ, His apostles or the primitive church, but also is manifestly contrary to the same, and contains many horrible blasphemies in it; and although many either unlearned or maliciously do not report that Mr. Peter Martyr, is unlearned, yet if the Queen's Highness will grant thereunto I with the said Peter Martyr, and other four or five which I shall choose, will by God's grace, take upon us to defend that, that not only our common prayers of the churches, ministrations of sacraments, and other rites and ceremonies, but also that all the doctrine and religion by our said sovereign Lord, King Edward VI is more pure and according to God's word, than any that had been used in England these thousand years; so that God's own word may be the judge, and that reason and proofs may be set in writing, to the intent as well that all the world examine and judge them, as that no man shall start back from their writing; and what faith there had been in the church these fifteen hundred years past.

And we shall prove that the order of the church set out at this present in this church of England by Act of Parliament is the same that was used in the church fifteen hundred years past, and so shall they never be able to prove theirs."

Shortly after this tirade against the Mass, Cranmer was summoned before the council of Bishops Bench and interrogated by Bishop Heath concerning his "declarations," and it was gently intimated that he was undoubtedly sorry he had written them, and inferentially assured that forgiveness might be forthcoming if he desired to recant. But Cranmer was adamant. He truculently declared: "As I do not deny myself to be the author of that letter, so must I confess here unto you that I am sorry that the said letter went from me in such sort as it did. For when I had written it, Master Scory got firstly the copy off me, and as it is come abroad, and as I understand, the city is full of it; for which I am sorry that it is so passed my hands for I had intended otherwise to have it in a more large and ample manner, and minded to have it set on St. Paul's door, and on the doors of all the churches in London, with mine own seal upon it."

The final chapter in Cranmer's life was written when Queen Mary took over the reins of government. She had deep-seated hatred for Cranmer, which is understandable, for, although a Queen ruling over millions of people, she also had a human hatred for those found guilty of attempting her destruction. She had two heart-rending experiences, and both seared her soul. She knew the double-dealing of Cranmer, in betraying her Father's trust to protect her interests in the succession to the throne; she also knew he had agreed to the devices of her half-brother, the boy-king, Edward VI, in his attempt to seat Lady Jane Grey upon the throne. Mary was a Queen, but she was also a firm believer in the age-old doctrine, "eye for an eye, tooth for a tooth."

So it was not surprising that Cranmer was summoned to appear before the Council to answer for his part in the treasonable plot against Mary. Most of the Council had supported Jane Grey, but they thoroughly absolved themselves from prosecution by agreeing to sit in judgment upon their former associate, Archbishop Cranmer. He was reprimanded by the Council and remanded to the Tower of London to await the Queen's action, on the 14th day of September 1553. His former associates, Bishops Ridley and Lattimer, were also confined there.

Queen Mary was determined to punish Cranmer, yet her respect for a Catholic Bishop would not permit her to sanction trial of a Bishop before a secular court. He was tried by an ecclesiastical court and found guilty of heresy. Because of his attitude against Holy Mass, he was judged contumaceous by the Holy Father. A commission from Rome was sent to publicly degrade him by stripping him of his episcopal robes. He was burned at the stake for heresy in November 1556. There is considerable controversy among English historians as to whether Cranmer died for treason or heresy. He was found guilty on both charges, and inasmuch as he was burned at the stake for heresy— there should be no doubt concerning it. If it was judgment on treason alone, he would have been beheaded. His present day defenders will argue until "the cows come home" that he was innocent on both counts, a victim of the hatred of "bloody Mary."

In many respects, Archbishop Cranmer was like Martin Luther. He was solemnly ordained a Catholic priest, and a consecrated Bishop. (Luther was not a bishop, though he consecrated several renegade priests who followed him.) Like Luther he violated his vows of chastity and celibacy. Like Luther he threw off his allegiance to the Vicar of Christ and persecuted his priesthood; like Luther he annulled valid marriages among so-called nobles to enlist their support in his struggle with Rome. Like Luther he abolished the Mass, and in imitation of Luther in posting his ninety-five theses upon the doors of St. Paul's church at Wittenburg, he proved to the world that misplaced ambition, rather than spiritual leadership motivated his rebellion against Holy Mother Church.

QUEEN MARY TUDOR

On October 1, 1553, Princess Mary Tudor was crowned Queen of England in Westminister Abbey by Stephen Gardiner, Bishop of Winchester. By tradition the crowning of an English Sovereign was reserved to the Archbishop of Canterbury, but Cranmer was in prison on charges of heresy and treason. The consecration and coronation by Bishop Gardiner was quite a reversal in the lives of both Queen and consecrating Bishop. Gardiner had been especially active in the attempt to force Queen Catherine to agree to an annulment of her marriage to Henry VIII going so far as the threat of death if she did not agree to the plans of Henry to divorce her. He later made public recantation of his bitter acts against Catherine, and was restored to the good graces of Queen Mary by her personal selection of him as Lord Chancellor of England; he remained loyal to her until she died.

Thursday October 15, 1553, the Parliament of Queen Mary met to effect the restoration of the ancient Faith as it was at the time of the death of Mary's father Henry VIII. The "Nine Articles" of Edward's reign were repealed. By so doing Parliament destroyed Cranmer's mixture of Catholicism, Lutheranism, Presbyterianism, and Calvinism. They were all outlawed as doctrines of the Church of England. The stage was set for the return of the Church of England to Papal obedience and supremacy in all things, spiritual and ecclesiastical.

To bring this about it was mandatory that the "Bill of Attainder" passed by Parliament against Reginald Pole, the Pope's Legate, be rescinded. This was done on the 12th day of November 1553, and on the twentieth day of November 1553, Pole arrived at Dover, England, where he was received with all the honors reserved for royalty.

On the following day (November 21st), both houses in session passed a resolution to return to the Catholic faith and Roman obedience. On November 23, 1553, Cardinal Pole pronounced the words of absolution "from all heresy and schism, and all judgments, censures, and penalties for that cause incurred" and restored them to the bosom and Communion of Holy Mother Church, in the name of the Father, Son, and Holy Ghost. (Journal of House of Commons, page 38, 1553.)

On the first Sunday of Advent, Cardinal Pole attended High Mass at St. Paul's Cathedral. Bishop Gardiner, Lord Chancellor of England, preached the sermon that reverberated throughout England. In his condemnation of those who were guilty of rebellion against their lawful Queen, and traitorous also to Christ's Vicar, he did not exclude himself. He made no attempt to deny his leadership in both fields; he asked God to pardon him for the dastardly part he had played in the plots to destroy his lawful Queen, and Christ's church. He welcomed the Pope's Legate, Cardinal Pole, assuring him of a great resurgence to allegiance to the Holy Father, and prayerfully besought the support of the Legate in their desire to be returned to membership in the Church of Christ. Thursday following, both Houses of Parliament called upon Cardinal Pole at Lambeth Palace, and humbly kneeling before him, received absolution "from all heresies, and schisms, and perjuries." An explanatory digression is in order here to clearly understand the status of Cardinal Pole, in these momentous happenings.

Cardinal Pole was appointed "Legate De Latere" to Queen Mary, on August 5, 1553. He was a Cardinal Deacon (not at this time an ordained priest). His Legatine powers were of such profound scope he was authorized under his "Letters Patent" from the Holy Father to use his own discretion in his approach to the settlement of the rebellion against Papal jurisdiction. Of course his policy was previously set at Rome insofar as valid or invalid ordinations and consecrations were concerned, but great latitude was given him.

One of the greatest problems confronting Cardinal Pole was rectifying the canonical standing of bishops and priests who had received "orders" or consecrations since the breach with the Apostolic See. He separated the clergy ordained into classes: one, containing those ordained in schism, but validly, according to the Roman Ordinal or Catholic Rite, and the other group consisting of those ordained or consecrated under the Rite of the "Edwardine Ordinal" drawn up by the Archbishop of Canterbury, Thomas N. Cranmer, which was enforced by Act of Parliament on April 1, 1550.

The first group, upon submission to Papal authority were absolved and penance imposed, and their faculties restored. Those of the second group, however, were considered as laymen, and dismissed without penance or absolution. They were acting as priests, but, possessing no valid orders, could violate none. Their crimes were mostly of deception and presumption but, acting as they did, they were guilty of sacrilegious conduct. These latter cases were entirely within the scope of Pole's discretion.

Dispute between Rome and the Anglican Church has gone on for four centuries as to Cardinal Pole's action concerning priests he found ordained under the "Edwardine Ordinal." The Anglicans maintain that there never was question as to orders and that Pole stated that Anglican orders were valid; but aver the only impediment Pole found was that many of the priests had married, and on those grounds alone he refused to permit them to perform their priestly functions, further stating that when these married priests agreed to set aside their wives and did, he would permit them to function, and restored their faculties. History, to the contrary, does not record one instance of a Protestant minister (as Anglican clergy ordained under the "Edwardine Ordinal" actually are) being allowed to officiate as priests or bishops without having Orders unconditionally conferred upon them by valid Catholic bishops.

Cardinal Pole meticulously carried out the orders contained in the declaratory brief of Pope Paul IV issued to him on October 30, 1555, to wit: he authorized Queen Mary to despose all bishops who had been ordained with the perverted Anglican Rite from their Sees, and to deprive them of their benefices. Many of the bishops had given great scandal to the people and their outrageously blasphemous outbursts against the Holy Eucharist and the Mass did not warrant their being validly advanced to Holy Orders in the Catholic Church.

The bishops consecrated under the "Edwardine Ordinal" were Robert Ferrar, bishop of St. David's, 1548; John Poynet, bishop of Winchester, 1550; John Scory, bishop of Rochester, 1551; Miles Coverdale, bishop of Exeter, 1551; John Taylor, bishop of Lincoln, 1552; John Harlow, bishop of Hereford, 1553, and John Hooper, bishop of Gloucester, 1552.

All these bishops were nominated by the privy-council to the boy king, Edward VI, under letters patent signed by the king. They were consecrated by schismatic bishops, under the Edwardine Rite, and all were deposed from their Sees by order of Queen Mary.

There were also two groups of validly consecrated Catholic bishops. One group had fallen into grievous sin by acquiescing in the king's "supremacy in the church of England." They repented, and proved their allegiance to the Vicar of Christ, by refusing later to accept Queen Elizabeth as "Supreme Governor of the Church of England," and suffered deposition from their Sees.

There were also other groups of clergy, validly ordained and consecrated whom Pole would not permit to remain in their

Sees because of their heretical acts and teaching, as their lives public and private were scandalous causing grave injury to religion and the Church.

There was no question of validity of orders, either as priests or bishops. The only issue was their refusal to renounce their heretical tendencies, and set aside their concubines. Their rebellion to Pole's orders resulted in the permanent vacancy of their Sees, and deprivation of their status as bishops of the Catholic Church.

The Queen's Decree, approved by the Pope's Legate Pole stated: "As to those who have already been promoted to any kind of 'orders' according to the newly fabricated method of ordaining, seeing that truly and as a matter of fact they have not been ordained at all, the diocesan Bishop, if he finds them fit and worthy, may supply what was wanting in the said persons—by their being unconditionally reordained as priests or bishops, according to the requirements of each case." This decree was issued on March 4, 1554.

As stated concerning Anglican priests ordained under the "Edward VI Ordinal" so too does it hold true relative to Anglican bishops, consecrated under the same Rite. Not one instance exists wherein a bishop consecrated under the "Edwardine Ordinal" was permitted to occupy his See during the reign of Queen Mary. And those schismatic bishops who were degraded, were degraded from the priestly office only as they had been ordained "ritu catholica"; that is, according to the Catholic rite of ordination.

This fact is further confirmed by the action of Rome in the cases of Archbishop Cranmer, Bishops Latimer and Ridley. When they were condemned to death, they were publicly stripped of all the insignia of their Episcopal office. They were validly consecrated bishops of the Catholic Church.

The decree of Queen Mary concerning the re-ordination of

Anglican clergy was strengthened by Pope Paul IV, when on June 20, 1555, he issued his "Authoritative Bull, Praeclara Carissimi" stating that the ministers of the Anglican church had to be reordained correctly, and until such time as they conformed they were not to perform any ecclesiastical duties in the restored Catholic Church.

Three years after the restoration of the Church of England to unity with Rome, Reginald, Cardinal Pole was preconized Archbishop of Canterbury. This exalted station, Primate of all England, necessitated sacerdotal powers. Accordingly on March 20, 1556, Pole was ordained priest at Lambeth Chapel, and on the 22nd of March 1556 (Sunday) he was consecrated Archbishop of Canterbury at Greenwich Friars Church, and on the following Wednesday the pallium was bestowed upon him in the Church of St. Mary's of the Arches (Bow Church in Cheaps) (Writhley's Chronicles, Vol. 2, page 134, 1556). Reginald, Cardinal Pole, passed away on November 17, 1558 at Lambeth Palace. He survived his great friend Queen Mary by one day; she died on November 16, 1558.

Two great souls went to their Maker. Each had rendered distinctive service to God, country, and Christ's church. Each left a legacy of loyalty and obedience to Christ's Vicar on earth of which the Catholic world is justly proud. Historians, partisan, bitter and prejudiced, attempt to belittle them and their accomplishments as Queen and Legate, but the recording Angel has the correct account of their stewardship, and while history is written and read their names will be emblazoned upon the walls of time. They belong to the ages, mortal, yet immortal.

Chapter Three

William Barlow, Consecrator of Matthew Parker, the designated first Anglican Archbishop of Canterbury, was one of the most important personalities in the establishment of the Elizabethan Anglican Church. He was chaplain to King Henry VIII, and by him was appointed in the "reformed" Church of England. He was confirmed by Thomas Cranmer, Archbishop and Primate of all England; but he was never *consecrated* a bishop in any church.

The validity of Anglican Orders must stand or fall upon the status of William Barlow as a validly consecrated Catholic Bishop in the years before the so-called "Reformation." It is of the utmost importance that thorough examination be made of the various stages in his career before his acceptance as a bishop in the Church of England, in which he served as such for more than thirty years.

William Barlow was duly ordained a priest in the Catholic Church; he was a professed Augustinian Friar, at St. Osith's Priory, in Essex; Henry VIII appointed him chaplain to Ann Boleyn, and he served her diligently until she became Queen of England. Just why a mistress of a married man (even though he be king) should require the attendance of a private chaplain is something that surely intrigues, and his attention to his spiritual responsibilities must have been patterned after the absentee landlords in Ireland. They collected the rents, but were never concerned about the leaks in the roof. In spite of the priestly presence, much to the embarrassment of the King, she was found to be with child.

Exhaustive research from every available source has been made to establish the valid consecration of William Barlow as a bishop in any church; Diocesan rolls, registers, writers of contemporary history, both civil and ecclesiastical, have been scrupulously examined, but no record of Barlow's "consecration," valid or invalid, can be found.

In 1847, over one hundred years ago, one Mr. Sergent Edward Bellasis published a volume, under the title of "WAS BARLOW A BISHOP?" In his investigations he apparently had access to the various registers in the dioceses concerned. In letters to prelates and clergy he delves quite deeply into the subject. He proves definitely that in the registers of St. Asaph, Bath and Wells, St. David's, or Chichester, no record of a consecration of Barlow as bishop could be found.

The chronology of Barlow as bishop can be briefly summed up in this wise: he was *presumed* to have been consecrated Bishop of St. David's; his first assignment was the bishopric of St. Asaph in 1536; shortly after he was translated to Bath and Wells, which See he resigned on the accession of Queen Mary; he went into hiding on the continent (as he stated) in fear of his life; but no proof of this statement was ever produced.

When Queen Elizabeth came to the throne, Barlow returned to England and shortly after he received the "Royal Mandate" to consecrate Matthew Parker as Archbishop of Canterbury.

No question was ever raised as to Barlow's occupancy of the Sees mentioned. The only question involved is, was *Barlow ever consecrated* bishop in any church?

The Anglican historian, Thomas Rymer states that Barlow was elected bishop of St. Asaph in January 1535, and the mandate for his consecration was dated February 2, 1536, but although Cranmer's register at Lambeth Palace is very meticulous about recording all consecrations of bishops during his Archepiscopate, *there is no record* of the consecration of Barlow; everything else appertaining to election, confirmation, is documented; but of consecration not a word is recorded. The king's mandate to Cranmer to consecrate Barlow was dated February 2, 1536; on the eighteenth day of the same month the bishop of St. Asaph died, and Barlow was translated to St. David's. The enigma is—was Barlow consecrated bishop before translation to St. David's, and if so, by whom?

The Roman position that Barlow was never consecrated is confirmed by the language in the licence to the Dean and chapter of St. Asaph, to proceed to the election of a successor to Barlow. He is referred to as "Bishop-elect," and the cause of the vacancy is described as his exchange. The exact words were "vacante transmutationem, Wilhelm Barlow ultimi-electi." The designation of "Bishop-elect" is used in all documents affecting the exchange and this would not be so had he been consecrated a bishop. The consecration of Robert Wharton as the successor to Barlow as bishop of St. Asaph is duly recorded in Cranmer's Register at Lambeth Palace, as well as in the Register of St. Asaph.

In "John Strypes Memorials, "Vol. I—page 347, it appears that Thomas Holcroft and William Barlow, "Bishop-elect" of St. Asaph, were sent by Henry VIII into Scotland to interest the King of Scotland to throw off the authority of the Pope of Rome in the church of Scotland, and Strype definitely proves it would be humanly impossible for Barlow to have returned from Scotland in time to be consecrated bishop under the mandate of February 2, 1536, and therefore he was *not consecrated* as bishop of St. Asaph. The statement is corroborated by the final entry in Cranmer's Register 196-B, concerning Barlow as "Bishop-elect." The sentence in the Register reads *"per liberam transmutationem*

D'ni Wilhi Barlow, ultimo Episcopo-electi, et confirmati."

The absence of any mention of consecration certainly supports the Roman position that Barlow was never consecrated Bishop of St. Asaph. Does a similar situation hold true as regards the See of St. David's?

Thomas Rymer presents the following facts which substantiate the Roman position on Barlow's non-consecration as a bishop in the Church of England. He states:

"The records in the register of St. David's show he was elected to St. David's, April 10, 1536, and election was confirmed April 21—eleven days later. He received the grant of 'temporalities' of St. David's on April 26, 1536, and from that day he styled himself as 'Bishop of St. David's.' The records in St. David's Register state he was summoned to Parliament as Bishop of St. David's April 27, 1536. He was enthroned Bishop of St. David's on May 1, 1536. No claim for consecration from that date has been made by any reliable Anglican ecclesiastical authority."

Because Barlow received his grant of "temporalities" on April 26, 1536, two of his defenders, namely, Father Courayer, a French apostate monk, and Dr. F. G. Lee, Anglican, maintain Barlow must have been consecrated on Sunday April 30, 1536. This statement has no support in Cranmer's Lambeth Register, for during 1536 the Episcopal consecrations were held on May 19, June 11, July 2, and October 22, 1536. (None were held on April 23, 1536. Stubb's Registrum Sacrum, pages 77-78.)

From the year 1534 when Papal Supremacy was abolished by Henry VIII, and during the reign of the boy-king Edward VI it was the law to recite in the grant of "temporalities," that all the conditions for a legal consecration had been complied with, namely, *congi d'elire,* election, royal assent, investiture with Episcopal insignia and the accepted homage and fealty of the nominee had been complied with. The fact of *consecration* was always mandatory. To prove consecration was insisted upon as the most vital act in the making of a bishop, Thomas Rymer, Anglican historian, quotes the mandate from the King concerning the consecration of Edward Fox, High Almoner of England, to the bishopric of Hereford. The mandate reads:

"By this Writ, We command that you confirm the election, and the person of the 'elect' with all convenient dispatch, and that you duly import to the same, and to his person, the gift of *consecration,* as it is meet; and that you do and execute all other and singular things pertaining to, or which in any way pertain together, or successfully, and successively to the conferring of such *confirmation and consecration.* Then follows the granting of the 'temporalities' of the See.

"Whereas, the Most Reverend Father in Christ, Thomas, Archbishop of Canterbury, hath consecrated Edward Fox a Bishop, and hath invested him with 'Episcopal Insignia' as it appeareth from his 'letters patent' directed unto US."

Different indeed is the mandate concerning Barlow's elevation to the See of St. David. It will be noted that it recites his nomination, election and confirmation, as Bishop of St. David's, but not a word as to his *consecration.* The Mandate reads:

"Henry the VIII, Defender of the Faith, Supreme Head of the Church of England, and in Earth, both spiritual and temporal.

"To all whom these 'Presents' concern;
Greetings:

"Know ye, that whereas the Cathedral church of St. David's by the death of Richard Rawlins, late Bishop of St. David's has been widowed, and deprived of pastoral care and comfort, and is thereby vacant and;

"Whereas:

On that account all the proceeds, and profits, farm rents, reversions, together with all the beneficial uses, and temporal emoluments of the said 'Bishopric' have belonged and accrued to US, by the right of our royal prerogatives, and the

same are known, and to belong and accrue, and
"Whereas:

The Precentor and Chapter of the said Cathedral church, after the death of the said bishop, with OUR approval, and previous licence have chosen for their bishop and pastor our well beloved and faithful William Barlow, named by US as their bishop, and,
"Whereas:

The most reverend Father in Christ, Thomas, Archbishop of Canterbury, hath accepted and confirmed that election; and hath set over the aforesaid church of St. David's the said bishop so elected, as appeareth to US directed by 'letter Patent' from the said Archbishop, We, now, for certain causes and considerations moving US, and for the sincere affection which WE have and bear towards him the aforesaid bishop have hereby, with special favor, and with certain knowledge and of OUR own free act, given and granted, and do by these Presents give and grant to the same NOW Bishop all and singular the issues and lands etc. during his life. In testimony wherefore, WE have set OUR hand, and caused the Great Seal to be affixed April 26, 1536."

This document clearly proves that Barlow had not been consecrated bishop up to April 26, 1536, and also furnishes the reason why he was not subsequently consecrated; the reason being Henry VIII took to himself all rights as "Supreme Head of the Church of England," respecting appointments of bishops, without further consecration by the Episcopacy. It is evident from writings and public utterances by Cranmer that he subscribed to the pretentions of King Henry VIII; he did not intend to suffer the king's wrath as did Cardinal Wolsey. In the vernacular of the street, he intended to "feather his own nest; feather it he did, but he also fouled it."

There is an old truism, that facts are stubborn things, difficult to circumvent; so, when the statement is made without malice, the Archbishop Cranmer was more interested in appeasing the king (that is to say agreeing rightly or wrongly to any of his acts) than he was in asserting his rights as Primate of England, his official subserviency to the acts lends confirmation to the assertion. In "Burnett's History of the English Reformation" Vol. I—page 201 it is recorded that Archbishop Cranmer speaking as Primate of England states:

"The ministry of God's word under His Majesty be bishops, parsons, and such other priests as be appointed by his Majesty, to that ministration, as for example, the bishop of Canterbury, the bishop of Durham, the parson of Winiwick, and such others; said officers be appointed, assigned and elected in any place by the laws and orders of kings and princes. In the admission of many of these officers, be comely ceremonies and solemnities, *and which be not of necessity,* but only for a good order and seemly fashion, for if such offices and ministrations were committed without such solemnities, they were nevertheless *duly committed;* and there is no more promise of God's grace given in the ecclesiastical office, than it is in the civil office."

This statement by Archbishop Cranmer is ecclesiastical recognition of the king's right and power to appoint any ecclesiastical official without further consideration by Episcopal authority. In a word it grants to a layman the authority and power vested solely in the Pope of Rome, Vice-regent of Christ on earth, chief pastor of the universal church, or some other ecclesiastical authority designated by him.

In the grant of temporalities given to Barlow in the mandate of his appointment as bishop of St. David's *without consecration,* we have as complete an example of "Erastianism" as history records. The king practically tells the Episcopacy "I have appointed Barlow a bishop; Cranmer has confirmed him, and no further consecration is necessary, and that now he is a bishop, and what are ye going to do about it?"

If any of the hierarchy dared question the validity of Barlow's appointment, it would be equivalent to challenging the king's supremacy, and none there were who would dare to expose themselves to the consequences of so rash an act. Unfortunately, there were too few Fisher's and More's among the Anglican hierarchy.

There is final proof that Barlow was never consecrated a bishop. It can be found in "Bramhill's Works," third volume, preface "Anglo-Catholic Library" in which the Rev. Dr. Haddon, editor of "Bramhill's Works" argues that Barlow must have been consecrated on June 11, 1536, along with bishop Repps of Norwich, because that was the day in June, 1536, on which any consecration is recorded to have taken place; so that if he was not consecrated on that day, he was not consecrated at all, and there is no record of Barlow being present at the consecration held on June 11, 1536.

Finally, both bishops Repp and Barlow took their seats in the House of Lords on June 30, 1536. If they had been consecrated together Barlow would have taken precedence, because he was "elected" April 10, confirmed April 21, and enthroned May 31, 1536, whereas bishop Repps was not "elected" until May 31, 1536.

The precedence given bishop Repps in the House of Lords proves they were not consecrated together. As fact, Barlow took his seat as *Custos Spiritualitatis* rather than as a consecrated bishop. The discovery of Barlow's "dyetts" in the office of the exchequer to the Garter-king-at-arms, is described as "bishop-elect" proves conclusively that Barlow was not consecrated on June 11, 1536. The date of the payment of Barlow's "dyetts" is given as June 12, 1536, and it is nowhere contended that he was consecrated, after taking his seat in the House of Lords.

Barlow's opinion of the necessity of consecration is best expressed in a sermon delivered by him in St. David's cathedral on November 12, 1536, and recorded in Strype's Memorials, volume I—page 184—record 77, wherein he said:

"If the king's grace, being Supreme Head of the Church of England, did choose, denominate and elect any man, being learned, to be a bishop, then he is chosen, without mention of any 'orders' should be as good a bishop as he is, or the best in England." It is also a matter of record, duly chronicled in John Strype's Memorials, that both Archbishop Cranmer and Barlow agreed that, for making a bishop, election or appointing by the king is sufficient. They jointly pronounce:

"Making of bishops hath two parts, appointing and 'ordering'; appointment, which the apostles by necessity made by common election, and sometimes by their own assignment, could not then be done by Christian princes, because at that time they were not; and now in these days, the power appertaineth to christian princes and rulers."

The king (Henry VIII) was quick to take advantage of this situation by reminding them that they confessed the apostles did occupy the one part that was now occupied by princes, so how could it prove that "ordering" was reserved to bishops. This attitude of the king was supported by Cranmer and Barlow. They agreed in the all-sufficiency of the royal power to create a bishop. The king, Barlow and Cranmer agreed there was no need for consecration, and in this position they were wholeheartedly supported by Lord Chancellor and Cromwell, Vicar-General.

The failure of any register to record the consecration of Barlow as bishop is admitted by Rev. Dr. Bailey in an article published in his book "Defense of Holy Orders in the Church of England" page 45—Vol. I wherein he states:

"We admit that in Cranmer's register the consecration of Barlow is not to be found, but his election and confirmation only; but, neither are those of many others whose consecrations have never been questioned by anyone"; he further states that after the word "confirmation" the whole half of the page was left vacant, suggesting the registrar forgot to fill it in. This statement is puerile and can not be seriously considered. The part played by Barlow in the consecration of Matthew Parker, the first "Elizabethan Anglican Archbishop," was too important to be frivolously accepted. The only reason Barlow's consecration was not recorded is—that *Barlow was never consecrated,* and no record could be made. Rev. Dr. Haddon, editor of Bramhill's Works, petulantly remarks that "the consecration of bishops Fox of Hereford, Latimer of Worcester, Sampson of Chichester, are not entered in Cranmer's register, and no one ever questioned their consecration.

There is nothing analogous in these two situations. The date of their consecration, and the names of the consecrator, and assistant consecrators, appear in their own diocesan registers, so their absence from Cranmer's register is of no significance.

In the light of the indisputable facts presented, it is impossible for the church of England to prove a valid consecration of William Barlow as a bishop *in any church.* But it is also true, that even if consecration could be established it still would have no effect upon the question of validity of Anglican orders, as a perverted rite had been in use during and after the reign of Edward VI, which definitely did not comprise the elements that the Catholic Church required for a valid consecration.

The opposite is also true. If a schismatical or heretical bishop or bishops, ordaining or consecrating, according to the Roman Pontifical had the intention to ordain sacrificing priests, and true bishops according to the requirements of the Roman Catholic Church, both ordinations and consecrations would be valid, but illicit.

Barlow had achieved all he desired, temporalities, possession of his see for life, and his seat in the House of Lords, and consequently was in no wise concerned with such a trivial thing as consecration.

The Barlow consecration is therefore a mystery, which four hundred years has failed to unravel. Until such time as the consecration of Barlow can be authoritatively established, the entire question of Apostolic succession in the church of England will remain as settled by Popes Clement VII, Julius III, Paul III, Paul IV, and Leo XIII. Each in succession declared: The Church of England is not in possession of the apostolic succession, and their orders are null and void from the beginning.

It is very strange, that Anglican clergy seem to evade discussing the status of Barlow's consecration. They content themselves by citing his long tenure of thirty years as bishop of St. David Diocese, and will observe that the Archbishop of Canterbury was responsible to God for the administration of His Church, and would not in conscience permit it.

Chapter Four

Queen Elizabeth ascended the throne of England in November, 1558, succeeding her half-sister Queen Mary Tudor, who during her reign restored England to unity with the Papal authority.

The repudiation of this re-union was the first serious business of the new Queen. She was definitely anti-Catholic. She was poignantly aware that Rome knew of her illegitimacy, and despite the action of her Parliament in enacting laws declaring her birth legitimate, the Pope would not accept her as legitimate.

Elizabeth revived all the anti-papal acts of her father, Henry VIII. She changed the title of Supreme Head of the Church to Supreme Governor of the Church of England, prayerfully admitting that "Jesus Christ was the Head of the Church," she was content to be recognized as the vice-regent in England, and supreme governor in all things, civil and spiritual.

When Elizabeth found there were ten vacancies among the hierarchy, she proceeded to fill them with clerics of her own choice who had renounced allegiance to the Vicar of Christ. There were also ten vacancies in ten other sees, caused by her action in deposing them.

There were five Catholic bishops in possession of their Sees, namely, Turnstall of Durham, Bourne of Bath and Wells, Pole of Peterborough, Furburville of Exeter, and Kitchen of Llandaff. With the exception of Kitchen all remained loyal to Rome.

In 1559, exercising her power as "Supreme Governor of the Church of England," she nominated Matthew Parker, former Dean of Lincoln to the See of Canterbury, to succeed Cardinal Pole who had died in November, 1558. She commanded bishop William Barlow to proceed with the consecration of Parker as Archbishop of Canterbury. The "Letters Patent" from the Queen were sent to Parker by Lord Chancellor Bacon, with a letter of the same date. Barlow had difficulty in procuring proper consecrators for the consecration of Parker. The Acts of Henry VIII required "that, a vacancy existing in the Archbishopric of Canterbury, the royal mandate must be addressed to any other archbishop and two bishops; or to any four bishops within the realm, or within any other of the king's dominions."

Besides the five Catholic bishops, there were also present the schismatic bishops (refugee's) Scory, Coverdale, Basle of Ossary, and several other suffragan bishops; but none answered to the requirements of "bishops within the realm."

The Queen was determined upon the consecration of Parker, and his enthronement as Archbishop of Canterbury but she also wanted validity in the consecration. She commanded that a commission be issued to the Catholic bishops Turnstall, Bourne, Pole and Kitchen, and for good measure she ordered the two schismatic bishops John Scory and Coverdale to participate also as co-consecrators.

The royal command to the Catholic bishops to consecrate Parker, a married priest, was a deliberately planned affront to these courageous servants of God. To accentuate the insult she also ordered two suspended excommunicated ecclesiasticals, Scory and Coverdale, be accepted as co-consecrators of Matthew Parker.

The Catholic bishops, as well as the Archbishop, refused to comply with the royal mandate to proceed with the consecration of Parker, and they were summarily deposed from their sees.

For four hundred years the question of the validity of Parker's consecration has been a controversial one. This does not mean that the Catholic church has any doubt or misgivings concerning validity; the uncertainty is all on the Protestant side of the issue; and it can best be ascertained which contention is supported, by factual recital of the various incidents which transpired prior to consecration. To clarify the question as to what ordinal was used in the consecration, facsimile of the Queen's letters patent which authorized the consecration of Parker is here reproduced, copied from "John Strype's Memorials," usually accepted as competent recordings of the events occurring during the establishment of the Elizabethan Anglican Church.

MANDATE TO CONSECRATE PARKER

1. Suite is to be made for the Queen's Letters Patent called "Significaverunt" to be addressed to the Archbishop of the province, for the confirmation of the "Elect," and for his consecration.

2. When the See Archiepiscopal is vacant then after election, like "Letters Patent" for the confirmation of the elect are to be directed to any other Archbishop within the Queen's dominions. If all be vacant, to four bishops to be appointed "BY THE QUEEN'S LETTERS PATENT" declaring her Grace's assent Royal with request for his consecration and pall.

3. The fealities for the temporalities of the See is to be made to Her Majesty; the oath also is to be given; and the ordinary fees to be paid to Her Majesty's officers.

4. The consecration is to be made on such Sunday as the consecrators and the consent of the consecrand shall accord.

5. The "Order of King Edward's Book" is to be observed for that there is none other "specially made" in the last session of Parliament.

The Queen's letters patent definitely establish two important defects in the Anglican Rite of consecration of a bishop, admitted by Parker in marginal notes, in his own handwriting.

1st—That there was not an Archbishop or four bishops to be had.

2nd—That the King Edward Book is to be used "for that there is none other specially made in the last session of Parliament."

During Queen Mary's reign, King Edward's Book, or more commonly called "Edwardine Ordinal," had been outlawed and the Roman Pontifical had been restored. With the advent of Elizabeth upon the throne, the Roman Pontifical was put out, and the Edwardine Ordinal was restored by the Queen, acting in her capacity as "Supreme Governor of the Church of England in all things spiritual and temporal." Parliament, however, at this time had not approved the restoration of the Edwardine Ordinal. Therefore the consecration of Matthew Parker was not in conformity with the laws of England, nor with the requirements of the Catholic Church.

Archbishop-elect Parker was keenly aware of this doubtfully valid situation and he placed the question before a group of eminent canonists and lawyers of the Anglican church for a decision. This commission was composed of William Day, Dean of St. Paul's, afterwards the Archbishop of York, Edwards Leeds, one of Parker's chaplains, Thomas Yale, Parker's Chancellor, Nicholas Burlingham, Counsellor, also Henry Harvey, Master of Trinity Hall, Cambridge, Robert Weston, later one of the "Lords Justices and Chancellor of Ireland."

These six eminent men drew up a commission for the confirmation and consecration of Parker, addressed to bishops Barlow, Scory, and Coverdale. To this commission they added a section dispensing with any disabilities in the persons addressed, or any illegalities in the acts done by them under it.

This commission drawn up by this group was not a valid instrument investing the consecrators with sacerdotal powers or jurisdiction. Even Kitchen had no canonical right to consecrate a bishop, and none of the remaining bishops had jurisdiction to perform any ecclesiastical act. The sole object of this group was to make certain that the Queen would include in her Dispensations by the largest words all the difficulties that might possibly arise. The "Act 8th, Elizabeth" in which is stated "that her Majesty the Queen in her said letters patent had used divers other general words and sentences whereby Her Majesty by her 'Supreme power and authority' had dispensed with all causes and defects, or doubts of any imperfection or disability" is definite proof of her intention to impose her will upon the hierarchy of the Church of England. The fact that Parliament by enactment had not restored the Edwardine Ordinal to use in the church did not concern her. Her determination to exercise her powers as "Supreme Governor of the Church" in their full plentitude was born in her pride and vanity, and her desire to be known as the one force in England that was strong enough to destroy the Catholic Church in England.

Matthew Parker was consecrated Archbishop of Canterbury on December 17, 1559. The consecration is described in a volume titled "Life of Parker" by William Kennedy, Anglican historian. It is such a recital of unprecedented secrecy in the consecration of a bishop that a reproduction of it should be of interest. He writes: "In the early hours of the morning of December 17, 1559, Parker entered Lambeth Chapel, his way being lighted by taperers. Within all was ready; Barlow, Scorey, Coverdale and Hodgkins, the consecrators, took their seats on the south side. The Archbishop-elect in his doctor's robes sat on the north side. The Matins, Scory preached 'a not inelegant sermon,' at the conclusion of which Parker and the bishops left the chapel to prepare for the Holy Communion. They returned by the north door, Parker in a surplice, Barlow in a cope, as he was to celebrate with Burlingham, archdeacon of Lincoln, and Guest, archdeacon of Canterbury, also in cope, to assist him; Scory and Coverdale in cassock, Hodgkins in surplice. After the Gospel, Barlow took his seat before the Holy Table, and three other bishops presented Parker to him in the usual manner. The writ was duly read, and the oath duly taken. The service proceeded according to the Edwardine Ordinal, the four bishops laying hands on Parker, repeating the crucial words of consecration in English.

"Take the Holy Ghost, and remember that thou stir up the grace of God which is in thee by the imposition of hands, for God hath not given us the spirit of fear, but of power, and love, and soberness."

The archbishop then communicated with the bishops and others who witnessed the ceremony. Parker's own record of his consecration is brief. He states: "On December 17, 1559, I was consecrated Archbishop of Canterbury. Alas, alas, O God for what time hast thou kept me. Now I am come into deep waters, and the flood hath overwhelmed me. O Lord I am oppressed, answer for me, and strengthen me with Thy free spirit, for I am a man, and have but a short time to live; give me of Thy sure mercies."

The Lambeth register makes no mention of the consecrating bishop Barlow or his assisting co-consecrators; it merely states "all four bishops imposed hands, reciting the words as used in the Edwardine Ordinal." It does not state that they, or any one of them did consecrate Parker, or that he was consecrated by them. This unusual departure from recognized practices in the recording of the consecration of a bishop is difficult of interpretation; it is easily understandable how failure to record so momentous an event might well lead to controversial conjecture.

However, the consecration of Parker by Barlow is admitted by Anglican and Catholic authorities. The sole question is validity of the consecration, and the continuing enigma is this: how can a consecration of a true bishop be accomplished when the chief consecrator himself was never consecrated a bishop in any church? And to further complicate the picture, the assistant co-consecrators possessed no legal or ecclesiastical competence, and employed a perverted rite which had not been sanctioned by parliament, and was not recognized by the Catholic Church as having the intention to consecrate a bishop who believed in a sacrificing priesthood. The assistant consecrators were John Scory, Miles Coverdale, and John Hodgkins. Both Scory and Coverdale were consecrated by schismatic bishops using the perverted ordinal, hence their consecrations were invalid. John Hodgkins had been duly and validly consecrated as bishop of Bedford, during the reign of Henry VIII, but his participation was of no value to a valid consecration, as he also acted under the Edwardine Ordinal. Incidentally, their names and the names of their consecrators appear in the registers of their respective Sees.

Every avenue of information has been exhausted to present the facts surrounding the consecration of Parker as Archbishop of Canterbury, and the continuance of the Apostolic succession. To be sure, a consecration took place, but for validity it might as well have been performed by civil magistrates.

Queen Elizabeth and her letters patent would suffice for the appointment of civil officers, but for making valid bishops in the church of God, she possessed no sacerdotal powers of any description.

Queen Elizabeth was no weakling. When she determined upon a plan to force her will upon her advisors she permitted nothing to stand in her way. She set her goal as the definite Protestantizing of England. She appointed a privy council, most of whom were Protestants under the leadership of Sir William Cecil as Secretary of State.

Cecil presented to the council a document titled "A device for the alteration of religion," which demanded rigid persecution of clergy who would not renounce allegiance to the Pope of Rome. Unanimously adopted by the "Privy Council," it was presented to the Parliament in 1559 and a new law called the "Act of Supremacy and Uniformity in Religion" was enacted.

The Act of Supremacy was originally passed by Parliament in 1534, and was directed against Catholics who refused to reject allegiance to Rome and persisted in practicing the old Catholic faith. The "Act of Uniformity" was passed to compel compliance by those citizens who did not accept "Anglicanism" although they rejected Catholicism, in other words the Puritans, Presbyterians, Calvinists, who were all deliberate nonconformists.

During this same session of Parliament (1534) the "Act of Succession" was passed. This Act outlawed the marriage of Henry VIII and Catherine of Aragon, "as against the laws of God and utterly void"; and at the same time they legitimatized the marriage of Henry VIII and Anne Boleyn. By this action the Parliament of 1534 removed the stigma of bastard from Elizabeth, and placed it upon the birth of Princess Mary, daughter of Henry and Catherine.

But, as all things, good or evil run their course, this situation was reversed in the minds of the people who were in possession of the facts, and the outstanding fact is that the parliament under Queen Mary did exactly the same thing, placing the bar sinister on Elizabeth, and restoring Mary to her natural birthright, the legitimate child of a valid Christian marriage, and so declared by the Holy Father gloriously reigning.

The passing of this Act to secure the throne to the children of Anne Boleyn was by implication an avowed denial of Papal authority since it stamped something valid which the Pope had ruled invalid. These laws were in effect until 1829 when the "Catholic Emancipation Act" was passed removing the hardships and penalties that had existed for two hundred and seventy years.

Elizabeth's venom against everything Catholic is understandable, but of course as Catholics we cannot condone her vicious assaults against the Catholic people and clergy of the realm. She was not responsible for the flagrant concupiscence of either parent. She carried the scar of her illegitimacy to the grave, and despite her queenly prerogatives and immense power and wealth, she was denied the one thing she desired most, an heir to carry on her policies. Her physical defects precluded the consummation of her desires, and in all probability this was responsible for many of her ruthless and violent acts. Tolerated mainly for her eminence as Queen of England with the power to elevate or destroy which she wielded as suited her fancy, she was a pathetic and desolate old lady in her declining years.

Elizabeth resembled her father Henry VIII in many ways: the same arrogant domineering manner; the same contempt for ecclesiastical usages or personalities. Bishops, obedient to her commands, were smiled upon and rewarded with wealthy benefices; contrariwise, they were eclipsed. She passed to her judgment before the "King of Kings" on March 24, 1603.

Chapter Five

ANGLICAN ORDERS

There were many French and Italian priests of great learning and sanctity who believed that Anglican Orders were valid.

Pope Leo XIII in 1895 issued an address to the Christian world to come back to "Unity of Faith" and action. Lord Halifax, a devout member of the High Church of England, through a distinguished French ecclesiastic, Abbe Portal, begged the Holy Father to reopen the cause of Anglican Orders to weigh new documents, hoping that further examination might result in reunion of Holy Mother Church with her estranged daughter, the Church of England.

The request was granted by Pope Leo XIII, and he appointed a commission of distinguished and able scholars, all brilliant churchmen, representing many different views upon the question.

This commission was composed of Cardinal Mazella, of Italian origin who taught many years at Woodstock, Maryland, and became a United States citizen. The secretary of the commission was Monsignor Merry del Val, a Spaniard, whose mother was a distinguished English lady. The balance of the commission was made up of Abbe Duchesne, Father De Augustinis, S.J., Abbot Gasquet, O.S.B., Father David, O.S.F., Monsignor Gasparri, later the renowned Papal Secretary of State, Canon Moyse of England, Father Scannell, and Father Llaveneras.

This commission can not be charged with being prejudiced against the Anglican Church since, in fact, the Anglican church had a slight advantage before the investigation started. Abbe Duchesne and Father De Augustinis, S.J., declared Anglican orders were certainly valid. Abbot Gasquet, O.S.B., Father David, O.S.F., and Canon Moyse held them positively invalid. Monsignor Gasparri thought they were probably valid. Father Scannell and Canon Moyse could not agree on the value of certain documentary evidence. Father Llaveneras would express no opinion on the subject before the commission began debating in session.

The commission conducted a most thorough inquiry into all phases of this momentous question. The decisions of previous commissions for three hundred years preceding were scrupulously scrutinized. Even the records of the Inquisition were overhauled for possible information. The Anglican defenders were granted every opportunity to prove their cause. The Holy Father, desirous of unity, was most solicitous in his attitude toward the proponents of the Anglican case.

The commission was composed of members of the Orders of St. Francis, St. Benedict, St. Ignatius Lloyala, the Roman Prelature, the secular clergy; history, canon law, dogmatic theology; all opposing schools of thought met in clashing debate, and it is recorded that the greatest disputes and oratorical clashes were between the two eminent Jesuits, Cardinal Mazella and Father De Augustinis.

In forming the commission to study Anglican orders, the Holy Father did not localize to Rome and Italy alone for decision: America, Ireland, England, Spain, France, and Italy were represented on it. The greatest theological talent available was employed in an effort to settle this grave question. The result of this investigation was not only of great importance to the Church of England; the whole Christian world awaited the findings of this commission; hence the Holy Father's cautious selection of its membership.

After every possible avenue of information had been probed, every argument, written or oral, assiduously analyzed, each member of the commission wrote his opinions and findings. They studied the findings of each other, so it could not be suspected there was collusion or an attempt to secret alignment for or against the merits of the controversy.

The results of the inquiry by the commission was placed before the "Suprema," the highest Commission of Cardinals presided over by the Pope in person—not Legate. After careful deliberation this "Suprema" Commission declared Anglican Orders were "null and void from the beginning."

On the Ides of September 1896, Leo XIII, Vicar of Christ, solemnly pronounced and declared that "Ordinations, according to the Anglican Rite, have been and are null and void from the beginning"; and on November 5, 1896, he wrote to the Archbishop of Paris, France, in a solemn brief that his decision was irrevocable.

It should be noted that in his decision on Anglican Orders, Pope Leo XIII was careful to specifically designate ordinations and consecrations according to the Edwardine Ordinal. He did not touch the question whether there might be some Anglican true priests and bishops; or whether some Anglicans may have been validly ordained priests by schismatical or heretical bishops, according to rites accepted by Rome. His decree regards only the *ordinations and consecrations according to the Edwardine Ordinal.*

It is canonically true that a sacrament to be valid must signify what it represents, and represent what it signifies, as in baptism, I baptize thee, in confirmation, I confirm thee, in penance, I absolve thee. In the Holy Eucharist the grace produced is the

"REAL PRESENCE," expressed by the words, "THIS IS MY BODY, THIS IS MY BLOOD."

The same rule applies to the Sacrament of Holy Orders; the grace produced is the diaconate, the priesthood, or the Episcopate; and the words of the form must express the effect. In the Anglican form – the Edwardine Ordinal does not express the grace produced. In the Anglican Ordinal (previous to 1662) the Anglican bishop ordaining an Anglican priest, imposing hands upon him says, "Receive the Holy Ghost; whose sins you shall forgive, they are forgiven; whose sins you shall retain, they are retained."

In this form of ordination, there is no mention of the priesthood, or the main objective of the priesthood – to consecrate the body and blood of our Lord – the Sacrament of Holy Eucharist – the Mass.

In the consecration of an Anglican bishop, the same deficiency in form and intention is apparent, as will be seen from the form in use up to 1662. The consecrating bishops, imposing hands on the consecrand, together say, "Receive the Holy Ghost and remember that thou stir up the grace of God that is given thee by the imposition of our hands; for God has not given us the Spirit of fear, but of love and soberness." In these words of ordination of priests, or consecration of bishops, there is no mention of either, therefore, failing to represent what it signifies, or signify what it represents, it is null and void from the beginning.

The ordination of priests and consecration of bishops up to 1547 under Henry VIII, and up to 1550 under Edward VI, were recognized by Rome as valid. They were conferred by real bishops, consecrated under and according to the Roman (Sarum) Pontifical.

This is not true of the orders conferred from 1550 to 1553, because, not only was the "Roman Missal" set aside for the "Anglican Communion Service," but also the "Roman Pontifical" was set aside for the "Edwardine Ordinal" which was defined by Rome to be defective in "Form and Intention."

The Edwardine Ordinal was in use from 1550 to 1662, when a change was made in the form of ordaining priests and consecrating bishops, to wit: after the words, "Receive the Holy Ghost," there was added the phrase "for the office and work of a priest," and in the consecration of a bishop, the words, "for the office and work of a bishop in the Church of God." The insertion of these words in the "Edwardine Ordinal" ceremonial of ordinations and consecrations was an official Anglican ecclesiastical recognition of the defect in the "form and intention" of ordinations and consecrations which took place during the period of 1550 to 1662.

As a cure for the deficiency of "form and intention" it might have sufficed, but it was of no value in establishing validity of orders as over one hundred years had elapsed since the omission, and no real bishops having been consecrated during that period, there were not then, and there are not now, validly consecrated bishops to validly ordain or consecrate; the "form and intention" has been revived – it is but shadow, without substance.

The inconsistency of the Anglican and Episcopal churches in claiming valid orders is proven in Article 25 of the "Thirty-nine Articles of Religion," accepted by both churches throughout the world. The said "Article" unequivocally states: "there are two sacraments ordained of Christ our Lord in the Gospel; that is to say, Baptism and the Lord's Supper"; they further assert; "those five commonly called sacraments, that is to say, Confirmation, Penance, *Holy Orders,* Matrimony, and Extreme Unction, are not to be counted for Sacraments of the Gospel, being such as have grown of the corrupt following of the Apostles, partly are states of life, allowed in the Scriptures, but yet have not the nature of sacraments with Baptism and the Lord's Supper, for they have not any visible sign or ceremony ordained of God."

Now be it noted; despite the strong assertion in "Article 25," that "there is *no Sacrament of Holy Orders,"* they insist that Anglican Orders have Apostolic Succession; that their priests have power to forgive sins and the power to offer up the Sacrifice of the Mass.

These claims are likewise at variance with "Article 31" of the "39 articles of Religion"; article 31, definitely states as a matter of faith to wit: "Wherefore, the sacrifices of Masses, in the which it was commonly said, "that the priest did offer Christ for the quick and the dead, to have remission of pain or guilt, were blasphemous fables, and dangerous deceits."

In this Article of Religion, the Anglican and Episcopal churches deny the sacrifice of the Mass; they likewise deny the power of the priest to forgive sin; they repudiate the Mass as a propitiation of the sins of men; yet in their services the Anglican and High Church Episcopal clergymen offer what they term a Mass.

The confusion of mind and faith is further shown by a study of "Article 28 of the 39 Articles." This article definitely sets forth, that transubstantiation, or the changing of the substance of bread and wine, into the substance of the Body and Blood of Jesus Christ, "can not be proved by Holy Writ, but is repugnant to the plain words of Scripture, overthroweth the nature of a Sacrament, and hath given occasion to many superstitions." Continuing, they assert: "The Body of Christ is given, taken, and eaten in the Supper, only after an heavenly and spiritual manner, and the mean whereby the Body and Blood of Christ is received and eaten in the Supper is faith."

This Article, accepted by the Anglican and Episcopal churches as a vital portion of their religious structure, is direct repudiation of the words of our Divine Lord, Who, at the Last Supper, stated to the Apostles: "Take ye and eat, This is My Body," and "This is the chalice of My Blood which shall be shed . . . for the remission of sin; drink ye all of it," and . . . blessing His apostles, He said, " Do THIS in commemoration of Me."

These words of Jesus Christ should be the alpha and omega of the doctrine of "transubstantiation." It was not a prophet speaking. It was the INFINITE GOD — THE INFALLIBLE TRUTH — WHO could neither deceive or be deceived.

In the Anglican and Episcopal churches there is no valid sacrificing priesthood, hence no "transubstantiation" and no amount of faith upon the part of Anglican or Episcopalian communicants can alter the substance of bread and wine into the Substance of the BODY and BLOOD of Christ.

The Apostles were given this power, and they transmitted to their lawful successors, the bishops of the Catholic church. For close to two thousand years, the bishops have handed down to their successors this same power, and so it will continue unfalteringly until eternity; for Christ has said "I shall be with you all days, even to the consummation of the world."

The Catholic church has always taught that a special grace is conferred in Holy Orders; an indelible mark is imprinted upon the souls of ordinands and consecrands. This belief is shared by all the ancient churches, whether in communion with Rome, or owing allegiance to Orthodox Patriarchs.

It is commonly understood among churchmen that the various Orders within the Church of England, such as "Cowley Fathers," or more strictly speaking, the "Society of St. John the Evangelist," the "Franciscans," the "Benedictines of London, England," the "Ritualists," or as they prefer to be called the "American Catholics," all claim and insist that their ordinations at the present time are derived from the ancient Catholic Rite. Historically, that is correct, as the Catholic Church Rite has never varied in its sacerdotal character. The Rite used in the Edwardine Ordinal has been badly mutilated and perverted by a definite heretical intention *not to do* what the Catholic church, the only true church of Christ requires for a valid consecration.

The Anglican hierarchy deny they accept the views of Archbishop Cranmer and Bishop Ridley in their rejection of the Mass. All these avowals are good as far as they go, but of themselves have no bearing upon their status as sacrificing priests. There is much verbiage and it sounds pleasant to the ear, but in no sense is it conducive to the establishing of the validity of Anglican and Episcopalian Orders.

The incorporation of the words *"Accipe Spiritum Sanctum"* does not constitute a valid consecration; but on the contrary, the context does exclude a sense of ordination or consecration according to the known forms of the Catholic Church.

No reasonable person denies that in Anglican, Episcopalian, and other Protestant groups there is faith and doctrine; but it is not the faith and doctrine of the Catholic church, founded by our Divine Lord, and guided by the Holy Spirit, God, and the Infinite Truth.

The Anglican and Episcopal churches embrace many of the errors of Martin Luther's doctrine, including his vicious assaults upon the Holy Father's person; the eminence of the Pope of Rome as the Vice-regent of Christ on earth has been challenged, and from the day of his rebellion against the church to the day he died, he was a violent opponent of all things Catholic, and to this day the Lutheran Evangelical Church has persisted in the spreading of hatred for the Chief Pastor of the Universal Church, the Pope now gloriously reigning, the successor of St. Peter the Prince of the Apostles — the Shepherd of our souls, under the power and authority given by Jesus Christ, when He said to Peter, "Feed My Lambs, feed My sheep." In passing, it might be observed that the High Lutheran Churches of Sweden, Finland, Denmark and Holland are again insisting that their clergy are validly ordained and consecrated, and that they possess Apostolic Succession. In the Swedish Cathedral at Stockholm the Latin Mass is sung without deviation from our own Catholic ritual.

In Archbishop Cranmer's renunciation of the Successor of St. Peter he flatly denies the necessity of the Sacrament of Holy Orders; he states "in the new Testament he that is appointed bishop of the church, needed no consecration by Scripture; for election or appointment thereto is all sufficient."

In an article published in the *National Review,* London, of September 1925, Anglican Bishop Knox, of the Diocese of Manchester, England, admits the action of the Holy Father rejecting the validity of Anglican Orders was justified. Bishop Knox states: "The Pope's refusal to recognize the validity of Anglican Orders was absolute, and was grounded on the fact that our church *does not ordain priests to offer the sacrifice of the Mass. . . .* In spite of our Archbishop's attempt to conceal *this defect,* the Pope from his point of view was unquestionably right. It is true that certain priests of the church of England offer so-called Masses, but as they were not ordained by the church with the intention that they should offer the Body and Blood of Christ to the Father, the sacrament of their ordination for this purpose is a failure; the Prayer Book and Ordinal are simply un-catholic, since they show no sign of fulfilling the most important of all Catholic functions."

If Bishop Knox was alone in his opinions concerning the quality of Anglican Orders, it might be glossed over as the action of a disappointed ecclesiastic, desirous of causing dissension; but the records show there were other outstanding members of the Anglican hierarchy who were unafraid to state the facts. Among this group none was more definite than John Charles Ryle, Bishop of Liverpool, England. In his article "Principles of a churchman" published in 1884, he makes this observation: "The reformers found the sacrifice of the Mass in our church, they cast it out as a blasphemous fable and dangerous deceit; the reformers found our clergy sacrificing priests, and made them prayer-reading, preaching ministers."

In a later article published in the "Liverpool Guardian" on November 4, 1896, page 176, Bishop Ryle states: "Our manner of conceiving the office of a minister of Christ is very different from that of the Pope. On the one hand, the ecclesiastic of the church of Rome is a real priest, whose principal duty is to offer the sacrifice of the Mass; on the other hand, the ecclesiastic of the Anglican Church is in no wise a priest, although we call him such; he is only an "Elder" whose sole duty or office *is not to sacrifice,* but rather to preach the word of God and administer the sacraments.

To these definite statements of Bishop Ryle of Liverpool, can be added the affirmation of Rev. Dr. Taylor, archdeacon of Liverpool, which appeared in the *Liverpool Tablet,* November 6, 1896 "that in the Edwardine Ordinal of 1550, not only was the sacrificial formula of ordaining 'Receive the power of offering sacrifice' expunged, but every trace of the sacerdotal and sacrificial idea was deliberately and of set purpose removed, and wholly eliminated from it. The word 'priest' is retained, but the priestly functions and expressions are gone."

The conclusions of both Bishop Ryle and Rev. Dr. Taylor are corroborated by the editor of *Church Times,* a high church magazine. In the issue of that magazine dated October 23, 1895, the editor makes this statement: "It is true that the Anglican reformers were not only in the 'Ordinal' lacking any intention to confer the power of sacrifice, but they actually cut out the reference to sacrifice, which the old 'Order' contained; to cut out is a more significant action than to refrain from putting in." The significance of this action was clearly to cease ordaining any sacrificing priests in the Church of England.

Canon Moyse of England, one of the commissioners appointed

by Pope Leo XIII to hear the plea of the Anglican church for recognition of their orders, completely covers the question in the report of the Eucharistic Congress of 1908, page 46. His comments were: "In the ordination service of the Catholic church, there are no less than sixteen different parts in which the *sacerdotium* or sacrificial character is clearly expressed: of these, not one was allowed to remain in the 'Edwardine Ordinal'; again, out of twenty-four passages in the Mass, which expresses the 'Real Presence' and sacrifice, not one was allowed to remain in the liturgy." It is easy to prove that statement.

Compare the Catholic Mass to the Anglican Communion Service; note the difference in the Anglican ordering of priests to the Catholic Pontifical. The comparison will show there are at least forty places where *something* is left out and that something expressed the Real Presence, or sacrifice of the Mass.

This cutting out of reference to the sacrificing priesthood, or the Real Presence was not done by laymen in the first instance, but by Archbishop Cranmer and Bishop Ridley with deliberate intention of excluding a sacrificing priesthood in the Church of England. This mutilation was approved by the English Parliament during the reign of the boy king, Edward VI; was abrogated under the Catholic Queen Mary Tudor, and restored by Queen Elizabeth, but not in time to receive legal sanction by Parliament when Matthew Parker was seemingly consecrated as Archbishop of Canterbury.

There were other Anglican leaders whose concept of the creation of bishops did not correspond to the views expressed by Archbishop Cranmer. One of the foremost among these leaders was the Reverend Dr. Haddon, editor of *Bramhall's Works.* He held a clearly defined belief in the sacrament of Holy Orders. Canon Estecourt in the volume *Anglican Orders* quotes him at great length. An excerpt of his writings is here presented; he states:

"My understanding of Holy Orders is: belief in the grace of God, as a supernatural dealing with the souls of men, and a gift of spiritual life; that these gifts of grace are intrusted to a corporate body, divinely constituted and visible as the appointed channels of grace, namely, the church; that in the church, there is a divinely constituted ministry, an order of men to whom God has intrusted certain authority and powers, and who possess exclusively the commission of Christ both to teach and administer sacraments deriving their power from God Himself, through those who have received authority to transmit such a supernatural gift, that is the grace of Orders, which office of administering the outward call and appointment is limited to bishops, through whom the gift of Orders so transmitted descended from the Apostles in an unbroken line, that is to say, the Apostolic Succession."

This statement by Dr. Haddon parallels Catholic belief in Holy Orders as the necessary agency for the creation of a sacrificing priesthood, but for comparative purposes is of no value, because of the following deficiencies:

1. Lack of any expressed belief of any divine gift being bestowed in ordination.

2. The Anglican form has been so mutilated and altered from the ancient forms with the express intention to exclude all semblance of power of sacrifice being conferred on a priest.

3. Because from the year 1554 to the present day, the Catholic church has refused to recognize Anglican Orders as valid.

4. Finally, because Anglican bishops and priests are themselves invalidly ordained and consecrated, possess no power to transmit Orders. It is not a bishop, it is the prescribed form of a church that is deficient in form, intention, and lack of a proper minister; hence the invalidity.

Chapter Six

"Rite of Anglican And Protestant Episcopal churches in the Ordering of Priests and Consecration of Bishops."

These forms are copied from the "Book of Common Prayer"; they have been in use in the Church of England since 1534, and in the Episcopal church in America since 1784.

"When the day appointed is come, this day being appointed by the bishop, after morning prayer is ended, there shall be a sermon or exhortation, declaring the duty and office of such as come to be admitted to the priesthood; how necessary that Order is in the church of God, and how also the people should esteem them in their office."

A priest shall present unto the Bishop sitting in his chair near to the Holy Table all those who are to receive the order of Priesthood that day, each of them being decently habited, and shall say:

"Reverend Father in God, I present unto you these persons present to be admitted to the Order of Priesthood."

The Bishop responds: "Take heed that the persons, whom ye present unto us, be apt and meet, for their learning and godly conservation, to exercise their ministry duly, to the honor of God and the edifying of His church."

The priest shall answer: "I have inquired concerning them, and also have examined them, and think them so to be."

Then the Bishop shall say to the people:

"Good people; these are they whom we propose, God willing, to receive this day unto the holy office of Priesthood; for, after due examination we find not to the contrary, but they are lawfully called to their function and ministry, and are persons meet for the same. But yet, if there be any of you who knoweth any impediment, or notable crime, in any of them for the which he ought not to be received into this holy ministry, let him come forward in the name of God, and show what the crime or impediment is." There being no objection raised against any of the candidates for ordination the clergy and the people recite the Litany. Then shall be said the service for the communion, with the Collect and Gospel as followeth:

The Collect:

"Almighty God, giver of all good things, Who by Thy Holy Spirit has appointed divers orders of ministers in the church; mercifully behold these Thy servants now called to the office of Priesthood; and so replenish them with the truth of Thy doctrine, and adorn them with innocency of life, that by word and good example they may faithfully serve Thee in this office, to the glory of Thy name, and the edifying of Thy church; through the merits of our Saviour Jesus Christ, Who liveth and reigneth with Thee and the Holy Ghost, world without end, Amen." Then followeth the Epistle, "Ephesus IV—7":

"Unto everyone of us is given grace according to the measure of the gift of Christ. Wherefore He saith, when He ascended up on high He led captivity captive, and gave gifts unto men. Now that He ascended, what is it but that He also descended first into the lower parts of the earth? He that descended is the same also that ascended up far above all heavens, that He might fill all things. And He gave some apostles; and some prophets, and some evangelists; and some pastors and teachers, for the perfecting of the saints, for the work of the ministry, for the edifying of the Body of Christ; till we all come in the unity of the faith, and of the knowledge of the Son of God, unto a perfect man, unto the measure of the stature of the fullness of Christ."

After this shall be read for the Gospel part of the ninth chapter of St. Matthew as followeth:

"When Jesus saw the multitude, He was moved with compassion on them, because they fainted, and were scattered abroad as sheep having no shepherd. Then saith He to His disciples, 'the harvest truly is plenteous, but the labourers are few; pray ye therefore the Lord of the harvest that He will send forth laborers into His harvest.' "

Then the Bishop shall say to them as followeth:

"Ye have heard, brethren, as well in your private examination, as in the exhortation which was now made to you, and in the holy lessons taken out of the Gospel, and the writings of the Apostles, of what dignity, and of what great importance this office is whereunto you are called. And now again we exhort you, in the name of Jesus Christ, that ye have in remembrance, unto how high a dignity, and to how weighty an office and charge ye are called; that is to say, to be messengers, watchmen, and stewards of the Lord; to teach and premonish, to feed and provide for the Lord's family; to seek for Christ's sheep that are dispersed abroad, and for His children who are in the midst of this naughty world, that they may be saved through Christ forever. Have always therefore printed in your remembrance, how great a treasure is committed to your charge, for they are the sheep of Christ, which He bought with His death, and for whom He shed His Blood. The church and congregation whom you must serve, is His Spouse and Body; and if it should happen that the same church, or any member thereof, do take any hurt or hindrance by reason of your negligence, ye know the greatness of the fault, and also the horrible punishment that will ensue. Wherefore, consider with yourselves the end of the ministry towards the children of God, towards the Spouse and Body of Christ; and see that ye never cease your labors, your care and diligence, until ye have done all that lieth in you, according to your bounden duty, to bring all such as are or shall be committed to your charge, unto that agreement in the faith and knowledge of God, and to that ripeness and perfectness of age in Christ, that there be no place left among you, either for error in religion, or for viciousness in life.

"For as much then as your office is both of such excellency, and of so great difficulty, ye see with what great care and study ye ought to apply yourselves dutiful and thankful unto the Lord, Who hath placed you in so high a dignity; as also to beware that neither yourselves offend, nor be occasion that others offend. Howbeit, ye cannot have a mind and will thereto of yourselves; for that which will and ability is given of God alone, therefore ye ought, and have need to pray earnestly for His Holy Spirit; and seeing that ye cannot by any other means compass the doing of so weighty a work, pertaining to the salvation of man, but with doctrine and exhortation taken out of the Holy Scriptures and with life agreeable to the same; consider how studious ye ought to be in reading and learning the Scriptures, and in framing the manners both of yourselves, and of them that specially pertain unto you, according to the rule of the same scriptures; and for the same cause, how ye ought to forsake and set aside as much as ye may, all wordly causes and studies."

"We have good hope that ye have well weighed these things with yourselves, long before this time; and that ye have clearly determined, by God's grace, to give yourselves wholly to this office, whereunto it hath pleased God to call you; so that, as much as lieth in you, ye will apply yourselves wholly to the work, and draw all your cares and studies this way; and that ye will continually pray to God the Father, by the mediation of our only Saviour Jesus Christ, for heavenly assistance of the Holy Ghost, that by daily reading and weighing the Scriptures, ye may wax riper and stronger in your ministry; and that ye may so endeavour yourselves, from time to time, to sanctify the lives of you and yours, and to fashion them after the rule and doctrine of Christ; that ye may be wholesome and goodly examples and patterns for the people to follow.

"And now, that this present congregation of Christ may also understand your minds and wills in these things, and that this, your promise may the more move you to do your duties, ye shall answer plainly to these things which we, in the name of God, and of His church, shall demand of you, touching the same."

Bishop to Ordinand:

"Do you think in your heart, that you are truly called, according to the will of God, and according to the canons of this Church, to the Order and ministry of Priesthood?"

Ordinands answer: "I think it."

The Bishop:

"Are you persuaded that the Holy Scriptures contain all doctrine required as necessary for eternal salvation through faith in Jesus Christ? and are you determined, out of the same Scriptures to instruct the people committed to your charge; and to teach nothing as necessary to salvation, but that which you shall be persuaded may be concluded and proved by Holy Writ?"

Answer: "I am so persuaded, and have so determined, by God's grace."

The Bishop:

"Will you give your faithful diligence always to minister the doctrines and sacraments and the discipline of Christ, as the Lord hath commanded, and as this church hath received the same, according to the commandments of God; so that you may teach

the people committed to your care and charge with all diligence to keep and observe the same?" Answer: "I shall do so, by the help of God."
The Bishop:

"Will you be ready, with all faithful diligence, to banish and drive away from the church all erroneous and strange doctrines contrary to God's word; and to use both public and private monitions and exhortations, as well to the sick as to the whole, within your cure as need shall require, and occasion shall be given?"

Answer: "I will endeavor so to do, the Lord being my helper."
The Bishop:

"Will you be diligent in prayers, and in reading the Holy Scriptures, and in such studies as help to the knowledge of the same, laying aside the study of the world and the flesh?"

Answer: "I will endeavor to do so, the Lord being my helper."
The Bishop:

"Will you be diligent to frame, and frame your own selves and your families, according to the doctrine of Christ's church; and to make yourselves and them, as much as in your power lieth, wholesome example and patterns for the flock of Christ?"

Answer: "I will apply myself thereto, the Lord being my helper."
The Bishop:

"Will you maintain and set forwards, as much as lies in you, quietness, peace, and love, among all Christian people, and especially among them that are or shall be committed to your charge?"

Answer: "I shall do so, the Lord being my helper."
The Bishop:

"Will you reverently obey your Bishop, and other chief ministers, who according to the canons of the church, may have the charge and government over you; following with a glad mind and will their godly admonitions, and submitting yourselves to their godly judgments?"

Answer: "I will do so, the Lord being my helper."

Standing up the Bishop shall say:

"Almighty God, Who hath given you this will to do these things grant also unto you strength and power to perform the same, that He may accomplish His work which He hath begun in you, through Jesus Christ our Lord. Amen."

After this the congregation shall be desired secretly in their prayers to make their humble supplications to God for all these things, for which prayers, there shall be silence for a time.

After which shall be sung the "Veni Creator," the Bishop beginning, and the persons to be ordained, together with the priests answering by verses as followeth:

Come Holy Ghost, our souls inspire,
And lighten with celestial fire,
Thou the anointing Spirit art
Who dost Thy seven fold gifts impart,
Thy blessed unction from above
Is comfort, life and fire of love.
Enable with perpetual light
The dullness of our blinded sight
Anoint and cheer our soiled face
With the abundance of Thy grace.
Keep far our foes, give peace at home
Where Thou art guide, no ill can come
Teach us to know the Father, Son,
And Thee of both, to be but One
That through the ages all along
This may be our endless song. Praise to Thy eternal Merit.
Father, Son, and Holy Spirit.

That done the Bishop shall pray in this wise and say:

"Let us pray;

"Almighty God and Heavenly Father, Who, of Thine Infinite love and goodness towards us has given to us Thy only and most dearly beloved Son, Jesus Christ, to be our Redeemer, and the author of everlasting life; Who, after He had made perfect our Redemption by His death and was ascended into heaven, sent abroad into the world His apostles, prophets, evangelists, doctors, and pastors; by whose labours and ministry He gathered together a great flock in all the parts of the world, to set forth the eternal praise of Thy Holy Name; for these so great benefits of Thy goodness, and for that Thou has vouchsafed to call these Thy servants here present to the same office and ministry, appointed for the salvation of mankind; we render unto Thee most hearty thanks, we praise and worship Thee; and we humbly beseech Thee, by Thy blessed Son, to grant unto all, which either here or elsewhere call upon Thy Holy Name, that we may continue to show ourselves thankful unto Thee for the benefits we have received from Thee; and that we may daily increase and go forward in the knowledge and faith of Thee and Thy Son, by the Holy Spirit; so that as well by these Thy ministers, Thy holy name may be forever glorified and Thy blessed kingdom enlarged; through the same, Thy Son, Jesus Christ our Lord Who liveth and reigneth with Thee in the unity of the same Holy Spirit, world without end. Amen."

When this prayer is done, the bishop with the priests present shall lay their hands severally upon the heads of every one that receiveth the Order of Priesthood; the receivers humbly kneeling, and the bishop saying:

"Receive the Holy Ghost for the office and work of a Priest in the Church of God, now committed unto thee by the imposition of our hands; whose sin thou dost forgive, they are forgiven; and whose sins thou dost retain, they are retained; and be thou faithful as a dispenser of the word of God, and of His holy sacraments, in the name of the Father, Son and Holy Ghost, Amen."

Then the bishop shall deliver to everyone of them kneeling; placing the bible in his hand saying:

"Take thou authority to preach the word of God, and to minister the holy sacraments in the congregation, where thou shall be lawfully appointed thereto."

When this is done, the Nicene Creed shall be said, and the bishop shall go on in the service of the Communion, which all they who receive Orders shall take together, and remain in the same place where hands were placed upon them until such time as they have received holy communion. The communion being done, after the last Collect, and just before the Benediction, shall be said this Collect:

"Most merciful Father, we beseech Thee to send upon these Thy servants Thy heavenly blessing; that they may be clothed with righteousness and that Thy word spoken by their mouths may have such success, that it may never be spoken in vain. Grant also, that we may have grace to hear and receive what they shall deliver out of Thy most holy word or agreeable to the same, as the means of our salvation; that in all things, words and deeds we may seek Thy glory, and the increase of Thy kingdom through Jesus Christ, Our Lord. Amen."

"The peace of God, which passeth all understanding, keep your hearts and minds in the knowledge and love of God, and of His Son Jesus Christ our Lord; and the blessing of God Almighty, Father, Son, and Holy Ghost be amongst you and remain with you forever."

This blessing concludes the ceremony of ordaining a priest in the Anglican and Protestant Episcopal Churches. At no place in this "Rite of Ordination" has mention been made of any intention to ordain a sacrificing priesthood, to offer the sacrifice of the Mass, without which no other powers can be given or bestowed.

In the Church of England before the Pontifical was abolished, and the Edwardine Ordinal substituted, the ordinands were reminded that, "the chalice with wine in it, and the paten with the host on it, were received in order that they would understand that they had conferred on them the power of offering up a sacrifice pleasing to God"; for it is the duty of a priest to effect the Sacrament of the Body and Blood of the Lord on the Altar.

It will be seen from this deletion in the Rite of Ordination that the intention not to ordain a sacrificing priest was deliberate and of set purpose.

Chapter Seven

Form of Consecration of Bishops
in the Anglican and Protestant
Episcopal Church in America.
(from Book of Common Prayer)

The form of ordaining and consecrating a bishop in the Anglican and Protestant Episcopal churches, differs from the Roman Pontifical both in form and intention.

The powers conferred on Anglican and Episcopal bishops are: "to govern, instruct, and exhort, to convince gainsayers, to drive away erroneous doctrine, to correct and punish."

The powers conferred on a Catholic bishop are "to govern, to interpret, to consecrate, to confirm, to ordain, to offer sacrifice of the Mass, to baptize."

It will be noted in this comparison of powers conferred, that all the duties which require the powers of the sacrament of Holy Orders are omitted in the Anglican and Episcopal Rites of ordination and consecration.

To clarify the lack of essential form and matter in the ritual of consecration of Anglican and Episcopal bishops, and to note the definite mutilation of the Roman Pontifical in the establishment of the Edwardine Ordinal, it is imperative that a comparison be made; and to that end the Book of Common Prayer is cited as the authority to prove the case.

In the Book of Common Prayer, the form of ordaining, or consecrating a bishop is thus provided.

"When all things are duly prepared in the church and set in order, after morning prayer is ended, the Presiding Bishop shall begin the 'Communion Service' in which this shall be the 'Collect.'

"Almighty God, Who, by Thy Son, Jesus Christ, didst give to Thy holy apostles many excellent gifts, and didst charge them to feed Thy flock; Give grace, we beseech Thee, to all bishops, the pastors of Thy church, that they may diligently preach Thy word, and duly administer the godly discipline thereof; and grant to Thy people, that they may obediently follow the same; that all may receive the crown of everlasting glory, through Jesus Christ, our Lord, Amen."

And another bishop shall read the Epistle:

I — Timothy III.

"This is a true saying; If a man desire the office of a bishop, he desireth a good work. A bishop then must be blameless, the husband of one wife, vigilant, sober, of good behaviour, given to hospitality, apt to preach, and teach; not given to wine, no striker, not greedy of filthy lucre; but patient, not a brawler, not covetous; one that ruleth his own household well, having his children in subjection with all gravity (for if a man know not how to rule his own house how shall he take care of the church of God); not a novice, lest being lifted up with pride, he fall unto the condemnation of the devil. Moreover, he must have a good report of them which are without; lest he fall into reproach, and the snare of the devil."

Another bishop shall read the Gospel:

St. John XX — 19.

"The same day at evening, being the first day of the week, when the doors were shut, for fear of the Jews, the disciples were assembled. Jesus came and stood in the midst of them, and said unto them: 'Peace be to you,' and when he had so said, He showed them His hands and His side; then were the disciples glad, when they saw the Lord, Then Jesus saith again, peace be to you; As My Father hath sent Me even so send I you; and when He had said this he breathed upon them saying: 'Receive ye the Holy Ghost, whose sin ye shall forgive, they are forgiven them, whose sins ye shall retain, they are retained.'" Or this Gospel:

St. Matthew XXVIII – 18.

"Jesus came and spake to them, saying: 'All power is given to Me in Heaven and in earth; Go ye therefore, and teach all nations, baptizing them in the name of the Father, and of the Son, and of the Holy Ghost, teaching them to observe all things whatsoever I have commanded you, and lo, I am with you all days, even unto the consummation of the world.'" Then follows the Nicene Creed, and after that the sermon; which being ended the bishop-elect, vested with his rochet, shall be presented by two bishops to the presiding bishop, sitting in his chair near the *Holy Table;* . . . the bishops presenting him saying:

"Reverend Father in God, we present you this godly and well learned man to be ordained and consecrated a bishop." Then shall the presiding bishop demand the testimonials of the person presented for consecration, and shall cause them to be read. He shall then require of him the following "Promise of Conformity to the doctrine, discipline, and worship of the Protestant Episcopal Church."

In the name of God, Amen;

"I .... chosen bishop of the Protestant Episcopal Church in .... do solemnly promise conformity and obedience to the doctrine, discipline, and worship of the Protestant Episcopal church in the United States of America, So help me God, through Jesus Christ." (If an Anglican is being consecrated, the term Anglican is used.)

Then the presiding bishop shall move the congregation present to pray, saying to them:

"Brethren, it is written in the Gospel of St. Luke, that our Lord and Saviour, Jesus Christ, continued the whole night in prayer, before he chose and sent forth His twelve apostles. It is written also, that the holy apostles prayed before they ordained Matthias to be of the number of the twelve. Let us, therefore, following the example of our Saviour Christ and his apostles, offer up our prayers to Almighty God, before we admit, and send forth this person, presented unto us to the work, whereunto we trust the Holy Ghost hath called him."

Then shall be said the Litany, save only that after this place "That it may please Thee to illuminate all bishops," etc., the proper suffrage shall be: "That it may please Thee to bless this our brother elected, and to send Thy grace upon him that he may duly execute the Office whereunto he is called, to the edifying of Thy church, and to the honor and glory of Thy name."
Answer: "We beseech Thee, to hear us, good Lord."

Then shall be said this prayer following.

"Almighty God, giver of all good things, Who by Thy Holy Spirit, hast appointed divers Orders of ministers in Thy church, mercifully behold this Thy servant, now called to the work of a Bishop (added 1662), and so replenish him with innocency of life, that, both by word and deed, he may faithfully serve Thee in this office, to the glory of Thy name, and the edifying and well governing of Thy church through the merits of our Saviour Jesus Christ, Who liveth and reigneth with Thee and the Holy Ghost, Amen."

Then the Presiding Bishop, sitting in his chair, shall say to him that is to be consecrated:

"Brother, forasmuch as the Holy Scriptures and the ancient canons command, that we should not be hasty in laying on hands, and admitting any person to government in the church of Christ which He hath purchased with no less price than the effusion of His own blood, before we admit you to this administration, we will examine in certain articles, to the end that the congregation present may have a trial, and bear witness, how you are minded to behave yourself in the church of God."

Bishop:

"Are you persuaded that you are truly called to this ministry, according to the will of our Lord Jesus Christ, and the Order of this church?"

Answer: "I am so persuaded."

Bishop:

"Are you persuaded that the Holy Scriptures contain all doctrine required as necessary for eternal salvation through faith in Jesus Christ? and are you determined out of the same Holy Scriptures to instruct the people committed to your charge; and to teach and maintain nothing as necessary to salvation, but that which you shall be persuaded may be concluded and proved by the same?"

Answer: "I am so persuaded, and determined by God's grace."

Bishop:

"Will you then faithfully exercise yourself in the Holy Scriptures and call upon God by prayer for the true understanding of the same, so that you may be able by them to teach and exhort by wholesome doctrine; and to withstand and convince the gainsayer?"

Answer: "I will do so by the help of God."

Bishop:

"Will you deny all ungodliness and worldly lusts, and live soberly, righteously, and godly in this present world; that you may show yourself in all things an example of good works unto others, that the adversary may be ashamed, having nothing to say against you?"

Answer: "I will do so, the Lord being my helper."

Bishop:

"Will you show yourself gentle, and be merciful for Christ's sake to poor and needy people, and to all strangers destitute for help?"

Answer: "I will so show myself with God's help."

Then shall the Presiding Bishop, standing up, say:

"Almighty God, our Heavenly Father, Who hath a good will to do all these good things; Grant unto you strength and power to perform the same, that He, accomplishing in you the good work which He hath begun, you may be found perfect and irreprehensible at the latter day, through Jesus Christ our Lord, Amen."

Then shall the bishop-elect put on the rest of the Episcopal habit; and kneeling down, "Veni Creator Spiritus" shall be said or sung over him; the Presiding Bishop beginning, and the bishops, with others that are present answers verses as followeth:

"Come Holy Ghost, our souls inspire," etc. as in the ordaining of a priest.

The "Veni Creator" being ended, the Presiding Bishop shall say:

"Let us pray;

"Almighty God, and most merciful Father, Who of Thine Infinite goodness, hast given Thine only and dearly beloved Son Jesus Christ to be our Redeemer, and the Author of everlasting life; Who after that He made perfect our Redemption by His death, and was ascended into Heaven, poured down His gifts abundantly upon men, making some Apostles, some prophets, some doctors, and pastors, to the edifying and making perfect His church; Grant we beseech Thee, to this Thy servant, such grace, that he may evermore to spread abroad Thy gospel, the glad tidings of reconciliation with Thee, and to use the authority given him not to destruction, but to salvation; not to hurt, but to help; so that as a wise and faithful servant, giving to Thy family their portion in due season, he may at last be received into everlasting joy, through Jesus Christ our Lord, Who, with Thee and the Holy Ghost, liveth and reigneth, One God, world without end, Amen."

Then the Presiding Bishop and bishops present shall lay their hands upon head of the bishop-elect, kneeling before them, the Presiding Bishop saying:

"Receive the Holy Ghost, for the office and work of a Bishop in the church of God (added 1662) now committed to thee by the imposition of our hands, in the name of the Father, and of the Son, and of the Holy Ghost, Amen; and remember thou shalt stir up the grace of God, which is given thee by this imposition of our hands; for God hath not given us the spirit of fear, but of power, of love, and soberness."

Then the Presiding Bishop shall deliver him the bible saying:

"Give heed unto *reading,* exhortation, and doctrine. Think upon the things contained in this book. Be diligent in them, that the increase may be manifest to all men; for by so doing, thou shalt both save thyself and them that hear thee. Be to the flock of Christ a shepherd, not a wolf; feed them, devour them not. Hold up the weak, heal the sick, bind up the broken; bring again the outcasts, seek the lost. Be so merciful, that ye be not too remiss; so minister discipline, that you forget not mercy; that when the Chief Shepherd shall appear you may receive the never fading crown of glory, through Jesus Christ. Amen."

Then the Presiding Bishop shall proceed in the Communion service, with whom the newly consecrated bishop with others shall also communicate. And for the last Collect, immediately before the Benediction shall be said the prayer.

"Most merciful God, Father, we beseech Thee to send down

upon this Thy servant Thy heavenly blessing; and so endue him with Thy Holy Spirit that he preaching Thy word, may not only be earnest to reprove, beseech and rebuke, with all patience and doctrine, but also may be, to such as believe a wholesome example in word, in conversation, in love, in faith, in chastity and in purity; that faithfully fulfilling his course, at the latter day he may receive the crown of righteousness, laid up by the Lord the righteous Judge, Who liveth and reigneth one God, with the Father, and the Holy Ghost, world without end. Amen."

"The peace of God, which passeth all understanding, keep your hearts and minds in the knowledge and love of God, and of His Son, our Lord Jesus Christ; and the blessing of God Almighty, the Father, the Son, and the Holy Ghost be among you and remain with you always."

With the imparting of the final blessing by the Presiding Bishop the ceremonial of consecration is ended.

A careful analysis of the Anglican and Protestant Episcopal Ordinal fails to elicit even one reference to the "Real Presence" or the creation of a sacrificing priesthood; in the consecration of the bishop, no mention is made or charge given that he shall ordain priests to offer up the sacrifice of the Mass, the main objective of the Catholic priesthood.

Other than creating a ministerial agency for the preaching of the word it is difficult to determine just what is intended in the ceremonial of ordaining and consecrating in the Anglican and Episcopalian churches. There are so many varying shades of thought in their theology that even the very devout members find difficulty in settling for themselves just what should be accepted as Anglican or Episcopalian belief.

A case in point will bring out this difficulty, from a Catholic viewpoint; and it must be as confusing to a member of either of these churches. The case is: In 1939, one Rev. Spence Burton, a member of the "Cowley Fathers" so-called, was elevated to the

Anglican Hierarchy and was consecrated by Presiding Bishop Tucker in Trinity Church, Boston. Ordinarily, Trinity church conducts services according to the tenets of the Low-Episcopal church, but it was transformed into a High-Church for this special occasion.

The difficult thing to understand is this: the bishop-elect is an Anglican priest who believes in and celebrates daily Mass; he insists he possess valid Orders, and the proper faculties for the celebration of the Eucharist. His consecrator, Bishop Tucker, and his co-consecrators reject the Mass as a "deceit and blasphemous fable," deny the "Real presence," and have no intention of ordaining a sacrificing priest or bishop.

With this conflict in vital theological beliefs how can a valid consecration take place? how can a contract be valid if there is no meeting of the minds; and there definitely is a wide breach between the dogmas of faith practiced by the Anglican church, and those of the Low-Episcopalian church; in truth it can be said, that even the ordinary layman unversed in theological matters would have no difficulty in discerning the incompatibility of beliefs, functions and ceremonials in the consecration of this Anglican bishop.

Recently in various Episcopalian magazines, articles have appeared intimating that there was a growing tendency to inter-communion between the Greek Orthodox and Anglican churches, even to the extent of celebrating the Eucharist at each other's altars. The author of this volume, accompanied by Thomas H. Murray, Past Grand Knight of Brighton Council, Knights of Columbus as witness, called upon his Grace Athenagoras Cavardas, at the Greek Orthodox Seminary in Brookline, Mass. on August 17, 1948, and during the visit the bishop was asked whether this inter-communion actually existed; specifically, he was asked as to the celebration of the Eucharist at their altars by Anglican priests. The bishop unequivocally stated: "under no circumstances could that occur, as the Greek church does not recognize the Anglican or Protestant Episcopal clergy as validly ordained sacrificing priesthood. The bishop had recently published a volume on the question of Anglican Orders setting forth the decisions of the Holy Synod concerning them. This statement by the bishop definitely settles the question of inter-communion between the two churches.

A rather interesting pamphlet is in distribution among the Episcopal churches in America; it is written by one C. P. S. Clarke, of England, formerly Archdeacon of Chichester. It contains many of the old assaults upon the Catholic church, and takes great consolation in the acquisition of the "Old Catholic" church and other dissident groups which for some reason have separated from the See of Rome. The prize fiction is this statement: "The Church of England is in full communion with the old Catholics of the continent, and *though full communion* is not yet established with the Orthodox Church of the East, is on friendly terms with it, and the orders of the Anglican church have been acknowledged as valid by the Patriarchates of Constantinople (1922), Jerusalem (1923), Alexandria (1930), and Roumania (1936), but for political reasons the subject has not yet been considered in full synod."

The good Archdeacon in his closing paragraph gives vent to this angelic observation: "If I seem to my Roman Catholic friends to have been unnecessarily hostile, I can only repeat the words of the French naturalist: 'this animal is vicious, if it is attacked it defends itself.'" (This pamphlet was published by A. R. Mobray & Co. Ltd., London.)

Despite the fanciful prognostications of the former Archdeacon Clarke of Chichester the Patriarchates of the ancient Oriental churches will continue to stand with the church of Rome, in the rejection of the Church of England's claim to possession of the Apostolical Succession.

Chapter Eight

Ritual of consecration of a bishop
in the Roman Catholic Church.

Ceremony of Consecration of His Excellency, the Most Reverend
Louis Francis Kelleher, D.D. – Auxiliary Bishop of Boston,
at Cathedral of the Holy Cross, Boston, June 8, 1945.

Consecrator
His Excellency, The Most Reverend
Richard James Cushing, D.D.
Archbishop of Boston

Assistant Consecrators
His Excellency, the Most Reverend
Francis Joseph Spellman, D.D.
Archbishop of New York
And
His Excellency, the Most Reverend
Edward Francis Ryan, D.D.
Bishop of Burlington.

Introductory Explanation:

The consecration of a bishop is the exclusive right of the Sovereign Pontiff, and cannot be performed without a mandate explicity given by His Holiness. When the consecration takes place outside of Rome, the necessary documents, known as "bulls," from the Latin word "bulla," signifying the leaden seal attached to them, are sent to the bishop-elect, notifying him of his appointment and authorizing him to select as his consecrator any orthodox bishop, with whom should be associated two other bishops as assistant consecrators. If the consecration occurs on a Sunday or a day other than the feast of an Apostle, special permission from the Holy See must be obtained by Apostolic brief allowing the choice of that day. The ceremony must take place in a church that is consecrated; that is, the church must be free from all encumbrances and solemnly dedicated in perpetuity to the service of God.

This translation of the Ceremony of Consecration was approved by the Archbishop of Boston, in accordance with the decrees of the Sacred Congregation of Rites.

At the appointed hour, the Consecrator, the Bishop-elect, the assistant consecrators and the others who are to be present at the consecration, proceed to the church, and the Consecrator, having prayed before the altar ascends to his throne near the Gospel corner, and there is vested as usual. The Bishop-elect, with the assistant consecrators, goes to his chapel and there puts on the necessary vestments, namely, the amice, alb, cincture, the stole, crossed as it is worn by priests, and the cope. The assistant consecrators, in the meanwhile, put on their vestments. All being ready, the Consecrator goes to the middle of the altar and there sits on the fald-stool with his back to the altar. The Bishop-elect, wearing his biretta, is led between the two consecrators, who are mitred. When he comes before the Consecrator, uncovering, he bows profoundly. The assistant consecrators, wearing their mitres, slightly incline their heads. Then they sit at a distance from the consecrator so that the Bishop-elect faces the Consecrator; the senior consecrator (assistant) sits at the right hand of the Bishop-elect, the junior at his left facing each other. When they are thus seated, after a short pause they rise, the Bishop-elect without biretta and the assistant consecrators without mitres.

Introduction.

The senior assistant consecrator, turned to the Consecrator says:

"Most Reverend Father, our Holy Mother the Catholic Church doth ask that thou promote this priest here present to the responsibility of the episcopate.

The Consecrator says:

"Have you the Apostolic mandate?"

The senior assistant consecrator answers: "We have."

The Consecrator says: "Let it be read."

Then the notary of the Consecrator, taking the mandate from the assistant consecrator, reads it from the beginning to the end; in the meanwhile all sit with heads covered.

Amleto Giovanni Cicognani, D.D.
By the grace of God and Favor of the Apostolic See
Titular Archbishop of Laodicea in Phrygia
And
Apostolic Delegate to the United States of America.

Decree.

A decree having already been executed by the Sacred Consistorial Congregation and sent under the seal of Apostolic Letters regarding the promotion of His Excellency, Most Reverend Louis Francis Kelleher to the See of Thaenae and Auxiliary Bishop to His Excellency, Most Reverend Richard James Cushing, Archbishop of Boston:

His Holiness, Pope Pius XII, by Divine Providence Supreme Pontiff, through the offices of the aforesaid Sacred Consistorial

Congregation has graciously decreed that despite the fact that these letters have not yet arrived, the above mentioned Most Reverend Louis Francis Kelleher having made his profession of faith, taken the necessary oaths and fulfilled all the requirements of the law, may be validly consecrated outside the City of Rome, on the Feast of the Most Sacred Heart of Jesus since this would be of benefit to the clergy and people.

Anything to the contrary notwithstanding.

In testimony whereof we have issued this decree under our hand and the seal of the Apostolic Delegation.

Given at Washington, from the office of the Apostolic Delegation on the fifteenth day of May, the feast of St. John the Baptist de la Salle, in the year of Our Lord, Nineteen Hundred Forty Five.

Signed: Amleto Giovanni Cicognani
Archbishop of Laodicea,
Apostolic Delegate.

The mandate having been read, the Consecrator says:

Thanks be to God.

As the Bishop-elect has already made his profession of faith and taken the oath in a private chapel, the Consecrator proceeds to the examination.

The Bishop-elect and the assistants sit, and the Consecrator reads in an audible voice the following examination. The assistant consecrators say in a lower voice whatsoever the Consecrator says.

Examination.

The Consecrator says:

The ancient rule of the Fathers doth teach and ordain that he who is chosen to the order of bishop, shall be with all charity examined carefully beforehand concerning his faith in the Holy Trinity, and shall be questioned concerning the various qualifications which befit the Episcopal office and which are regarded as essential, according to the word of the Apostle: "Impose hands hastily on no man." This is done in order that he who is ordained may be instructed how it behooveth one placed under this rule to conduct himself in the Church of God, and also that they may be blameless who impose on him the hands of ordination. Therefore, by the same authority and commandment, with sincere charity, we ask thee, dearest brother, if thou desirest to make thy conduct harmonize, as far as thy nature doth allow, with the meaning of the divine Scripture.

Then the Bishop-elect, rising, with uncovered head, answers:

"With all my heart I wish in all things to obey."

He will act in like manner when making all the other responses that follow.

The Consecrator interrogates:

"Wilt thou teach the people for whom thou art ordained, both by words and by example, the things thou understandest from the divine Scriptures? The Bishop-elect answers: I will.

C.—Wilt thou receive, keep and teach with reverence the traditions of the orthodox Fathers and the decretal constitutions of the Holy and Apostolic See?

B.—I will.

C.—Wilt thou show in all things fidelity, submission, obedience, according to canonical authority, to blessed Peter the Apostle, to whom was given by God the power of binding and loosing, and to His Vicar, our Holy Father Pope Pius XII, and to his successors, the Roman Pontiffs?

B.—I will.

C.—Wilt thou refrain in all ways from evil and, as far as thou art able with the help of the Lord, direct them to every good.

B.—I will.

C.—Wilt thou observe and teach, with the help of God, chastity and sobriety?

B.—I will.

C.—Wilt thou, as far as thy human frailty shall allow, always be given up to divine affairs and abstain from wordly matters or sordid gains?
B.—I will.
C.—Wilt thou thyself observe, and likewise teach others to observe, humility and patience?
B.—I will.
C.—Wilt thou for the Lord's sake be affable and merciful to the poor and to pilgrims and all those in need?
B.—I will.
Then the Consecrator says to him:

"May the Lord bestow upon thee all these things and every other good thing, and preserve thee and strengthen thee in all goodness."

All answer: Amen.

C.—Dost thou believe, according to thy understanding and the capacity of thy mind, in the Holy Trinity, the Father, and the Son, and the Holy Ghost, one Almighty God, and the whole Godhead, in the Holy Trinity co-essential, consubstantial, co-eternal, and co-omnipotent, of one power, one will and majesty, the Creator of all creatures, by Whom are all things, through Whom are all things, and in Whom are all things in earth and in heaven, visible and invisible, corporeal and spiritual?
B.—I do assent and do believe.
C.—Dost thou believe each single Person of the Holy Trinity is one God, true, perfect?
B.—I do believe.
C.—Dost thou believe in the Son of God, the Word of God eternally begotten of the Father, consubstantial, co-omnipotent and co-equal in all things with the Father in Divinity, born in time of the Holy Ghost from Mary ever Virgin, with a rational soul, having two origins, one eternal from the Father, the other temporal from the mother, true God and true Man, proper and

perfect in both natures not the adopted nor the fantastic, but the sole and only, Son of God, in two natures and of two natures, yet in the singleness of one Person, incapable of suffering and immortal in His divinity, but Who in His humanity suffered for us and for our salvation, with real suffering of the flesh, and was buried, and rising on the third day from the dead in a true resurrection of the flesh, on the fortieth day after the resurrection, with the flesh wherein He rose and with His soul, ascended into heaven and sitteth at the right hand of the Father, thence to come to judge the living and the dead, and to render to everyone according to his works as they shall have been good or bad?
B.—I assent and so in all things do I believe.
C.—Dost thou believe also in the Holy Ghost, full and perfect and true God, proceeding from the Father and the Son, co-equal and co-essential, co-omnipotent and co-eternal in all things with the Father and Son?
B.—I do believe.
C.—Dost thou believe that this Holy Trinity is not three Gods, but one God Almighty, Eternal, Invisible and Unchangeable?
B.—I do believe.
C.—Dost thou believe that the Holy, Catholic and Apostolic Church is the one true church in which there is but one true Baptism and the true remission of all sins?
B.—I do believe.
C.—Dost thou also anathematize every heresy that shall arise against this Holy Catholic Church?
B.—I do anathematize it.
C.—Dost thou believe also in true resurrection of this same flesh of thine, and in life everlasting?
B.—I do believe.
C.—Dost thou believe also that God, the Lord Almighty, is the sole origin of the New and Old Testament, of the Law, and of the Prophets and of the Apostles?

B.—I do believe.
Afterward the Consecrator says: "May this faith in thee by the Lord be increased, unto true and eternal happiness." All answer, Amen.

The examination being finished, the assistant consecrators lead the Bishop-elect to the Consecrator, whose hand is reverently kissed by the Bishop-elect kneeling. Then the Consecrator, standing before the altar, the Bishop-elect at his left, begins the Mass with his ministers, saying in the usual manner the confession. The assistant consecrators standing in their proper places do likewise with their chaplains.

The Solemn Mass of the Sacred Heart of Jesus
is then begun.

The Consecrator begins the Mass, makes his public confession. The Bishop-elect and assistant ministers make their public confessions, after which, the assistant consecrators lead the Bishop-elect to his chapel. After he has laid aside the cope, acolytes put on his buskins and sandals. He receives the pectoral cross, and is vested with the tunic, dalmatic, chasuble and maniple. He advances to his altar and standing between the two consecrators reads the usual part of the Mass up to the alleluia of the gradual. The Consecrator, going up the altar with his ministers, says:

"Take away from us, we beseech Thee, O Lord, our iniquities, that we may be worthy to enter with pure minds into the Holy of Holies through Christ, our Lord. Amen.

Kissing the altar, the Consecrator says:

"We beseech Thee, O Lord, by the merits of Thy saints whose relics are here, and of all the saints, that Thou wouldst vouchsafe to forgive me all my sins. Amen.

Then the Consecrator kisses the Book of Gospels, then he blesses the incense, which he puts in the thurible, saying: "Be thou blessed by Him in Whose honor thou art about to burn."

The altar is incensed by the Consecrator, and he in turn is incensed by the deacon he then goes to the throne and reads the Introit: Psalm 32.

The Consecrator then recites and the choir sings the "Kyrie." At the conclusion of the "Kyrie" the Consecrator intones the "Gloria in Excelsis Deo"; when this is finished the Consecrator sings:

"Peace be to you," and the choir responds, "And with Thy Spirit";

The Consecrator then sings the following Oration and prayer for the Bishop-elect.

"Hear our prayers, O Almighty God, so that the work of our humble ministrations may be given fulfillment by Thy power, through our Lord Jesus Christ, Thy Son, Who liveth and reigneth with Thee in the unity of the Holy Ghost. Amen."

The sub-deacon chants the Epistle, after which he goes to the throne, where he kisses the Consecrator's ring, and receives his Blessing. Immediately the Consecrator reads the Epistle and the Gradual up to the Alleluia. The Epistle is of St. Paul to the Ephesians 3-8-19.

"Brethren: To me the least of all the saints, is given the grace to preach among the Gentiles the unsearchable riches of Christ, and to enlighten all men, that they may see what is the dispensation of the mystery, which hath been hidden from eternity in God, Who created all things: that the manifold wisdom of God may be made known to the principalities and powers in heavenly places throughout the world through the Church according to the Eternal purpose, which He made in Christ Jesus, our Lord: in Whom we have boldness and access with confidence by the faith of Him. Wherefore I pray you not to faint at my tribulation for you, which is your glory. For this cause I bow my knees to the Father of our Lord, Jesus Christ, of Whom all paternity in heaven, and earth is named, that He would grant you, according to the richness of His glory, to be strengthened by His Spirit, which might unto the inward man, that Christ may dwell in faith in your hearts: that being rooted and founded in charity, you may be able to comprehend with all the saints, what is the breadth and length, and height, and depth: to know also the charity of Christ, which surpasseth all knowledge, that you may be filled unto all the fullness of God."

The Gradual; Psalm 24-8-9.

"The Lord is sweet and righteous; therefore He will give a law to sinners in the way. V.—He will teach the meek His way, alleluia, alleluia. V.—Take My yoke upon you, and learn of Me, because I am meek and humble of heart; and you shall find rest to your souls, alleluia."

The Consecrator goes to the faldstool before the middle of the altar, and then sits, wearing his mitre. The assistant consecrators again lead the Bishop-elect to the Consecrator, to whom the Bishop-elect, having laid aside his biretta, bows profoundly. The assistants, with their mitres on, bow slightly to the Consecrator. All sit as before. The Consecrator says:

"A bishop judges, interprets, consecrates, ordains, offers, baptizes and confirms."

Then, all rising, the Consecrator with his mitre on says:

"Let us pray, dearest brethren, that the kindness of Almighty God, providing for the good of His Church, may bestow the abundance upon this Elect, through Christ, our Lord, Amen."

The Consecrator before his faldstool, and the assistant consecrators before theirs, with mitres on, kneel. The Bishop-elect prostrates himself at the left of the Consecrator, the ministers and all others kneel. Then the choir sings the Litany of the Saints.

At almost the end of the Litany, the Consecrator rises, turns toward the Bishop-elect and taking in his left hand, the staff, sings

C.—That Thou wouldst vouchsafe to bless this Elect here present.

R.—We beseech Thee, hear us.

C.—That Thou wouldst vouchsafe to bless and sanctify and Elect here present.

R.—We beseech Thee, hear us.

He sings the third time;

C.—That Thou wouldst vouchsafe to bless and sanctify and consecrate this Elect here present.

R.—We beseech Thee, hear us.

Meanwhile the Consecrator makes the sign of the cross three times over the Bishop-elect: the assistant consecrators do and say the same, remaining kneeling; the Consecrator again kneels, and the chanters continue the Litany to the end.

The Litany finished, all arise; the Consecrator stands with mitre on, before his faldstool; the Bishop-elect kneels before him. Then the Consecrator saying nothing, lays the open book of the Gospels upon the neck and shoulders of the Bishop-elect, so that the printed page touches his neck. One of the chaplains kneels behind, supporting the book until it is given into the hands of the Bishop-elect.

Then the Consecrator and the assistant consecrators touch with both hands the head of the Bishop-elect, saying:

"Receive the Holy Ghost."

This being done, the Consecrator standing without mitre sings:

"Be propitious, O Lord, to our supplications, and bestowing the abundance of sacerdotal grace upon this Thy servant, pour upon him the power of Thy blessing, through our Lord, Jesus Christ, Who liveth and reigneth in the unity of the Holy Ghost, God, Amen.

Then extending his hands before his breast, sings:

The preface.

C.—World without end. R.—Amen.

C.—The Lord be with you. R.—And with thy spirit.

C.—Lift up your hearts. R.—We have lifted them unto the Lord.

C.—Let us give thanks to the Lord, our God. R.—It is meet and just.

C.—"It is truly meet and just, right and salutary that we should at all times and places, give thanks unto Thee O Lord Father Almighty Eternal God, worthy of all dignities that serve unto Thy glory in sacred Orders; to thee O God, Who in private conversation didst instruct Moses Thy servant, concerning (among other branches of divine worship) the nature of sacerdotal vesture, and didst order Aaron Thy chosen one should be clothed in mystic vestments during the sacred functions, so that succeeding generations might be enlightened by the example of their predecessors. This is done lest the knowledge derived from Thy instructions should be wanting in any age. Since with the ancients the very appearances of symbols doth obtain reverence, so also with us the realization of the things symbolized doth mean more than the symbols themselves. For the adornment of our minds doth fulfill what was expressed by the vestments of that ancient priesthood and now brightness of souls, rather than splendor of rainment doth commend the Pontifical glory unto us. For even those things which then were slightly unto the eyes of the flesh, demanded rather that the eyes of the spirit should understand the things they signified. And therefore we beseech Thee Lord bountifully to give this grace to Thy servant whom Thou hast chosen to the ministry of the supreme priesthood so that whatever things those vestments signify by the refulgence of the gold, the splendor of jewels and the variety of diversified handiwork, these may shine forth in his character and his actions. Fill up in Thy priest the perfection of

Thy ministry and sanctify with the dew of Thy heavenly ointment this Thy servant decked out with the vestments of all purity."

One of the chaplains binds the head of the Bishop-elect with a long cloth; the Consecrator facing the altar, prostrate on both knees, intones the "Veni Creator Spiritus," the choir continuing it to the end. At the conclusion of the first verse, the Consecrator rises and sits with mitre on: with Holy Chrism he anoints the head of the Bishop-elect kneeling before him, making first the sign of the cross on the crown, and then anointing the rest of the crown saying in the meanwhile: "May thy head be anointed and consecrated by heavenly benediction in the Pontifical Order"; and making the sign of the cross three times over the head of the "Elect" he says: In the name of the Father, and of the Son, and of the Holy Ghost, Amen.

C.—Peace be to you. R.—And with thy spirit.

Having completed the anointing, the Consecrator cleansed his thumb with bread crumbs, he rises without mitre, and continues in the same tone singing:

"May this O Lord flow abundantly upon his head: may this run down his cheeks; may this spread unto the extremities of his whole body, so that inwardly he may be filled with the power of Thy Holy Spirit, and outwardly clothed with that same Spirit. May constant faith, pure love, sincere piety abound in him. May his feet by Thy sight be beautiful for announcing the glad tidings of Thy good things. Grant to him, O Lord, the ministry of reconciliation in word and deed, in the power of signs and of wonders. Let his speech and his preaching be not in the persuasive words of human wisdom, but in the showing of the spirit and power. Give to him, God, the keys of the kingdom of heaven, so that he may make use of, not boast of, the power which Thou hast bestowed unto edification, not unto destruction. Whosoever he shall bind upon earth, let it be also likewise bound in heaven; whose sins he shall loose on earth, let them be loosed also in heaven. Whose sins he shall retain, let them be also be retained in heaven; and do Thou forgive the sins of whomsoever he shall forgive; let him who shall curse him, be also accursed; and let him who shall bless him, be filled with blessings. Let him be the faithful and prudent servant for Thee to set over Thy household, so that he may give them food in due season, and prove himself a perfect man. May he be untiring in his solicitude, fervent in spirit. May he detest pride, cherish humility and truth, and never desert it, overcome either by flattery or by fear. Let him not put light for darkness nor darkness for light; let him not call evil for good, nor good for evil. May he be a debtor to the wise and to the foolish, so that he may gather fruit from the progress of all. Grant to him, O Lord, an Episcopal Chair for ruling Thy Church, and the people committed to him. May he have authority; may he have power; may he have strength. Multiply upon him Thy blessing and Thy grace, so that by Thy gift he may be fitted always obtaining Thy mercy, and by Thy grace may he be faithful, through our Lord Jesus Christ, Thy Son, Who liveth and reigneth with Thee in the unity of the Holy Ghost, God, world without end. Amen."

The Consecrator begins, and the choir takes up the antiphon:

"The ointment upon the head which ran down upon the beard of Aaron which descended on the border of his vestments; The Lord hath commanded blessing for ever.

"Behold how good and pleasant it is for brethren to dwell in unity."

"Like the precious ointment on the head that ran down upon the beard, the beard of Aaron. Which ran down to the skirt of his garment, as the dew of heaven, which descendeth upon Mount Sion."

"For there the Lord had commanded blessing and life for

evermore. Glory be to the Father, and to the Son, and to the Holy Ghost; as it was in the beginning, is now, and ever shall be, world without end."

Then the whole antiphon is repeated.

"The ointment upon the head," etc.

The antiphon before the Psalm having begun, a long cloth is placed on the neck of the Bishop-elect; the Consecrator sits down with mitre on, and the Bishop-elect kneels before him his hands joined. Then the Consecrator anoints with chrism the hands of the Bishop-elect in the form of a cross, by drawing two lines with the thumb of his right hand, namely, from the thumb of the right hand to the index finger of the left hand, and from the thumb of the left hand to the index finger of the right hand; afterwards he anoints the entire palms of the Bishop-elect saying: "May these hands be anointed with the sanctified oil and the chrism of sanctification, as Samuel anointed David to be King and Prophet so may they be anointed and consecrated." And making the sign of the cross thrice over the hands of the Bishop-elect, he says:

"In the name of the Father, and of the Son, and of the Holy Ghost, making the image of the Holy Cross of our Saviour Jesus Christ, Who hast redeemed us from death and led us into the kingdom of heaven: hear us we beseech Thee, O loving, Almighty Father, eternal God, and grant that we obtain what we ask for through the same Christ, Our Lord." He continues: "May God and the Father of our Lord Jesus Christ, Who hath Himself willed to elevate thee to the dignity of the Episcopate, bedew thee with chrism and with the liquor of mystic ointments and make thee fruitful with richness of spiritual benediction. Whatsoever thou shalt bless, may it be blessed: and whatsoever thou shalt sanctify, may it be sanctified; and may the imposition of this consecrated hand or thumb be profitable in all things unto salvation. Amen."

After this the consecrand joins both hands, the right resting upon the left, and places them upon the cloth hanging from his neck. The Consecrator cleanses his thumb with bread crumbs, and without mitre, rises and blesses the Pastoral Staff, saying:

"Let us pray: O God Who dost sustain human weakness, bless this staff: and in the clemency of Thy merciful kindness, effect inwardly in the character of Thy servant, what it outwardly designates, through Christ, our Lord." R. Amen.

He sprinkles Staff with holy water, and sitting down with mitre on, he hands the Staff to the Consecrated who is kneeling before him. He receives it between the index and middle finger, the hands remain joined, while the Consecrator says:

"Receive the Staff of the Pastoral Office, so that in the correction of vices thou mayest be lovingly severe, giving judgement without wrath, softening the minds of thy hearers whilst fostering virtues, not neglecting strictness of discipline, through love of tranquility. Amen."

After which the Consecrator, without mitre rises and blesses the ring, saying:

"Let us pray; O Lord, Creator and Preserver of the human race, Giver of spiritual grace, Bestower of eternal salvation, do Thou send forth Thy blessing upon this ring so that whosoever shall be adorned with this sign of holiest fidelity, it may avail him by the power of heavenly protection unto eternal life, through Christ our Lord. Amen."

The Consecrator then sprinkles the ring with holy water, placing it on the finger of the right hand, saying:

"Receive the ring, the symbol of fidelity, in order that, adorned with unspotted faith, Thou mayest keep inviolably the Spouse of God, namely, His Holy Church." Then the Consecrator takes the Book of Gospels from the shoulders of the consecrated, and with the aid of the assistant consecrators, hands it, closed, to him, the latter touching it without opening his hands, the Consecrator saying in the meanwhile:

"Receive the Gospel, and go forth and preach to the people committed to your care for God is powerful to increase His grace in thee, He that liveth and reigneth, world without end, Amen."

Finally, the Consecrator receives the consecrated with the kiss of peace. The assistant consecrators do likewise, each saying to the consecrated: "Peace be to you"; he answers to each, "and with thy spirit."

The newly consecrated Bishop, between the assistant consecrators, returns to his chapel, where, while he is seated, his head is cleansed with bread crumbs, and with a clean cloth. He washes his hands, and the Consecrator washes his at his faldstool. He then goes to the throne and the Mass is resumed: the newly consecrated Bishop likewise resumes the Mass in his chapel.

Prayer before the Gospel.

"Cleanse my heart and my lips O God Almighty, Who didst cleanse the lips of the Prophet Isais with a burning coal, vouchsafe of Thy gracious mercy so cleanse me that I may worthily proclaim Thy holy Gospel, through Christ, our Lord, Amen."

The Gospel is from St. John, 19-31-37.

The deacon places the book of Gospels on the altar, goes to the throne where he kisses the Consecrator's ring, then kneeling on the lowest step of the Altar, says the prayer "cleanse my heart and lips O God," etc.

After the Gospel, the altar is incensed and then the "Credo" is intoned by the Consecrator, and the choir sings:

The Credo.

"I Believe in God the Father Almighty, Maker of heaven and earth, and of all things, visible and invisible: and in one Lord,

Jesus Christ, the only begotten Son of God, born of the Father before all ages, God of God, Light of Light, true God of true God, begotten, not made; consubstantial with the Father by Whom all things were made, Who for us came down from heaven (the Consecrator genuflects, and adores the Word made flesh) and was incarnate by the Holy Ghost of the Virgin Mary, and was made man. He was crucified for us, suffered under Pontius Pilate and was buried. And the third day, he rose again from the dead, according to the scriptures, and ascended into heaven, and He shall come again with glory to judge the living and the dead; and His kingdom shall have no end; and in the Holy Ghost the Lord and giver of life, Who proceedeth from the Father and the Son Who together with the Father and the Son is adored and glorified; Who spoke by the Prophets; and one holy, Catholic and apostolic church. I confess to the remission of sin; and I await the resurrection of the dead; and the life of the world to come."

The Mass is continued in the regular order; at the Post-Communion the Consecrator offers this prayer for the newly consecrated Bishop: "We beseech Thee, O Lord, to fulfill in us Thy mercy, moreover graciously grant us to be such, and so cherish us that we may be able to please Thee in all things, through Jesus Christ, The Son, Who liveth and reigneth with Thee in the unity of the Holy Ghost." Amen.

At the canon of the Mass, during the commemoration of the living the Consecrator offers a prayer for the newly consecrated Bishop: "We beseech Thee, O Lord, to be appeased and to accept this offering which we Thy servants, and likewise Thy whole family make to Thee. We make it also on behalf of this Thy servant Whom Thou hast chosen to raise to the Order of Bishop. Mercifully keep him in Thy gifts, so that by divine grace he may fulfill what by divine grace he has received; order our days in Thy peace, and bid us to be delivered from eternal damnation, and received into the fold of Thine elect, through Christ our Lord, Amen."

The newly consecrated Bishop recites the following prayer: "We beseech Thee, O Lord, to be appeased and to accept this offering which we Thy servants, and likewise Thy whole family make to Thee; We make it also on behalf of me Thy servant whom Thou has vouchsafed to raise to the Order of Bishop. Mercifully keep me in Thy gifts, so that by divine grace I may fulfill what by divine grace I have received. Order our days in Thy peace, and bid us to be delivered from eternal damnation, and received into the fold of Thine elect, through Christ our Lord. Amen."

The Consecrator makes the sign of the cross over the bread and wine, and prays they become the Body and Blood of Christ.

Then follow the prayers incidental to the Consecration. The canon is again interrupted by the Consecrator to pray for the dead, and he then recites the commemoration of the Church suffering, militant, and triumphant. The Mass then continues—the Lord's prayer is sung by the Consecrator, and then follows the Agnus Dei, and the administration of Holy Communion.

The Consecrator gives the newly consecrated Bishop the kiss of peace, saying, "Peace be with you." R.—And with thy spirit. The consecrated Bishop gives his kiss of peace to his assistant consecrators saying, "Peace be with thee." R.—And with thy spirit.

After Communion, the Consecrator with his mitre sits on the faldstool, the newly consecrated Bishop kneels before him; the master of ceremonies places the zucchetta on the head of the consecrated Bishop. The Consecrator blesses the zucchetta, saying: "Let us pray: O Lord God, Father Almighty, Whose goodness is wonderful and Whose power is immense, from Whom is every best and every perfect gift, the ornament of all beauty, vouchsafe to bless and sanctify this mitre to be placed on the head of Thy prelate, Thy servant, through Christ, our Lord, Amen."

The Consecrator sprinkles the mitre with holy water, blesses it, and aided by the assistant consecrators, he places it on the head of the consecrated, saying:

"O Lord, place on the head of this, Thy Bishop and champion, the helmet of defense and salvation, so that, his face being adorned and his head armored with the protection of both testaments, he may seem formidable to the opponents of truth, and through the plenteous bestowal of Thy grace may be their sturdy adversary. Thou, Who didst mark with splendor and truth, the countenance of Moses, Thy servant, ornamented from his fellowship with Thy word; and didst command the tiara be placed on the head of Aaron Thy High Priest, through our Lord. Amen."

The Consecrator, without mitre, rises and blesses the gloves of the Consecrated, saying:

"O Almighty Creator, Who hast given to man, fashioned after Thine image, hands notable for the formation, as an organ of intelligence for correct workmanship: which Thou hast commanded to be kept clean, so that the soul might worthily be carried in them, and Thy mysteries worthily consecrated by them, vouchsafe to bless and sanctify these hand coverings; so that whosoever of Thy ministers, the holy Bishops shall humbly wish to cover his hands with these, Thy mercy shall accord to him cleanness of heart, as well as of deed through Christ, our Lord. Amen."

The Consecrator sprinkles the gloves with water; the pontifical ring is taken from the finger of the Consecrated Bishop; the Consecrator, with the assistance of the assistant consecrators, places the gloves on the hands of the consecrated saying:

"Encompass, O Lord, the hands of this Thy servant and minister with the cleanness of the new Man Who descended from heaven, so that as Thy beloved Jacob, his hands covered with the skins of young goats, implored and received the paternal benediction, having offered to his Father most agreeable food and drink, so also the one may desire to implore, and to receive the benediction of Thy grace, by means of the saving Host offered by his hands: through our Lord Jesus Christ Who in the likeness of sinful flesh, offered Himself to Thee for us."

The Consecrator then places the Episcopal ring on the finger of the consecrated and aided by the assistant consecrators, assists the Consecrator to the faldstool. The Consecrator places the Staff in his left hand. Then the Consecrator turns to the altar, and intones this hymn of thanksgiving, which is sung by the choir:

"Te deum Laudamus."

At the conclusion of the hymn, the consecrated Bishop, accompanied by the assistant consecrators and chaplains, goes down the center aisle blessing the congregation; the Consecrator remaining at the centre of the altar. The Bishop returning to the faldstool sits until the end of the "Laudamus" is sung.

The Consecrator intones the following antiphon:

"May thy hand be strengthened and thy right hand be exalted; justice and judgement be the preparation of thy throne. Glory be to the Father, and to the Son, and to the Holy Ghost; as it was in the beginning, is now, and ever shall be, world without end, Amen." The antiphon is repeated, the Consecrator sings;

C.—O Lord, hear my prayer
R.—And let my cry come unto Thee
C.—The Lord be with you
And with Thy spirit.

Let us pray: "O God the pastor, and Ruler of all the faithful, look down in Thy mercy upon this, Thy servant, whom Thou hast appointed over Thy church, and grant, we beseech Thee, that both by word and deed, and by example he may edify all those who are under his charge, so that with the flock entrusted to him, he may attain unto life everlasting, through Christ our Lord, Amen."

Taking the pastoral staff in his hand the Consecrator turns to the people and blesses them thrice "in the name of the Father, and of the Son, and of the Holy Ghost, Amen." The Consecrator and assistant consecrators put on their mitres; the consecrated Bishop goes to the Epistle side of the altar, with mitre on, and holding his staff, facing the Consecrator, he kneels, and sings, "for many days"; then going to the middle of the altar, he again kneels and sings in a higher voice, "for many days"; he then approaches the Consecrator and kneeling the third time sings in a still higher voice, "for many years."

The consecrated Bishop then receives the kiss of peace from the Consecrator and assistant Consecrators, The Consecrator says in a low voice: The Lord be with you. R. — and with thy spirit

Gospel of St. John.

"In the beginning was the Word, and the Word was with God, and the Word was God. The same was in the beginning with God. All things were made by Him, and without Him was made nothing that was made. In Him was life, and the life was the light of men; and the light shineth in darkness, and the darkness did not comprehend it. There was a man sent from God, whose name was John. This man came for a witness, to give testimony of the Light, that all men might believe through him. He was not the Light, but was to give testimony of the Light. That was the true Light, that enlighteneth every man that cometh into the world. He was in the world, and the world was made by Him, and the world knew Him not. He came to His own, and His own knew him not; but as many as received Him He gave them power to be made sons of God: to them that believe in His name who are born not of blood, nor of the will of the flesh, nor of the will of man, but of God. And the Word was made Flesh, and dwelth amongst us, and we saw His glory, as it were glory of the only begotten Son of the Father, full of grace, and truth."

Thus is finished the beautiful and solemn ceremonial of consecrating a new Bishop in the Catholic Church – the Church of Christ, God, founded by Christ on Peter. The newly consecrated Bishop takes upon himself a new mantle, emblazoned – "Successor to the Apostles – the companions of our Lord and Saviour, Jesus Christ"; and like them he has become filled with the Holy Ghost, the third person of the Holy Trinity, true God, Who will guide his every act in the administration of his sector of God's Kingdom on earth.

The Bishops office is the fullness of Christ's Holy Priesthood: the most exalted position to be attained by man, being to sinners the fulfillment of Christ's promise: "whatsoever they loose upon the earth shall be loosed in heaven."

Truly indeed, the Episcopacy of the Catholic Church is a solemn and awe-inspiring responsibility, sublime beyond conception, and the crowning glory of all earthly pursuits.

Chapter Nine

The ceremonial of Ordination of Catholic Priests.

With his mitre on the Bishop sits on the faldstool before the middle of the altar. The Archdeacon calls the ordinands. "Let those who are to be ordained to the Order of Priesthood come forward."

Then the Archdeacon presents them to the Bishop saying: "Most Reverend Father, our Holy Mother the Church (Catholic) ask that you ordain the deacons here present, to the office of the holy priesthood." The Bishop inquires: "Dost thou know them to be worthy?" The archdeacon answers: "As far as human frailty alloweth me to know, I doth, and bear witness that they are worthy of this office." The Bishop replies: "Deo Gratias."

The Bishop addresses the clergy and people as follows:

"Dearly beloved brethren: The captain of a ship as well as the passengers are in the same condition as to safety or danger. Their cause is common, therefore they ought to be of the same mind. Indeed, not without reason did our Fathers ordain that in the election of candidates for the service of the altar the people also should be consulted. For it happens here and there that, as to the life and conduct of a candidate some few know what is unknown to the majority. Necessarily also the people will render obedience to one more readily after he is ordained if they have approved of his ordination. Now with the help of the Lord, these deacons are to be priests.

"As far as I can judge their life has been of recognized goodness and pleasing to God, and in my opinion, merits for them promotion to a higher ecclesiastical honor. However, one or a, few may be mistaken in their judgment, or deceived by affection, we must heed the opinion of many. Therefore, whatever you know of their lives or character, whatsoever you think of their worthiness, freely make it known. Testify as to their fitness for the priesthood, according to merit rather than according to affection. If anyone has anything against them before God and for the sake of God let him come confidentially and speak. However, let him be mindful of his condition."

The Bishop makes a short pause. Then he addressess the ordinands the following admonition.

"Dearly beloved sons: you are about to be ordained to the Order of Priesthood. Strive to receive it worthily, and after receiving it perform its duties in a praiseworthy manner.

"The office of the priest is to sacrifice, to bless, to govern, to teach and to baptize. Truly it must be with great fear that you ascend to so high a station: and care must be taken that heavenly wisdom, and irreproachable character, and long continued righteousness shall commend the candidates chosen for it.

"It is for this reason, that the Lord when commanding Moses to select from the whole people of Israel, seventy men to assist him, and to impart to them a share in the gifts of the Holy Spirit, added this direction:

"Take whom thou knowest to be elders amongst the people. Now you have been typified by the seventy elders: you elders, if you assisted by the seven gifts of the Holy Ghost, observe the then commandments of the Law, and prove yourselves to be worthy, mature in mind, and likewise in works.

"In fulfillment of the same mystery and figure, the Lord chose seventy two disciples, whom He sent two by two, to go before Him, preaching. Thus we wished to teach by word and deed, that the ministers of the church should be perfect in the practice of their faith: in other words, they should be as well grounded in the two-fold virtue of charity which is the love of God and one's neighbor.

"Therefore, endeavor to be such, that, by the grace of God, you may be worthy to be chosen as helpers of Moses, and the twelve Apostles, that is, of the Bishops of the Catholic church, who are signified by Moses and the twelve Apostles."

"Truly wonderful is the variety with which the church is endowed, adorned and governed. Its ministers are men ordained to various Orders, some bishops, some priests, some deacons, and sub-deacons. Thus out of many members distinguished as to dignity, the one Body of Christ is formed."

"Therefore, dearly beloved sons, chosen by our brethren, to be our helpers in the ministry, maintain in your deportment inviolate purity, and holiness of life; understand what you mean and what you do, imitate what you administer. In as much as you celebrate the mystery of the Lord's death, you should endeavor to mortify in your members all sin and concupiscence. Your preaching must be a spiritual medicine for the people, and the sweet odor of your lives a joy to the church of Christ. May you thus build up by word and example the House of God, so that your promotion may not be a cause of eternal damnation for me, nor the reception of this Order for you, but rather of reward. May He in His grace and mercy, grant our prayer."

Then follows the touching ceremony of prostration. The ordinands prostrate themselves upon the floor of the sanctuary as a sign of their unworthiness, and the need of divine guidance. The Bishop and all others assisting kneel; the chanters begin the Litany of the Saints, the choir answering. After the Litany the ordinands arise. The most solemn moment of the Ordination

Rite has arrived: the moment in which the transformation takes place in the soul of the ordinand, which makes him, "Priest forever according to the Order of Melchizedek." The Bishop imposes his hands upon each ordinand without saying any prayer, and after all this, the priests present do the same. Then the Bishop and all priests raise their right hands and hold them over the candidates.

All is hushed in silence: it is as if the heavens opened, and the Holy Spirit came down in visible form to take possession of His elect. "The Spirit of the Lord is upon me, because the Lord hath anointed me." (Isais, 6-I) With his arms extended, the Bishop prays:

"Let us dearly beloved brethren, beseech God the Father Almighty, to bestow in abundance heavenly gifts upon these His servants whom He has chosen for the Priesthood. May they by His help accomplish what they undertake in following His gracious call, through Christ, our Lord. Amen."

The Bishop turns to the altar and says: "Let us pray: The ministers respond: "Let us bend our knees. R. – Arise.

Again the Bishop turns to the ordinands saying:

"Hear us, we beseech Thee, Lord our God, and pour on these Thy servants the blessings of the Holy Spirit and the power of priestly grace. Sustain them forever with the bounty of Thy gifts whom we present to Thy mercy to be consecrated: through our Lord, Jesus Christ, Thy Son, Who liveth with Thee in the unity of the Holy Ghost."

The following is said by the Bishop with arms extended.

B. – "Forever and ever"

R. Amen

B. "The Lord be with you."

R. – And with thy spirit.

B. – "Lift up your hearts;"

R. – We have lifted them to the Lord.

B. — "Let us give thanks to the Lord our God"
R. — It is meet and just.
Bishop: "It is truly meet and just, right and profitable to salvation to give thanks to Thee, Holy Lord, Father Almighty, Eternal God, Giver of honors and dispenser of all dignities. Through Thee all things prosper: by Thee they are maintained; through Thee the endowments of our rational nature are continually raised to a higher perfection, all according to a wisely appointed plan.

"There have come into existence priestly Orders, and the office of Levites, instituted amid sacred mysteries. When Thou didst appoint High Priests to govern the people, Thou didst also choose men of lower rank and dignity to be at their side to assist them in their work. Thus in the desert, Thou didst instill the spirit of Moses in the minds of the seventy judicious men, so that with their help, he easily governed the countless multitudes of the people.

"In like manner, Thou didst transfer to Eleazar and Thamur, the sons of Aaron, the fullness of their father's priesthood, so that there would be a sufficient number of priests for the salutary sacrifices, and the performance of the numerous sacred Rites. By the same Providence, Thou hast joined to the Apostles of Thy Son, teachers of the Faith, and with their help they have filled the whole world with the glad tidings of the gospel.

"Therefore, we beseech Thee, O Lord, give also to us in our infirmity: we need it the more, as our weakness is so much greater than theirs. We beseech Thee O Lord, Almighty Father, invest these Thy servants with the dignity of the Priesthood. Do Thou renew in them the spirit of holiness, so that they may persevere in this office, which is next to ours in dignity, since they have received it from Thee, O God.

"May the example of their lives lead others to mortal uprightness, and may they ever be faithful fellow watchers and labourers, and assist us in our Episcopal office: and may they, setting the example of a holy life in every respect, be able to give a good account of their stewardship entrusted to them, and thus attain the prize of eternal glory, through the same Christ our Lord, Jesus Christ, Who liveth and reigneth in the unity of the Holy Ghost, world without end, Amen."

The Bishop imposes the Stole upon each candidate, saying:

"Receive the yoke of the Lord, for His yoke is sweet, and His burden light."

Then the Bishop vests the candidates with the chasuble, in such a manner that only the front part hangs down, and the back part, remains folded, saying at the same time:

"Receive the priestly garb by which priestly charity is signified: for God is powerful to increase your charity, and the perfection of your work." The ordinands answer "Thanks be to God:"

While all are kneeling the Bishop prays:

"O God, Author of all goodness and holiness, from Whom comes true consecration and the fullness of benediction, do Thou, O Lord, pour out Thy gracious blessing upon these Thy servants, upon whom we confer the honor of the Priesthood. May they, by gravity of demeanor, and strictness of life prove themselves to be Elders, trained according to the principles which Paul set down for Titus and Timothy. May they keep Thy laws before their minds day and night, believe what they read, teach what they believe, and live according to what they teach. May they show forth justice, constancy, fortitude and other virtues, be leaders by their example, inspire strength by exhortation, and preserve the grace of their ministry, pure and undefiled. And thus, as ministers of Thy people, may they by a spotless benediction change bread and wine into the Body and Blood of Thy Son. And having kept their conscience clear, pure and true their faith in charity, may they rise on the day of God's just and final judgment, full of the Holy Ghost a perfect man in the fullness of the manhood of The Son, Who liveth and reigneth with Thee in the unity of the Holy Ghost, God, forever and ever, Amen."

The Bishop kneels before the altar, and intones the hymn "Veni Creator Spiritus."

After the first stanza the Bishop sits on his faldstool, takes off his gloves: the candidates kneel before him, and he anoints their hands while doing this, he pronounces this prayer: "Vouchsafe O Lord, to consecrate and sanctify these hands by our unction and our blessing.

"That whatsoever they shall bless, may be blessed, and whatsoever they shall consecrate, be consecrated and sanctified, in the name of our Lord, Jesus Christ, Amen."

By previous imposition of hands, the candidates have been made Priests, possessing all the powers of the priesthood. But the power to change bread and wine into the Body and Blood of our Divine Lord, is such a tremendous gift that a special Rite is employed to express its bestowal. The hands of the ordinands having been anointed, the Bishop closes them and one of the assisting priests binds them together with white cloth, leaving the fingers free. The ordained priests approach and kneel before the Bishop: a chalice containing some wine and water, and the paten with a host upon it, is presented to each; whereupon the ordained takes the paten between the index and the middle finger, touching with the latter the cup of the chalice, while the Bishop says: "Receive the power to offer the Sacrifice of the Mass, for the living and the dead."

The Bishop washes his hands and continues the Mass: after the Offertory the Bishop puts on his mitre, and takes his seat before the middle of the altar. All the ordained approach, and kneeling before the Bishop offer to him a burning candle, kissing the Bishop's ring. Having received this offering, the Bishop washes his hands and the Mass continues. All the newly ordained priests say the Mass together with the Bishop, and all prayers are said aloud. From the Offertory on, the concelebration of the Mass continues. This is really the first Mass of the newly ordained priests; concelebration in the Latin Mass takes place only at ordination to the priesthood.

At the communion the Bishop consumes the sacred species; the newly ordained priests receive Holy Communion from the Bishop, in one species only. After receiving, those who have received major offices partake of some wine. One of the priests standing at the Epistle side near the corner of the altar, holds a chalice and a purification for the purpose. When all have received Holy Communion the Bishop purifies the paten and chalice, saying together with the newly ordained priests;

"May we keep O Lord, with a pure heart what we have received with the mouth, and may this temporal gift be to us a remedy to life everlasting."

"May Thy Body O Lord, of Which I have taken, and Thy Blood Which I have drunk cleave unto my soul: and grant that no stain of sin may remain in me after I have been refreshed with this pure and holy sacrament. Who livest and reigneth forever, Amen."

After the Bishop has taken the absolution he washes his hands, and then reads the following responsories on the Epistle side.

"From now on I shall call you servants no longer, but my friends, for you know all things whatsoever I have wrought in the midst of you. Allelulia.

"Receive in you the Holy Ghost, the Paraclete. He it is the Father will send you. Alleluia: you are my friends, if you do the things I command you. Receive in you the Holy Ghost, the Paraclete. Glory be to the Father, and to the Son, and to the Holy Ghost. He it is the Father will send to you: Alleluia."

Having said this responsitory the Bishop turns to the newly ordained priests: they recite the Apostles Creed, thus publicly confessing the faith they are about to preach.

At the conclusion of the Credo, the Bishop bestows upon the newly ordained priests the power to forgive sins: By the imposition of hands of the Bishop the priests were given all priestly powers. Because of the excellence of the power to forgive sins, a special ceremony is employed to express its bestowal on the priest. The newly ordained kneel before the Bishop, who lays his hands on each and says:

"Receive the Holy Ghost, whose sins you forgive, they are forgiven, and whose sins you shall retain, they are retained."

The Bishop unfolds the chasuble, which up to this point the ordained has worn upon the back, saying: "May the Lord clothe thee with the role of innocence." Then the Bishop taking both hands of the ordained into his own asks for the promise of obedience. "Dost thou promise me and my successors reverence and obedience? Answer: I promise."

"Dost thou promise to the Bishop (or prelate) who will be the Ordinary for the time being, reverence and obedience? Answer: I promise."

Then the Bishop still holding the hands of the ordained, kisses him on the cheek, saying "the peace of the Lord be always with thee." The priests answer: Amen. The newly ordained return to their places, and the Bishop addresses to them the following exhortation:

"Dearly beloved sons: The office which you shall perform in the future is not without danger. Therefore I exhort you to learn carefully from other well informed priests the order of the whole Mass, the consecration, the breaking of the Host and communion before you begin to say Mass." The Bishop rises, and blesses the priests kneeling before him "The blessing of Almighty God the Father, and the Son, and the Holy Ghost, descend upon you, that you may be blessed in the Priesthood, and that for the sins of the people, you may offer up the Sacrifice of propitiation to the Almighty God, to Whom be honor and glory, forever, Amen." The Bishop delivers the final admonition to the newly ordained priests.

"Dearly beloved sons: earnestly reflect upon the ordination which you have received today, and the burden which has been laid upon your shoulders. Endeavor to live holy and godly lives, and to be pleasing to Almighty God, that you may obtain His grace. May He in His mercy design to bestow it upon you. All those who have been promoted to the tonsure, or the minor Orders, say the seven Penitential Psalms, with the Litany, versicles and orations. Deacons, say the nocturn of the day.

"Those who have been ordained to priests say after your first Mass, three other Masses, one to the Holy Ghost, one to the Blessed Virgin, and one for the poor souls, and finally one in memory of me." The Bishop then turns to the altar, and together with the newly made priests says the last Gospel according to St. John: In the beginning; was the Word, and the Word was with God, and the Word was God; etc., etc.

Thus ends the Rite of ordination of a priest in the Catholic Church. The newly ordained priest clothed in the precious vestments of Christ's Holy Priesthood is empowered to take His place in the world as a shepherd of souls, the awe inspiring power of absolving from sin: the keys of the kingdom of heaven are in his hands: and the majestic privilege of offering the Body and Blood of Jesus Christ to the Father as a propitiation for the sins of men. Truly is the Catholic priest especially endowed.

Our divine Lord loved His Blessed Mother above all created beings, sinless, immaculate, "tainted natures unblemished boast," yet He did not give to her this tremendous power, conferred upon sinners. She is our greatest intercessor before the throne of her divine Son, yet, she cannot absolve sin, nor offer up the Body and

Blood of her divine Son.

As said of the Catholic Bishopric, so too can it be said of the Catholic priesthood: "it is a solemn responsibility, sublime beyond conception, and the crowning glory of all earthly persuits."

"Juravit dominus et non puenatabit eum, tuae sacerdos in aeternum secundam ordinem Melchizedek" (the Lord has spoken and He will not repent, thou art a priest forever according to the Order of Melchizedek).

Chapter Ten

Ancient Liturgies, and Rites of Ordinations of Priests and Deacons; also Consecration Rites of Bishops not in communion with the Holy See, but recognized by the Catholic Church as possessing valid Orders, and valid sacraments.

Many Anglican prelates and Anglican laity have asserted that Rome was determined to destroy all Christian churches not in communion with the See of Peter, by declaring their priestly Orders to be invalid.

These assertions are not in line with history, as study of the various Rites will determine. All ancient churches preserve their liturgies from the Apostolic days to the present. Their bishops though schismatic, adhere to the ancient forms of ordaining priests and consecrating bishops. The Liturgies of the primative churches are very careful to identify in no uncertain language the office to which men are to be ordained and consecrated. The prayers for the grace of the Holy Ghost definitely proclaim the intention of the Consecrator to consecrate a sacrificing priesthood, and true bishops. The first to be presented in this study is the Nestorian Church.

Nestorius was a Syrian ecclesiastic; the date of his birth is unknown, though his death is recorded as the year 451. He was consecrated Patiarch of Constantinople in December 427, upon the death of Sisinius. Previous to his elevation to the Patriarchate by Theodosius II he had been engaged as a missionary, and was held in great esteem, due to his forensic brilliance. Like many others before him and since, the adulation poured upon him succeeded in establishing in his own mind his pre-eminence as a leader in the theological field. He denied the Blessed Virgin Mary to be the Mother of God, and, accordingly at the Council of Ephesus in the year 431 he was deposed from his See. After his deposition the church gradually fell into error and separated from Roman obedience. As a matter of fact the Nestorian church has no communication with any other separated churches. The Rites of the Nestorian church seem to be a mixture of Apostolic Traditions and Greek Rites. There is no doubt their Rites of Ordination of priests and consecration of bishops, antedated the Council of Ephesus held in 431. In both Rites of ordination and consecration of bishops, it will be noted that the prayer accompanying the laying on of hands, contain words which definitely describe the Orders conferred, to wit:

Ordination of Bishop:

The Consecrator puts his right hand on the head of the consecrand and says: "We offer before Thy Majesty, this Thy servant, whom we believe Thou hast set aside, and chosen, that he may be a bishop."

Ordination of Priest:

The Bishop places his right hand on the ordinand saying in a low voice; "Do Thou O Lord, great God of strength, look upon these Thy servants, and choose them to the Priestly office."

Ordination of Deacon:

The Bishop places his right hand on the head of the candidates, extending his left hand in the manner of prayer, saying over their heads: "Lord God, Who didst choose Thy Holy Church, and didst raise up in her, prophets, priests and doctors, and did also place in her deacons, even as Thou didst choose

Stephen and his companions, so now also, O Lord, give to these Thy servants, the grace of Thy Holy Spirit, that they may be chosen ministers."

The ancient churches of Antioch, Armenia, Greece, Asia Minor, and Alexandria all possessed different forms of ordination and consecration. The Maronites, Jacobites, Copts, Syrian Chaldeans also have their own established forms of ordination and consecration: some agreeing that imposition of hands is all sufficient, accompanied by the proper prayers to bestow the grace desired and required in a valid consecration of a sacrificing priesthood.

The Liturgy of the Apostolic Constitutions for the making of a Bishop is as follows:

One of the first bishops, with two others standing near the altar while the other bishops and priests silently praying, and while the deacons holding the divine Gospels on the head of the bishop-elect, shall say to God: "Give, O Lord to this Thy servant whom Thou hast chosen to the Episcopal office to feed Thy people, and discharge the office of Pontiff." Then follows the long prayer discriptive of the Bishopric.

Ordination of a Priest: "When Thou O Bishop will ordain a priest lay thy hand upon his head, and with the circle of priests and deacons standing by thee, say thou thyself in prayer: 'Lord Almighty our God, do Thou now look down upon this Thy servant, who by the vote and judgment of the whole clergy is admitted to the Priesthood.' "

Ordination of a Deacon: "Thou shalt make a deacon O Bishop, by laying hands upon him, while the whole body of priests and deacons stand by thee, and say in prayer: 'O Almighty God, show Thy countenance upon this Thy servant chosen to Thee in the deaconite, and fill him with the Holy Ghost and with strength, as Thou didst fill Stephen the first martyr.' "

After laying on of hands of priests and deacons the long prayer invoking the Holy Ghost to fill the ordinands and deacons with grace is recited. These prayers are similar to those used in Catholic ceremonies of priests and bishops consecrations and ordinations. Ancient Roman Liturgy — Consecration of a Bishop:

Two bishops place and hold the book of Gospels upon his head, and while one bishop says over him the blessing, all the other bishops who are present touch his head, and the Consecrator says the usual long prayer concerning the responsibility of a bishop as successor of the Apostles, and then the words of consecration: "And therefore to this Thy servant whom Thou hast chosen to the High Priesthood."

Ordination of a Priest: The bishop blesses him, lays his hands upon his head, and also all the priests: "Grant we beseech Thee, Almighty Father, in this Thy servant, the dignity of the priesthood."

Ordination of a Deacon: The Bishop alone who blesses him, lays hands upon his head, and consecrates him thusly: "Look mercifully, we beseech Thee O Lord also upon this Thy servant whom we humbly dedicate to the office of deacon to serve in Thy sanctuary."

Consecration of Greek Bishops:

The Archbishop laying hands upon him to be consecrated, prays thus "Do Thou, O Lord of all, strengthen and confirm this Thy servant, that by the hand of me a sinner, and of the assisting ministers and fellow bishops, and by the coming, the strength and the grace of the Holy Ghost he may obtain the Episcopal dignity."

Ordination of a Priest:

The Archbishop laying hands upon him prays thus:

"O God, who by the title of priest dost honor those who are judged worthy to administer in that rank with holiness the words of truth, make perfect Thy servant, that he may deport himself worthily in that greatly priestly honor."

Ordination of a Deacon:

The Archbishop having laid hands upon him prays in this wise:

"Do Thou O Lord, this man whom it has pleased Thee that I should promote to the office of deacon — preserve him in all gravity of conduct: give him the grace which Thou hast given to Blessed Stephen, the proto-martyr."

Coptic Rite:

Consecration of a Bishop:

The Patriarch lays his right hand on the head of the newly called. The bishops extend their hands and touch his neck and shoulders. The Patriarch says the prayers of Ordination:

"O Lord God, Almighty, Ruler, bestow therefore this same grace upon Thy servant whom Thou hast chosen as Bishop."

Ordination of a Priest:

The Bishop lays his right hand upon the head of the ordinand and prays:

"O Lord, God Almighty, look upon this Thy servant, who is presented to Thee for the Priesthood."

Ordination of a Deacon:

The Bishop lays his right hand on him in the usual manner, and prays:

"O Lord God Almighty, we beseech Thee, that Thou wouldst show Thy countenance on this Thy servant who is presented to Thee for the Deaconite. Fill him with the Holy Ghost, and with wisdom and strength, as Thou didst fill Blessed Stephen."

Armenian Rite of Ordination of a Bishop:

The Archbishop says:

"The divine grace calleth this Thy servant from the priesthood to the Episcopate: I impose hands. Pray that he may be worthy of the rank of Bishop." Then follows the long prayer invoking the Holy Ghost on him.

Armenian priest ordination:

The Bishop imposes hands on the ordinand and prays:

"O Lord God, give grace to this Thy servant, that he may possess the rank of Priesthood." The bishop again places his hand on the head of the ordinand and further prays: "O Lord, Thou hast chosen and received him to the Priesthood. Preserve this Thy servant now ordained inmovable in this priesthood."

Armenian ordination of a Deacon:

The Bishop lays his hand for the second time on the head of the new deacon, saying, "O Lord God, make the grace of Thy Spirit to rest on this Thy servant, who approaches to the ordination of the ministry of Thy Holy Church" the Bishop lays his hand for the third time on the head of the candidate, praying: "The divine and heavenly grace calleth this man, thy servant from the sub-deaconate to the deaconate." Again laying hands on him saying: "O divine and heavenly grace, which always supplies the needs of the ministry of the Apostolic Church, call — from the sub-deaconate to the deaconate."

"Give him the grace to follow, and the strength, to be like St. Stephen, the proto-martyr and first deacon."

Ancient Gallican Rite:

Ordination of a Bishop:

Two bishops place and hold the Book of Gospels upon the head of the bishop-elect, and while one says over him the blessing, all the other bishops touch his head. The prayer of consecration follows: the final prayer to God is offered by the Consecrator — "And therefore to this Thy servant whom Thou hast chosen to the ministry of the High-Priesthood give grace."

Ordination of a Priest:

When a priest is ordained the bishop blesses him and lays hands upon the head of the ordinand, and the priests present do likewise. Then the bishop pronounces the words of consecration

"Grant, we beseech Thee, Almighty God, in this Thy servant the dignity of the Priesthood."

Ordination of a Deacon:

When a deacon is ordained the bishop alone who blesses him, lays hands upon his head, and offers this prayer: "Look mercifully O Lord, and we beseech Thee, upon this Thy servant whom we humbly dedicate to the office of deacon, to serve at Thy altar."

In the administration of these ancient "Rites" there is a slight difference in the ceremonial practices, for example: it will be noted that in the Greek Liturgy it is the Archbishop and assisting bishops who administer the "Rite." In the ancient Roman and Gallican Rites, two bishops confer and consecrate; but in the Armenian Rite it is the Archbishop alone who consecrates a bishop, and in the ordination of a priest the Bishop without priests ordains the ordinand.

In the conferring of these Rites of ordination and consecration there is a *definite intention* to ordain sacrificing priests; and the invocation to the Holy Ghost to sanctify the ordinand and the consecrand is present in all forms of ordinations.

The recognition of the validity of these various Rites by the Church of Rome (despite their schismatic background) is the convincing answer to Archbishop Cranmer's pronouncement "that the See of Peter denies validity of Orders in churches not in communion with and obedient to the Roman See."

For centuries these schismatical churches have ordained priests and bishops; During these centuries the sacrifice of the Mass has been offered as a propitiation for the sins of men; all the majestic and great powers of the priesthood are possessed by them. The strange thing about these churches (schismatic) is this. They stand wtih the Roman Church in refusing to recognize Anglican Orders as valid, and when the Anglican Archbishop Benson in 1886 made an attempt to effect an understanding with them, "not to Anglicanize, but to aid an existing church to strengthen an ancient church" their overtures were not successful. This campaign was particularly directed to the Nestorian and Greek churches, but both have remained adamant to the pleas of the Church of England.

Among the ancient churches there is one that remained in communion with the See of Peter, known as the Maronite Church. The Maronites are found mostly around Mt. Lebanon, although they have spread in small numbers through the country surrounding Antioch, in Galilee, and on the Syrian coast. In America, colonies have been established in Scranton, Pennsylvania, New York, and Massachusetts has several communities presided over by Chor-bishops. The present Chor-bishop in Boston, is the Rt. Rev. Stephen el-Douaihy, for many years secretary to His Beatitude the Patriarch of Lebanon. He belongs to a celebrated family in Lebanon, and numbers among his ancestors distinguished Archbishops, and renowned soldiers. He has been in this diocese for thirty years, and the church greatly progressed under his administration. Despite many attempts to divert them from Papal allegiance, they have remained faithful to the Vicar of Christ. They retain their ancient Liturgy, carried on in the same tongue used by our Divine Lord.

Ancient Maronite Rites;
Consecration of a Bishop.

The bishop raises his hands and extends his arms, and lowers them thrice upon the head of the consecrand, saying; "Thou Who canst do all things, adorn with all virtues, this Thy servant Thou hast made worthy to receive from Thee the sublime Order of Bishop."

Ordination of a Priest; The bishop places his right hand on the head of the ordinand, praying, "Choose O Lord, and this Thy

servant to the Priesthood and grant him to discharge worthily the priesthood of Thy kingdom."
Ordination of a Deacon; The bishop lays his right hand on the ordinand's head saying orally in a loud tone the prayer: "Do Thou O Lord, look upon Thy servant and send down upon him the grace of the Holy Ghost, and as Thou didst give grace to Blessed Stephen, whom Thou didst first call to this ministry."

Chapter Eleven

"Oxford" and other movements towards unity with Rome.

In the year 1833 the so called "Oxford" movement was inaugurated. Its sponsors were Edward B. Pusey, John Keble, and John Henry Newman. Together they wrote and published the pamphlets known as "Tracts for the Times". It is admitted that the practice of confession in the Church of England of today dates from Pussey's essay on the "entire absolution of the penitent". It was a return to Catholic belief before the so-called "Reformation"; and it created a definite upheavel at the time. In many respects Pusey was responsible for the re-instatement of Roman practices in the Church of England which are still observed by the High-churchmen. He died in the Anglican faith on September 16, 1882, and is buried in Oxford Cathedral, where for 54 years he had been Canon.

John Keble, the second member of this illustrious group was the son of an Anglican clergyman, a vicar of St. Aldwyn. John Keble was ordained a priest in the Church of England in 1816, and remained as tutor at Oxford University as a public examiner and teacher in Oriel till 1823.

The Catholic Emancipation and reform bills had created heated discussions not only in the political life of England, but also at Oxford University. Earl Grey's reform ministry had suppressed the Irish bishops and Keble preached the assize sermon in the

University. Cardinal Newman in his "apologia" writes of the sermon "I have ever considered and kept the day as the start of the religious movement of 1833".

The Irish bishops were Anglicans sent over to Ireland to occupy Sees which had been vacated by Catholic bishops, and the ministry treated them like serfs. As a consequence of Keble's sermon on "National Apostasy" the tractarian movement grew apace; the tendency towards High Church with leanings toward Rome was greatly accelerated: the publication of tract 90 by John Henry Newman in 1841, brought such an outburst of Protestant wrath that further publication was forbidden by ecclesiastical authority. Keble had no part in the writing of the Tract, although he had read and approved of it before it was published. He came forward and took his share of the condemnation heaped upon Newman. It never was Keble's or Pusey's intention to leave the Church of England: they were content to fight abuses within the church, and both were saddened by Newman's entry into the Catholic church. Despite Newman's secession from the church of England there was always a kindly feeling for him personally; but they made every effort to stem the tide to a re-union with Rome, and Papal obedience.

For twenty years following Newman's conversion Keble participated in every movement which sought to restore Catholic doctrine and practices in the Church of England. He retired to Bournemouth, and spent his days in caring for his wife who had been an invalid for many years. He died on the 20th of March 1866, and one month later his wife was buried beside him in the churchyard at Hursley, England.

John Henry Newman the towering figure in the "Oxford" movement was born in London on February 21st 1801, the eldest son of John Newman and Jemima Foudrinier, a lady of Huguenot ancestry. He entered Trinity College at the age sixteen. In his twenty-first year he was elected a fellow of Oriel, at that time the center of intellectual life at Oxford University. He was ordained priest in the Anglican Church in 1824.

He went on a voyage with Froude, an intimate friend, and on the return journey homeward was taken violently ill. During his convalescence he was much concerned about the status of his religious inclinations. It was during these moments of uncertainty that he composed his beautiful hymn, "Lead Kindly Light" which has brought comfort to millions of harassed souls, and at the present writing is one of the great hymns of the Christian churches.

About 1843 Newman had decided that the day was drawing near when he would become a convert to the Catholic faith. In his "Apologia" he speaks of being engaged in writing an "essay on the development of doctrine" in the beginning of 1845, and continued until October of that year when he laid aside his "essay" and determined to enter the Catholic church. One of his very close friends had been received into the Church on Michaelmas Day by Father Dominic, Superior of the Passionist House at Aston near Stone, England. Father Dominic was passing through London on his way to Belgium and he stopped off at Oxford on the evening of October 8, 1845. Father Dalgairns was sent by Newman to meet Father Dominic and to ask him to receive him (Newman) into the Catholic church.

On October 9, 1945, Newman made his profession of faith, was conditionally baptized, and on the following day with his friends received Holy Communion from Father Dominic. A year later (1846) he went to Rome and was ordained into the Catholic Priesthood, and was signally honored by Pope Pius IX with the degree of Doctor of Divinity.

With the permission and blessing of Pope Pius IX, he established a community of Religious known as the "Oratory of St. Philip" with house at London, Birmingham, and Edgbaston. For forty years he remained a recluse spending his time in writing books upon theological matters, and discipline. During his long eventful life he had encountered opposition both within and outside the church, but he accepted them all as part of the life he had elected.

Shortly after his ascension to the throne of Peter, Pope Leo XIII raised Father Newman to the Sacred College. This was a most unusual happening and had no counterpart in the modern history of the Church; no simple priest outside of the Roman Curia had ever been raised to the Cardinalite.

Cardinal Newman dedicated his life to the salvation of souls: he was always conscious for his own frailties, and took every possible means to ask for prayers for his own spiritual guidance. Illustrative of this attribute was his request from his old Bishop Dr. Ullathorne who was visiting the aging Cardinal at Edgbaston; as the bishop was leaving the Cardinal was on his knees requesting the bishop for his blessing. The bishop recites the incident thus: "rule of the church orders that the lower dignatary kneel before the higher: what could I do? there he was on his knees before me: I could not refuse without giving him great embarrassment. So, I laid my hand on his head and said, 'My dear Lord Cardinal, notwithstanding all the laws to the contrary, I pray God to bless you, and that His Holy Spirit may be full in your heart.' I felt annihilated in his presence: there is a saint in that man."

Cardinal Newman's ending was a beautiful one, in character of his entire life. The night before he died, gathering his Brothers of the Oratory around his bed, he requested them to sing Father Faber's hymn "The eternal years" remarking reminiscently, "Many people speak well of my hymn, 'Lead Kindly Light,' but Father Faber's hymn is the eternal 'Light.'" This holy man passed peacefully to his Maker on August 16, 1890. With deep humility and reverence he wrote his own epitaph, "Ex umbris et imaginibus in veritatem," (from the shadows and the symbols into truth).

The passing of Cardinal Newman created a void not only in the church of God in England, but throughout the Christian world. Two great religious bodies called him their defender, and took great pride in his membership. The conversion of Newman to the Catholic faith, lost to the Church of England a brilliant and devoted churchman, but gained for the Church of Christ, an able, yet humble defender of the faith.

Cardinal Newman was buried on the quiet Lychey Hills, beside his faithful companion and disciple, Ambrose St. John. He had gained all he desired: he was alone with "The Alone."

After Cardinal Newman's death the movement towards reunion with Rome grew apace, and during the past seventy years more than fourteen hundred Anglican clergy have been received into the church and were re-ordained into the Catholic Priesthood. Verily indeed his saintly shadow lingers.

The publication of Pope Leo XIII's "Apostolicae Curae" Encylical Letter, thoroughly quenced the talk concerning recognition of Anglican Orders as valid by the Apostolic See. Naturally there was bitter feeling among the Anglican hierarchy and inferior clergy, who felt their Orders were valid, so for almost three quarters of a century no definite attempt was made at reconciliation with Rome. However, in 1921 another effort was made to interest Rome to reopen the discussion. Through various stages the question was agitated till 1925, when Lord Halifax, through his devoted friend Abbe Portal prevailed upon the late Cardinal Mercier of Belgium to preside over a conference. This movement was known as the "Maline Conversations."

In justice to the Anglican side it must be stated that the "Maline Conversations" were initially in answer to the appeal of the Anglican bishops for a "general meeting" of all Christians throughout the world to çonsider the possibility of general unity and doctrinal agreement, that might prove acceptable to the

Church of Rome, and all other groups not in communion with the See of Peter. History records that this effort (as of all previous) was unsuccessful, for the very explicit reason that the Catholic Church — the center of all Christendom — founded by Jesus Christ, true God and true man, could not enter into any discussion concerning "Revealed Religion," unless all parties participating would admit the authority of the Pope of Rome, Christ's Vicar, in all phases, namely, possession of the true faith — jurisdiction over the Universal Church, the eminence of the Bishop of Rome, as the successor of the St. Peter, Apostle, the Rock and foundation — the Prince of the Apostles.

The interesting element in all these attempts to discuss reconciliation was the universal challenge which accompanied the petition. As recent as the reign of Benedict XV, Lord Halifax, the most articulate lay intercessor, and ardent defender of the Anglican Establishment, writing in his article "Further considerations in behalf of Re-union," page 32, states:

"Englishmen will never consent to anything which in their eyes would seem to invalidate the Orders conferred by the Episcopate of the Church of England, and to deny the claim of the Anglican Church apart from the question how far the Church of England was in schism, or not, to be a church in the sense of that word as used in the creed." Continuing he propounds this question: "May not Anglicans ask, whether by the 'church' Roman Catholics always mean the members of a body, with an external jurisdiction, and subject to a visible head; or whether they do not also mean those who by the gift of the Holy Ghost, and the possession of the sacraments are incorporated in Christ?" (Reunion and the Roman Papacy, page 27).

In view of this definite statement that "Englishmen will never agree to admit the invalidity of the 'Orders' in the Church of England" the natural reaction would be to question the sincerity of the petitioners: obviously, if they will not agree to accept an adverse decision, nothing is to be gained by a conference on the disputed question.

The query by Lord Halifax has no bearing upon the validity of Anglican Orders or the Apostolic succession of their Hierarchy: the decision of Pope Leo XIII, namely, "no sacrificing priesthood; no valid bishops, therefore no valid sacraments which can convey the gift of the Holy Ghost, and no sacramental incorporation in Jesus Christ." In a word the only sacrament in the Church of England is that of Baptism, and that sacrament can be administered by anyone having the use of reason, and the attention and intention to do what the church requires for a valid baptism.

Inasmuch as this study is a factual recital of Anglican and Protestant Episcopal church history, especially concerning validity of Orders and related subjects, it is in keeping with the purpose of this thesis to present the various invitations to unity offered by Pope Leo XIII, and succeeding Pontiffs, not only to the English people but to all those Christians, who, for many reasons were separated from the only true church of Jesus Christ — the Holy Catholic and Apostolic Church.

Chapter Twelve

To maintain continuity, the Encyclical Letter of Pope Leo XIII to the English People will be presented first.
(Encyclical Letter, "Amantissima Voluntatis")
(Written on April 14, 1895.)

Leo XIII, to the English People who seek the Kingdom of Christ in the Unity of the Faith, health and peace in the Lord.

Some time since, in an Apostolic Letter to Princess and peoples, We addressed in common with other nations, but We have greatly desired to do this by a special Letter, and thus give to the illustrious English race a token of Our sincere affection. This wish had been kept alive by the hearty good will We have always felt towards your people, whose great deeds in olden time the history of the Church declares. We were yet more moved by not infrequent conversation with your countrymen, who testified to the kindly feelings of the English towards Us personally, and above all to their anxiety for peace and eternal salvation through Unity of Faith. God is Our witness how keen is Our wish that some effort of Our's might tend to assist and further the great work of obtaining the re-union of Christians in England, and We render thanks to God, Who so far has prolonged Our life, that We make an endeavour in this direction. But, since as but right, We place Our confidence of a happy issue principally and above all in the wonderful power of God's grace, We have with full consideration determined to invite all Englishmen who glory in the Christ given Faith to join Us in this, and We exhort them to lift up their hearts to God with us, to fix their trust in Him, and to seek from Him the help necessary in such a matter by assiduous diligence in prayer.

The love and care of the Roman Pontiffs for England have been constant and perpetual. It may be instanced by Our predecessor, Gregory the Great. His religion and humanity have rightfully led your race to have a special reverence for him. Although prevented, by the Divine call to yet higher duty, from himself undertaking the apostolic labour of converting the Anglo-Saxons, as he proposed to do whilst a monk, his mind remained intent upon this great and salutary design (Joan Diac. in vita ejus C-11, 33) nor did he rest until it was accomplished. For from that monastic family which he had formed in learning and holiness of life in his own house, he sent a chosen band under the leadership of Augustine to be the messengers of grace, wisdom, and civilization to those who were still buried in paganism. And relying as he did on Divine help, his hope grew stronger under difficulty, until at length he saw his work crowned with success. He himself writes of this in tones of triumphant joy in reply to St. Augustine, who had sent him the news of the happy result: "Glory be to God on high and peace on earth to men of good will."

To Christ be the glory in whose death we live: by whose weakness we are getting strong, in the love we seek in Britain those brethren whom We know not; by whose mercy We have found those whom knowing not what We sought.

Who can tell what gladness filled the hearts of all here to know that the English race, by the workings of the grace of God

Almighty, and by your labours, my brothers have been illuminated by the light of our Holy Faith, having cast out the darkness of error, and now with freedom treads under foot those idols to which aforetime they were subject in foolish fear. (Epistle cxi-28-aluis cxi 58.)

And congratulating Ethelbert, King of Kent, and Bertha his Queen in a letter of affection, in that they had imitated "Helen" of illustrious memory, and Constantine the devout Emperor (ibid, c.XI, 66, al.c.XI, 50: c.XI, 29, al c.XI, 59) he strengthens them and their people with salutary admonitions. Nor did he cease for the rest of his life to foster and develop their faith in instructions dictated by holy prudence. Thus Christianity, which the Church had conveyed to Britain, and spread defended there against rising heresy, after having been blotted out by the invasion of heathen races, was now by the care of Gregory happily restored.

We have begun by recalling these things, not only because they are in themselves great and glorious events in the history of the Church of Christ, but also because their commemoration will be pleasing to the English people, who were the subject of them. Moreover, it is noteworthy that the same proofs of love and solicitude were manifested by the succeeding Pontiffs, to whom Gregory thoughtfully transmitted them as an inheritance. This they showed by their constant care in choosing worthy pastors, and capable teachers in learning, human and divine, by their helpful counsels, and of their providing in abundant measure whatever was necessary for establishing and developing that rising Church. And very soon was such care rewarded, for in no other case perhaps, did the Faith take root so rapidly, nor was so keen and intense a love manifested towards the See of Peter. That the English Church, and race, in those days were devoted to this center of Christian unity divinely constituted in the Roman Bishops, and that in the course of ages men of all ranks were united to them by ties of loyalty, are facts too abundantly and plainly testified by the pages of history to admit of doubt or question.

But in the storms that devastated Catholicity throughout Europe in the XVI century, England, too, received a grievous wound; for it was unhappily wrenched from communion with the Apostolic See, and then was bereft of that holy Faith in which for long centuries it had rejoiced and found liberty. It was a sad defection; and Our predecessors, while lamenting it in their earnest love, made every prudent effort to put an end to it, and to mitigate the many evils consequent upon it. It would take too long, and it is not necessary to detail the sedulous and increasing care taken by Our predecessors in those circumstances. But by far the most valuable and effective assistance they afforded lay in their having so repeatedly urged on the faithful the practice of special prayer to God that He would look with compassion on England. In the number of those who devoted themselves to this special work of charity there were some venerable and saintly men, especially St. Charles Borromeo, and St. Philip Neri; and in the last century, Paul the founder of the Society of the Passion of Christ, who, not without a certain Divine impulse, was it is said, instant in application "at the throne of Divine grace" and this all the more clearly earnest because the times seemed less favourable to the realization of his hopes. We OURSELVES, indeed, long before being raised to the Supreme Pontificate, were deeply sensible also of the importance of holy prayer offered for this cause, and heartily approved of it. For, as We gladly recall, when We were the Nuncio in Belgium, We became acquainted with an Englishman, Ignatius Spencer, himself a devoted disciple of the same St. Paul of the Cross, who laid before Us a project he had already initiated for extending a society of pius people to pray for the return of the English nation to the Church (for this purpose, he specially recommended the recital of the "Hail Mary," and at his request, this prayer was made a rule for the members of his congregation, by a general rule in Rome 1857).

We can hardly say how cordially We entered into the design, wholly inspired by faith and charity, and how We helped forward this cause, anticipating that the English nation would obtain abundant assistance thereby. Although the fruits of Divine grace obtained by prayer had already manifested themselves previously, yet as that holy league spread, they became much more abundant. Very many were led to answer the Divine call, and among them not a few men of distinguished eminence, and many too who in doing so had to make personal and heroic sacrifices. Moreover, there was a wonderful drawing of hearts and minds towards the Catholic faith and practice, which rose in public respect and esteem, and many a long cherished prejudice yielded to the force of truth.

Looking at all this, We do not doubt that the united and humble supplications of so many to God are hastening the time of further manifestations of His merciful designs towards your Nation when the Word of the Lord may run and be glorified (2 Thess. III, I). Our confidence is strengthened by observing the legislative and other measures, which, if they do not, directly, still do indirectly help forward the end We have in view, by ameliorating the conditions of the people at large, and by giving effect to the laws of justice and charity.

We have heard with singular joy of the great attention which is being given in England to the solution of the social question of which We have treated with such care in Our Encyclicals, and of the establishment of benefit and similar societies, whereby on a legal basis the condition of the working classes is improved. And We have heard of the vigorous and persevering efforts made to preserve for the people at large an education based on religious training and teaching, than which there is no firmer foundation for the instruction of youth, and the maintenance of domestic life and civic polity; of the zeal and energy with which so many engage in forwarding opportune measures for the repressing of the degrading vice of intemperance: of societies formed among the most natable young men for the promotion of purity of morals and for the maintenance of the honor due to womanhood. For, alas, in regard to the Christian virtue of continence pernicious views are subtly creeping in, as though a man was not so strictly bound as a woman.

Moreover, reflecting men are deeply concerned at the spread of Rationalism and Materialism, and We Ourselves have often lifted up Our voice to denounce these evils which weaken and paralize not religion only but the very foundation, and springs of thought and action. The highest credit is due to those who fearlessly and increasingly proclaim the rights of God and of our Lord Jesus Christ, and the laws and teachings given by Him for the establishing of the Divine Kingdom here on earth; in which teachings alone, strength, wisdom, and safety are to be found. The various and abundant manifestation of care for the aged, for orphans, for incurables, for the destitute, reformatories, and other forms of charity, all which the Church as a tender Mother instituted, and from the earliest times have ever inculcated as a special duty, are evidences of the spirit which animates you.

Nor can We omit to mention the strict public observance of Sunday and the general respect for the Holy Scriptures. Every one knows the power and resources of the British Nation, and the civilization influence, which, with the spread of liberty accompanies its commercial prosperity even to the utmost regions. But, worthy and noble as are all these varied manifestations of activity, We now turn Our minds to the origin of all power and the perennial source of all good things, to God, our most heavenly beneficient Father. For the labours of man, whether public or private, will not attain to their full efficacy unless we appeal to God in prayer and obtain the Divine Blessing. Indeed "happy is that people whose God is the Lord" (Ps. cxl, iii-15).

For the mind of the Christian should be so fixed and turned that he places and rests the chief hopes of his undertakings in the Divine help obtained by prayer, where human effort is intensified, and made more generous, and the desire of doing good, as though quickened by a heavenly fire, manifests in more vigorous and serviceable actions. In this power of prayer God has not merely dignified man, but with Infinite mercy has given him a protection and help in the time of need, ready at hand to all, easy and void of effect to no one who has confident recourse to it. Prayer is our powerful weapon, our great protection, our storehouse, our port of refuge, our place of safety. (St. Chrysostom Homilies in Genesis No. 30.)

But if the prayer of the righteous man avail so much with God even in earthly things, how much more will it not avail one who is destined to an eternal existence for the obtaining of those spiritual blessings which Christ has procured for mankind, by the sacrament of His mercy.

For He Who of God is made unto us wisdom, and justice, and sanctification and redemption, (I Cor. 1-30), in addition to what He taught, instituted, and effected, gave also for the purpose salutary precept of prayer and in His great goodness confirmed it by His example.

These simple truths are known to every Christian, but still by many they are neither remembered nor valued as they should be. It is for this reason that We insist the more strenuously on the confidence which should be placed in prayer, and recall the words and example of the Fatherly love of the same Christ, our Lord; words of deepest import and highest encouragement; words also which show how, in the counsels of God prayer is at the same time the expression of our helplessness, and the sure hope of obtaining the help we need. "And I say to you, ask and it be given you, seek and you shall find, knock and it shall be opened to you; for everyone who asketh, receiveth, and he that seeketh, findeth; and to him that knocketh, it shall be opened" (Luke, XI, 9-10). And the Son of God Himself shows us that if our prayers are to be acceptable to the Divine Majesty they must be united with His name and merits.

"Amen, Amen, I say unto you, if you ask the Father anything in My name, it shall be given you. Hitherto, you have not asked anything in my Name. Ask and you shall receive it, that your joy may be filled (John XVI, 23, 24). And He confirms this by reference to the tender love of parents to their own children. If you, then, being evil, He says "know how to give good gifts to your children, how much more will your Father from heaven give the good Spirit to them that ask Him" (Luke, XI, 13). And how abundant are not the choice gifts contained in that hidden power of which Christ spoke, when He said; "No man comes to the Father except through Me."

It is impossible that men grounded in this teaching should not feel drawn, and even compelled to the habit of faithful prayer. With what steady perseverance will they not practice it; with what fervor pursue it, having before them the very example of Christ Himself, Who, having nothing to fear for Himself and needing nothing, for He was God, yet He passed the whole night in prayer (Luke VI-12), and with a strong cry and tears offered up prayers and supplications (Hebrews-V-7), and during the prayer he expressed a desire to stand pleading before His Father as if remembering at that time He was our "teacher" as Venerable Bede, that ornament of your nation, wisely comments (on St. John's Gospel XVIII). But nothing proves so clearly and forcibly with the precept and the example of our Divine Lord in regard to prayer as His last discourse during those sad moments that preceeded His Passion and death, when raising His eyes to heaven, with a heart of love, He again and again entreated His

Holy Father, praying that there would be a union of His disciples and followers in the truth, so that this union should appear to the eyes of the nations, a most convincing proof of His own Divine mission (John XXII, 21).

And here no thought is more welcome to Our minds than that unity of Faith and will for which our Redeemer and Divine Master prayed in that earnest application — a unity which, if useful at all times even for temporal interests, both at home and abroad is shown to be more needful by the very divisions and confusions of these days. We on Our part, watching the signs of the times, exhorting, and taking thought for the future, urged thereto by the example of Christ, and the duty of the Apostolic Office, have not ceased to pray, and still humbly pray for the return of Christian nations, now divided from Us from the unity of other days.

We have more than once in late years given expression to the object of Our desires, and have devoted sedulous care to its realization. The time cannot be far distant when We must render an account of Our stewardship to the Prince of Pastors, and how happy We should be if We could bring to Him some fruit — some realization of these Our wishes which He has inspired and sustained.

In these days Our thoughts turn with love and hope to the English people, observing as We do the frequent and manifest works of Divine grace in their midst; how to some, it is plain, the confusion of religious discussions and dissensions which divide them is a cause of deep concern; how others see clearly the need of some sure defence against the roads of modern errors which only too readily humour the wishes of fallen nature and depraved reason, how the number of these religious and discreet men, who sincerely labour much for the reunion with the Catholic Church, is increasing. We can hardly say how strongly these and other signs quicken the charity of Christ in us, and redoubling Our prayers from Our inmost soul, We call down a fuller measure of Divine grace, which, poured out on minds so well disposed may issue in the ardently desired fruit, the fruit, namely, that we may all meet in the unity of Faith, and of the knowledge of the Son of God (Eph. IV-13), careful to keep the unity of the Spirit in the bound of peace, one body and one Spirit; as you are called in one hope of your calling — One Lord, one Faith, one Baptism, (ibid, 3, 5).

With loving heart, then, We turn to you all in England, to whatsoever community or institution you may belong, desiring to recall you to this holy unity. We beseech you, as you value your eternal salvation, to offer up humble and continuous prayer to God, our heavenly Father, the Giver of all Light, Who with gentle power, impels to the good and the right; and to implore without ceasing, light to know the truth in all its fullness, and to embrace with all fidelity the designs of His mercy, calling upon the glorious name of Jesus Christ Who is the Author and finisher of our Faith (Heb. XII-1), Who loved the Church and delivered Himself for it that He might sanctify it and might present it to Himself a glorious Church (Eph., V-25-27). Difficulties there may be for us to face, but they are not of a nature which should delay Our Apostolic zeal or stay your energy. Ah, no, doubtless the many changes that have come about, and time itself, have caused the existing divisions to take deeper root. But is that reason to give up all hope of remedy, reconciliation and peace? By no means, if God is with us. For we must not judge of such great issues from a human standpoint only, but rather must we look to the power and mercy of God.

In great and arduous enterprises, provided they are undertaken with an earnest and right intent, God stands by man's side, and it is in precisely these difficulties that the action of His Providence shines forth with greatest splendour. The time is not too far distant when thirteen centuries will have been completed since the English race welcomed those Apostolic men, sent as We have said, from this very city of Rome, and casting aside the pagan deities, dedicated the first fruits of its faith to Christ our Lord and God. This encourages Our hopes. It is indeed, an event worthy to be remembered with public thanksgiving, because of the greatness of the benefit and the fullness of the Christian name which you then obtained. Would that this occasion might bring to all reflecting minds the memory of the faith then preached to your ancestors, the same which is now preached—Jesus Christ, yesterday, today, and the same forever as the Apostle says, (Heb. XIII-8) who also most eloquently exhorts you, as he does all, to remember those first preachers who have spoken the word of God to you, will follow, considering the end of their conversation, (Ibid, 7).

In such a cause, we call first of all to Our assistance as our allies the Catholics of England, whose faith and piety We know by experience. There can be no doubt that weighing earnestly the prayers, the virtue of which We have truly declared, they will strive by every means to succor their fellowmen and brethren by invoking in their behalf the divine clemency. To pray for one's self is a need, to pray for others is a counsel of brotherly love: and it is plain that it is not prayer dictated by necessity so much as that inspired by fraternal charity, which will find most favor in the sight of God. Certainly Christians have taken up this practice from the beginning. The early ages set us a striking example, especially in all that pertains to the gift of faith. Thus it was the custom to pray to God with ardor, that relations, friends, rulers, and fellow citizens, might be blessed by a mind obedient to the Christian Faith. (St. Augustine, Dedone perser-verante) (CXIII-63).

And in regard to this there is another matter which gives Us anxiety. We have heard that in England there are some who being Catholics in name, do not show themselves to be Catholics in practice; and that in your great towns there are vast numbers of people who know not the elements of the Christian Faith, who never pray to God, and live in ignorance of His mercy and His justice. We must pray to God, and pray more earnestly in the sad condition of things, since He alone can effect a remedy. May He show the measures properly to be taken; may He sustain the courage and strength of those who labor at this arduous task; may He deign to send labourers into His harvest.

Whilst We so earnestly press upon Our children the duty of prayer, We desire at the same time to warn them that they should not suffer themselves to be wanting in anything that pertains to the grace and the fruits of prayer, and they should ever have before their minds the precept of the Apostle Paul to the Corinthians — "Be without offense to the Jews and the Gentiles, and to the Church of God" (I- Cor- X-32). For besides those interior dispositions of soul necessary for rightly offering prayer to God, it is also needful that they should be accompanied by actions and by words befitting the Christian profession. The exemplary observance of uprightness and justice, compassion for the poor, penance, peace—these are what will give force and efficacy to your prayers.

Mercy favors the petitions of those who in all justice study to carry out the precepts of Christ according to His promise; "If ye abide in Me, and My works and words abide in you, you shall ask whatever you will, and it shall be done unto you" (John XI-7).

And therefore do We exhort you that, uniting your prayers with Our's your great desire may now be that God will grant you to welcome your fellow citizens and brethren in the bond of perfect charity. Moreover, it is profitable to implore the saints of God, the efficacy of whose prayers, especially in such a cause as this, is shown in that pregnant remark of St. Augustine to St. Stephen; "If holy Stephen had not prayed the Church today would not have had a Saint Paul." (sermo in nat. St. Stephen, VI-N-5.)

We therefore humbly call upon St. Gregory, whom the English people have ever rejoiced to call the Apostles of their race, on Augustine his disciple and his messenger, and on those other saints of God, through whose wonderful virtues and no less wonderful deeds, England has merited the tile of "Island of the Saints;" on St. Peter the Apostle, and St. George, their special patrons, and above all on Mary the Most Holy Mother of God whom Christ Himself from the Cross gave to be the Mother of mankind, to whom your Kingdom was dedicated by your forefathers under the glorious title "the dowry of Mary." All these, We with full confidence call upon to be our pleaders before the throne of God, that renewing the Faith of other days, He may "fill you with all joy and peace in believing," that you may abound in hope and power of the Holy Ghost (Romans 15-16). Care should be taken that the prayers for unity already established among Catholics on certain fixed days should be made more popular and recited with greater devotion and especially that the pious practice of the Holy Rosary, which We Ourselves have so strongly recommended, should flourish, for it contains as it were a most salutary institution for the people at large. Moreover, We are pleased of Our own will and authority to add still another to the sacred indulgences which have been granted from time to time by Our predecessors. We grant, that is, to all who piously recite the prayer appended to this letter, to whatever nation they may belong an indulgence of three hundred days; moreover, a plenary indulgence once a month on the observance of the usual conditions to those who have recited it daily.

Finally, may the Divine prayer of Christ Himself for Unity fill up the full measure of Our desires, a prayer which on this day, celebrating the Mystery of His most Holy Resurrection, We repeat with the utmost confidence. "Holy Father, keep them in

Thy Name whom Thou hast given Me; that they may be one as We also are One: sanctify them in truth. Thy word is truth. And not only for them do I pray, but for them also who through their word shall believe in Me, that all may be one, as Thou Father, in Me, and I in Thee, that they may be one in Us, I in them, and Thou in Me; that they may be made perfect in One; and the world may know that Thou hast sent Me, and hast loved them as Thou hast also loved Me." (St. John, II-17 XVII-21-22.)

Finally, We desire all manner of blessings from God for the whole of the British people, and with all Our heart We pray that those who seek the Kingdom of Christ and salvation in the Unity of Faith, may enter on the full realization of the desires.

Given at St. Peter's in Rome, on the 11 of April, 1895, in the eighteenth (18th) year of Our Pontificate.

Pope Leo XIII.

Chapter Thirteen

The Encyclical Letter of Pope Leo XIII,
on the Re-union of Christendom.
(Praeclara Gratulationis)
written on his golden Jubilee as a Bishop
June 20th 1894.

The preceding chapter was a Letter directed especially to the Church of England, inviting the people of England to return to unity with the See of Peter.

This Encyclical was issued to the world, (Praeclara Gratulationis) to all schismatical churches to return to Rome. It is presented to again prove the fallacy of Anglican Archbishop Cranmer's statement that the Pope of Rome "desired to destroy all religious bodies not in union with Rome; who would not accept the yoke of anti-christ,—the Pope of Rome."

The Encyclical Letter.

Since We are the Vice-regent on Earth of Almighty God Who will have all men to be saved and to come to the knowledge of the truth, and now that Our advanced age and the bitterness of anxious cares urges Us on towards the end common to every mortal, We feel drawn to follow the example of Our Redeemer and Master, Jesus Christ, Who when about to return to Heaven, implored of God His Father, in earnest prayer, that His disciples and followers should be of one mind, and of one heart; 'I pray that they all may be one, as Thou Father in Me and I in Thee; that they may be one in Us' (John XVIII, 20-21). And as this Divine prayer and supplication embraces not only the souls of those who went henceforth to believe in Him, it gives Us an excellent reason for confidently expressing Our hopes, and for making all possible endeavors, that the men of every race and clime may be called and moved to embrace the unity of Divine Faith.

Conversion of Pagans.

Pressed on to Our intent by charity, which hastens fastest where the need is greatest, We direct Our first thoughts to those most unfortunate of all nations who have received the light of the Gospel, or who after possessing it lost it through neglect or the vicissitudes of time, and who in consequence are ignorant of God, and live in the depths of error. Now, as all salvation comes from Jesus Christ, for there is no other name given to men whereby we must be saved (Acts IV-2), the most ardent of Our desires is that the Most Holy Name of Jesus Christ should rapidly pervade and fill every land.

"And this is indeed a duty which the Church, faithful to the Divine mission entrusted to her, has never neglected. What has been the object of her labours for more than nineteen centuries? Is there any other work she has undertaken with greater zeal and constancy, than that of bringing the nations of the earth to the truth, and principles of Christianity? Today, as ever by Our authority, the heralds of the Gospel constantly cross the seas to reach the farthest corners of the earth: and We pray God daily that in His Goodness He may deign to add to the numbers of His ministers of holy things, men worthy of this Apostolic office, and who are ready to sacrifice their comfort, their health and their very life if need be, in order to extend the frontiers of the Kingdom of Christ.

Ah, but Thou, above all, Saviour and Father of mankind, Jesus Christ, delay not to bring about what Thou didst once promise to do when lifted up from the earth Thou wouldst draw all to Thyself. Come then, and speedily manifest Thyself to the immense multitude of souls who have not felt as yet the ineffable blessings which Thou hast provided for men by Thy Blood: rouse those who are sitting in darkness, and in the shadow of death, that, enlightened by the rays of Thy wisdom and virtue, in "Thee and by Thee" they may be made perfect in one.

As We consider the mystery of this unity, We see before Us all those peoples which long ago passed, by the mercy of God, from their time-worn errors to the wisdom of the Gospels. Nor could We, indeed, recall anything more pleasing or better calculated to restore the work of Divine Providence than the memory of the days of yore, when the Faith that had come down from heaven was looked upon as the common inheritance of one and all; when civilized nations separated by violence, distance, character, and habits, in spite of frequent disagreements and warfare on other points, were united by Christian Faith in all that concerned religion.

The recollection of that time causes Us to regret all the more deeply that, as the ages roll by, the waves of suspicion and hatred arose, and great and flourishing nations were dragged away, in an evil hour, from the bosom of the Roman Church. In spite of that, however, in Him alone Who can fix the hour of His benefits, and Who has the power to incline man's will as He pleases; and We turn to those same nations, exhorting and beseeching them with Fatherly love to put an end to these dissensions and return again to unity.

The Eastern Churches.

First of all then, We cast an effectionate look upon the East, from whence in the beginning came forth salvation to the whole world. Yes, and the yearning desire of Our hearts bids Us conceive the hope the day is not far distant when the "Eastern Churches," so illustrious in their ancient faith and glorious past, will return to the fold they have abandoned. We hope it, all the more, because that which divides them from Us is not so great: nay, with some exceptions, we agree so entirely on other heads that, we often have recourse to arguments and testimonies from the teaching, the Rites, and customs of the East.

The principal subject of dissension is the Primacy of the Roman Pontiff. But let them consider the sentiments entertained by their forefathers, and examine what the oldest traditions testify, and it will indeed, become evident to them that Christ's divine utterance, "Thou art Peter, and upon this Rock I will build My Church," has undoubtedly been realized in the Roman Pontiffs. Many of these latter, in the first ages of the Church, were chosen from the East, and foremost among them Anacletus, Evaristus, Anicetus, Eleutherius, Zogwinus, and Agatho; and most of them, after governing the Church in wisdom and sanctity, consecrated their ministry by the shedding of their blood. The times, the causes, and the authors of these discords are known to all.

Before the day when separated what God had joined together, the name of the Apostolic See was held in reverence by all the nations of the Christian world; and the East, like the West, agreed together unhesitatingly in obedience to the Pontiff of Rome, as the legitimate successor of St. Peter, and therefore the Vicar of Christ here on earth.

And accordingly, if we go back to the beginning of this dissension we shall find that Photius himself was careful to send his advocates to Rome on matters that concerned him; and Pope

Nicholas I sent his legates to Constantinople from the Eternal City, without the slightest opposition, in order to examine the case of Ignatius the Patriarch with all diligence, and to bring to the Apostolic See a full and accurate report; so that the history of the whole negotiations is a manifest confirmation of the Primacy of that Roman See from which they then began to dissent. Finally, in two great Councils, the second of Lyons, and that of Florence Latins and Greeks, as is well known easily agreed, and all unanimously proclaimed as a dogma, the Supreme power of the Roman Pontiffs.

We have recalled these things intentionally because they constitute an invitation to peace and reconciliation; and with all the more reason because in Our own days We seem to see a more conciliatory spirit towards Catholics on the part of the Eastern Churches, even some degree of kindly feeling. To mention an instance, those sentiments were lately made manifest when some of Our faithful travelled to the East on a holy enterprise, and received so many proofs of courtesy and good will.

Therefore, Our mouth is open to you, "to you all of Greek or other Oriental Rites who are separated from the Catholic Church. We earnestly desire that each and every one of you should meditate upon the words, so full of gravity and love, addressed to Bessarion to your forefathers." What answer shall We give to God when He comes to ask why We have separated from Our brethren; To Him Who, to unite us and bring us into one fold, came down from heaven, was Incarnate, and was crucified? What will Our defense be in the eyes of posterity? Oh, my venerable brethren, we must not suffer this to be, we must not entertain this thought, we must not thus so ill provide for ourselves and for Our brethren.

Weigh carefully in your minds and before God the nature of your request. It is not for any human motive, but impelled by Divine charity and a desire for the salvation of all, that We urge your reconciliation and union with the Church of Rome; and We mean a complete and perfect reunion, such as could not subsist in any way if nothing else were brought about but a certain degree of agreement in the tenets of belief and an exchange of fraternal love. The true union between Christians and that which Jesus Christ, the Author of the Church instituted and desired, consists in oneness of Faith and government.

Nor is there any reason for you to fear that We, or any of Our successors will ever diminish your rights, the privileges of your Patriarchs, or the established Ritual of any of your churches. It has been and will always be the intent and discipline of the Apostolic See, to allow a just and good place to the primative traditions and special customs of every nation. Indeed, if you return to communion with Us, you will see how much, by God's bounty the glory and dignity of your church will be increased. May God then, in His mercy and goodness hear the prayer that you, yourselves address to Him "make the schisms of the Churches to cease, (Liturgy of St. Basil), and "assemble those who are dispersed, bring back those who err and unite them to Thy Holy Catholic Church," (ibid). May you then return to that one Holy Faith which has been handed down to Us and to you from time memorial; which your forefathers preserved untainted, and which was enhanced by the competing splendor of the virtues, the great genius, and the sublime learning of Saint Athanasius and Saint Basil, Saint Gregory, of Nazianum and Saint Chrystom, the two saints who bore the name of Cyril, and so many other men whose glory belongs to us as a common inheritance to the East and to the West.

And now, suffer that We should address you more particularly, nations of the Slavonic races, you whose glorious name and deeds are attested by many an ancient record. You know full well how much the Slaves are indebted to the merits of St. Cyril and St. Methodius, to whose memory We Ourselves rendered due honors only a few years ago. Their virtues and their labors were to great numbers of your race the source of civilization and salvation. And hence the admirable interchange which existed so long between the Slavonic nations and the Pontiffs of Rome, of favours on the one side and of filial devotion on the other. If in unhappy times many of your forefathers were separated from the Faith of Rome, consider what a priceless boon it would be for you to return to Unity. The Church is anxious to welcome you also to her arms, that she may give you manifold aids to salvation, prosperity, and grandeur.

To Protestant Nations.

With no less affection do We now look upon the Nations who, at a more recent date, were separated from the Roman Church by an extraordinary revolution of things and circumstances. Let them forget the various events of times gone by, let them raise their thoughts above all that is human, and seeking only truth and salvation, consider in their minds the Church as it was constituted by Christ. If they will but compare that Church with their own communions, and consider what the actual state of religion is in these, they will easily acknowledge, that, forgetful of their early history, they have drifted away, on many points into the novelty of various errors; nor will they deny that of what may be called the patrimony of Faith and Truth, which the authors of these innovations carried away with them in their desertion, there now remains to them scarcely any formula that is really certain and supported by authority.

Nay more, things have already come to such a pass that many do not even hesitate to root up the very foundation upon which alone rests all religion, and the hope of men, to wit, the Divine Nature of Jesus Christ our Saviour.

And again, whereas formerly they used to assert that the books of the old and new testaments were written under the inspiration of God, they now deny them that authority; this, indeed, was an inevitable consequence when they granted to all the right of private interpretation. Hence, too, the acceptance of individual conscience as the sole guide and rule of conduct to the exclusion of any other; hence those conflicting opinions and numerous sects that fell away so often into the doctrines of Naturalism and Rationalism.

Therefore is it, that having lost all hope of an agreement in their convictions, they now proclaim and recommend a mere union of brotherly love. No doubt we should all be united by a bond of mutual charity: Our Lord Jesus Christ enjoined it most emphatically, and willed that this mutual love for each other should be the mark of His disciples. But how can hearts be united in perfect charity, where minds are not joined by Faith?

It is on this account that many of those to whom We allude, men of sound judgment, and seekers after truth, have looked to the Catholic Church for the sure way of salvation; for they understood clearly that they could never be united to Jesus Christ as their Head if they were not united to His Body, which is the Church; nor really acquire the true Christain Faith if they reject the legitimate teaching authority confided to Peter and his successors. Such men as these have recognized in the Church of Rome, the form and image of the true Church, which is clearly made manifest by the marks that God her Author has placed upon her, and not a few were possessed with penetrating judgment and a special talent for historical research, have shown forth in their remarkable writings the uninterrupted succession of the Church of Rome from the Apostles, the integrity of her doctrine, and the consistency of her rule and discipline.

With the example of such men before you, Our heart appeals to you even more than Our words; to you, Our brethren, who for three centuries and more have dissented from Us on the Christian Faith; and to you all likewise, who in later times, for any reason, have turned from us, "let us all come together in the unity of faith, and of the knowledge of the Son of God" (Eph. IV-13). Suffer Us to invite you to that unity which has ever existed in the Catholic Church, and can never fail; suffer Us lovingly to hold out Our hand to you.

The Church, as the common Mother of all has long been calling you back to her; the Catholics of the world await you with brotherly love that you may render holy worship to God together with us, united in perfect charity by the profession of one Gospel, one Faith, and one Hope.

Were governments and states restored to the unity of Faith, it is wonderful what efficacious remedies for evil and abundant stores of benefits would ensue. We will touch upon the principle ones.

The first regards the dignity and office of the Church. She would receive the honor which is her due, and she would go her way, free from envy, and strong in her liberty, as the minister of Gospel truth and grace, to the notable welfare of states. For as she has been by God as a teacher and guide to the human race, she can contribute assistance which is peculiarly adapted to direct even the most radical transformation of times, to the common good, to the happy solution of the most complicated questions, and to the promotion of uprightness and justice, which are the most solid foundations of the Commonwealth. Moreover there would be a marked increase of union among the nations, a thing most desirable at this time to ward off the horrors of war.

We behold the conditions of Europe. For many years past, peace has been rather an appearance than a reality. Possessed with mutual suspicions, almost all the nations are vieing with one another in equipping themselves with military armaments. Inexperienced youths are removed from parental direction and control, to be thrown amid the danger of a soldier's life; robust young men are taken from agriculture or ennabling studies, or

trade, or the arts, to be put under arms. Hence the treasury o
states are exhausted by the enormous expenditures, the nationa
resources are fritted away, and private fortunes impaired; an
this armed place, so to speak, which now exists, cannot last much
longer. Can this be the normal condition of human society? Ye
we cannot escape from this situation, and obtain true peace, except by the aid of Jesus Christ. For to repress ambition, and cov-
etousness, and envy — the chief instigators of wars — nothing
is more powerful than the Christian virtues of justice; for by their
exercise, both the laws of nations and the faith of treaties may be
continued inviolate, and the bonds of brotherhood continue unbroken and men realize that "Justice exalteth a Nation."

As it is in external relations, so in the internal life of the State
itself, the Christian virtues will provide a guarantee of the common weal much more sure and stronger far than any which
laws or armies can afford. For there is no one who does not see
that the dangers to public security and order are daily on the
increase, since seditious societies continue to conspire for the
overthrow and ruin of States, as the frequency of their atrocious
outrages testifies.

Let us, one and all, then, for the sake of the common good,
labour with equal assiduity to restore the ancient accord, and
concord. In order to bring about this concord, and spread abroad
the benefits of the Christian revelation, the present is the most
seasonable time; for never before have the sentiments of human
brotherhood penetrated so deeply into the souls of men, and
never in any age has man been seen to seek out his fellowman
more eagerly, in order to know them better and to help them.
Immense tracts of land and sea are traversed with incredible
rapidity, and thus extraordinary advantages are afforded, not only
for commerce and scientific investigations, but also for the propagation of the Word of God, "from the rising of the sun, to the
going down of the same."

May God Who is rich in mercy, and in Whose power are the times and moments, grant Our wishes and desires, and in His great goodness hasten the fulfillment of that Divine promise of Jesus Christ; "there shall be one fold and one Shepherd." (John X-16.)

Given at Rome at St. Peter's on the 20th day of June, 1894, in the seventeenth year of Our Pontificate.

Pope Leo XIII.

Chapter Fourteen

Encyclical Letter of Pope Leo XIII, (Satis Cognitum),
On the Unity of the Church,
Written on the occasion of the Commission of Enquiry
Into Anglican Orders.
June 29, 1896.

To Our Venerable Brothers, the Patriarchs, Primates, Archbishops, Bishops, and other Ordinaries, in Peace and Communion With the Apostolic See, Leo XIII.

Venerable Brethren, Health and Benediction. It is sufficiently well known to you that no small share of Our thoughts and of Our care is devoted to Our endeavours to bring to the fold of, and the guardianship of Jesus Christ, the Chief Pastor of souls, sheep that have strayed. Bent upon this, We have thought it most conductive to this salutary end and purpose to describe, as it were, the features and lineaments of the Church. Among these most worthy of Our consideration is Unity. This the Divine Author impressed on, as it is a perpetual sign of truth and of unconquerable strength. The essential beauty and comeliness of the Church ought greatly influence the minds of those who consider it. Nor is it improbable that ignorance might be dispelled by its contemplation; that false ideas and prejudices may be dissipated from the minds especially of those who are involved in error without fault of theirs; and that even a love for the Church may be stirred up in the souls of men, like unto charity wherewith Christ loved and united Himself to that Spouse redeemed by His Precious Blood. "Christ loved the Church and gave Himself for it" (Eph. V-2-5). If those about to come back to their most loving Mother (whether not yet known fully to them, or else culpably abandoned) should find that their return involves, not indeed the shedding of their blood (at which price nevertheless the Church was bought by Jesus Christ), but by some lesser trouble and labor, let them at any rate clearly understand that their burden and duty has been laid on them not by the will of man, but by the will of command of God. They may thus, by the help of heavenly grace, realize and feel the truth of the Divine saying, "My yoke is sweet and My burden light" (Matthew XI-30), Wherefore, having put all Our hope in the "Father of Lights," from Whom "cometh every best and perfect gift" from Him, namely, Who alone gives the increase, (I Cor, iii-6) We earnestly pray that He will grant Us the power of bringing home to men, conviction.

Although God can do by His own power whatever is effected by created beings, nevertheless in the counsels of His loving Providence He has preferred to help man by human instrumentality. And, as in the natural order, He does not give full perfection except by means of man's work and action, so also He makes use of human aid for that which lies beyond the limits of nature, that is for the sanctification and salvation of souls.

But it is obvious that nothing can be communicated amongst men save by means of external things which the senses can perceive. For this reason human nature was assumed by the Son of God, "Who being in the form of God," emptied Himself, taking the form of a servant, being made in the likeness of man

Phil. II-6-7), and thus, living on earth He taught us His doctrine, and gave His laws by conversing with men.

Now, since it was necessary that His divine mission should be perpetuated to the end of time, He joined to Himself a few Disciples trained by Himself, and made them partakers in His power. And when He had called down upon them from heaven, the Spirit of Truth, He bade them go through the whole world and faithfully preach to all nations what He had taught and commanded, so that by the profession of His doctrine, and the observance of His laws, the human race might attain to holiness on earth, and never ending happiness in heaven. In this wise and on this principle, the Church was begotten. If we consider the chief end of this Church and the proximate efficient causes of salvation it (the church) is undoubtedly spiritual; but in regard to those who constitute it, it is external and necessarily visible. The Apostles received a mission to teach by visible and audible signs, and they discharged their mission by words and acts which certainly appealed to the senses. And thus, their voices feeding upon the ears of those who heard them, begat faith in souls. "Faith cometh by hearing, and hearing by the word of Christ" (Romans, X-17). And Faith itself, that is, assent given to the first and supreme truth, must be manifested by outward profession. For with the mind we believe unto justice, but with the mouth profession is made unto salvation. In the same way in man, nothing is more internal than heavenly grace which begets sanctity; but the ordinary, and chief means of obtaining grace are external; that is to say, the sacraments which are administered specially for that purpose, by means of certain ordinances.

Jesus Christ commanded His apostles and their successors to the end of time to teach and rule the nations. He also ordered the nations to accept their teaching, and obey their authority. But this correlation of rights and duties in the Christian commonwealth, not only could not have been made permanent, but could not even have been initiated except through the senses, which are of all things the messengers and interpreters. For these reasons the Church is so often called in Holy Writ a body, and even the "Body of Christ." Now you are the Body of Christ (I Cor. 12-27). And precisely because IT is the body of Christ It is living and energizing, inasmuch as by the infusion of His power Christ guards and sustains it, just as a vine gives nourishment and renders fruitful the branches united to it. And as in living the vital principle is unseen and invisible, and is evidenced and manifested by the movements and actions of the members, so the principle of supernatural life in the Church is clearly shown by that which is done by it.

From this it follows that those who arbitrarily conjure up and picture to themselves a hidden and invisible Church are in grievous and pernicious error, as also are those who regard the Church as a mere human institution which possesses a certain discipline and external Rites but is without the perennial communication of the gifts of Divine grace, and without all that which testifies of constant and undoubted signs to the existence of that life which is drawn from God.

It is assuredly impossible that the Church of Jesus Christ can be one or the other, as that man should be a body alone, or a soul alone. The connection and union of both elements is as absolutely necessary to the true Church as the intimate union of the soul and body is to human nature. The Church is not something dead; it is the Body of Christ, endowed with supernatural life, as Christ, the Head and Exemplar, is not constituted solely by His invisible Divine Nature, as the Monophysites hold; nor is He constituted solely by His Divine invisible human nature as the Photians and Nestorians assert, but is One from and in both natures; so the mystical Body of Christ is the true Church, only because its invisible parts draw life and power from the supernatural gifts and other things whence spring their very nature and other things (essence). But since the Church is such by Divine Will and constitution, such it must uniformly remain until the end of time. If it did not, then it would not have been founded as perpetual and the end set before it would have been limited to some certain place, and to some certain period of time; both of which are contrary to the truth.

Hence this union of visible and invisible elements, inasmuch as it harmonizes with the natural order, and by God's will belongs to the very essence of the Church, must necessarily remain so long as the Church itself shall endure. Wherefore Chrysostom writes; "Secede not from the Church; for nothing is stronger than the Church, Thy hope is in the Church, thy salvation is the Church, thy refuge is in the Church. It is higher than the heavens, and wider than the earth. It never grows old, but is ever full of vigor." Wherefore Holy writ pointing to its strength and stability calls it a mountain (Homilies De Capto Eutropia, N. O.). Also Augustine says: "Unbelievers think that the Christian religion will last for a time, a certain period in the world, and will then disappear. But it will remain as long as the sun — as long as the sun rises and sets, that is as long as the ages of time shall roll, the Church of God, the true Body of Christ, will not cease to be (Psalm 21-m-8). And in another place, "The Church will totter if its foundations shake; but how can Christ be moved? Christ remaining immovable it (the Church) shall never be shaken. Where are they that say that the Church has disappeared from the world, seeing it can not be even shaken?" (Enmaratio in Psalm Ciii, sermo II, n-5). He who seeks the truth must be guided by the following fundamental principles. The Church was instituted and founded, and formed by Christ the Lord; If we want to know what its nature is, the main thing is to see what Christ willed and what in fact He did, It is by such a criterion that the unity of the Church must be principally considered; and of this, for the general good, it has seemed to speak in this Encyclical."

The Unity of the Church.

It is so evident from the clear and frequent testimonies of Holy Writ, that the true Church of Jesus Christ is one that no Christian can dare to deny it. But in judging and determining the nature of this unity many have erred in various ways. Not only the origin, but the whole constitution of the Church belongs to the class of things effected by the will, and free choice. For this reason the entire case must be judged by the facts and what was actually done. We must consequently investigate, not how the Church might possibly be One, but how He, Who founded it, willed that it should be One.

Christ instituted only *one Church.*

Now when we consider what was actually done, we find that Jesus did not, in point of fact, found and institute a Church to consist of many communities similar in kind, but distinct from each other, and lacking these bonds which render the Church unique and indivisible in accordance with the Article in the Creed; "I believe in one Church." The Church in respect of its units belongs to the category of things indivisible by nature, though heretics try to divide it into many parts. . . . We say therefore, that the ancient Catholic Church is unique in its essence, in its doctrine, in its origin, and in its excellence. Furthermore, the eminence of the Church arises from its unity, as the principle of its constitution a unity surpassing all else, and having nothing like unto it, or equal to it. (Clement of Alexandria, Stromatum, lib.-CVII-17). For this reason Christ, speaking of this mystical edifice, which we call His own "I will build My Church;" hence any other church beside this one has not been founded by Christ, and therefore cannot be the true Church.

This becomes even more evident when the purpose of the Divine Founder is considered. For what did Christ the Lord seek? What did He intend in regard to the Church to be founded, or when founded? This: to transmit to it the same mission and the same mandate to continue it, which He had received from His Father. This He clearly resolved to do; this He actually did. "As the Father hast sent Me into the world, I also send you into the world" (John XVIII-18). But the whole human race, without distinction of time or place. "The son of Man came into the world, that the world might be saved by Him, (John, 3-17)." For there is no name under heaven given to man whereby we must be saved, (Acts 3-12). The Church must therefore without stint to all men, and transform, and transmit all ages the salvation effected by Jesus Christ and the blessings flowing therefrom. Wherefore, by the will of its founder, it is necessary that this Church should be one in all lands and at all times. To justify the existence of more than one Church it would be necessary to go outside this world, and to create a new and unheard of race of men. That the one Church should embrace all men everywhere and at all times was seen and foretold by Isaais when, looking into the future, he saw the appearance of a mountain conspicuous by its all surpassing altitude, which set forth the image of "the House of the Lord," that is, of the Church "And in the last the mountain of the Lord shall be prepared on the top of the mountains." (Isaais II-1).

But this mountain which towers over all other mountains is one; accordingly, the House of the Lord to which all nations shall come to seek the rule of living is also ours, and all nations shall flow into it. And many peoples shall go and say; come let us go up to the mountain of the Lord, and to the House of the God of Jacob, and He shall teach us His ways, and we will walk in His paths. (ibid II-2-3). Explaining this passage, Optatus of Melevis says; "It is written in the Prophet Isaais; From Sion the law shall go forth, and the word of the Lord from Jerusalem. For it is not on Mt. Sion that Isaais sees the valley, but on the holy mountain, that is, the Church, which has raised itself conspicuously throughout the entire Roman world under the whole heavens.

"The Church is therefore, the spiritual Sion in which Christ has constituted King of God the Father, and which exists throughout the entire earth in which there is but one Catholic Church." (DeSchisn, Donatist, lib iii, n. 2). And Augustine says; "what can be so manifest as a mountain, or so well known?" There are, it is true, mountains which are unknown because they are situated in some remote part of the earth. But this mountain is not unknown, for it has filled the whole face of the world, and about this it is said that "it is prepared on the summit of the mountains" (In Eph. Joan tract, I-n-13). Furthermore, the Son of God said that the Church should be His Mystical Body, and with which He should be united as the Head, after the manner of the human body which He assumed, to which the natural head is physiologically united. As He took to Himself one only mortal body, which He gave to suffering and death in order to pay the price of man's redemption, so also He has only one Mystical Body, in which and through which He renders men partakers of holiness and of eternal salvation. God "hath made Him (Christ) head over all the Church, which is His Body." (Eph. I-22-23). Scattered and separated members cannot possibly cohere with a head so as to make one body. But St. Paul says; "All the members of the body, whereas they are many, yet are one body, so also is Christ." (I Cor. XII-12.)

Wherefore the Mystical Body, he declares is "compacted and fitly joined together, by what every joint supplieth according to the operation in the measure of every part." Thus, dispersed members, separated one from the other, cannot be united with one and the same head. "There is but One God, and One Christ,

and His Church is one, and the Faith is one, and one the peopl
joined together in the solid unity of the body in the bond
concord. This unity cannot be broken, nor the one body divide
by the separation of its constituent parts." (St. Cyprian, D
Catholicae Ecclesia Unitate, n-28). And to set forth more clear
the unity of the Church, St. Cyprian makes use of the illustratio
of a living body, the members of which cannot possibly liv
unless united to the head and drawing from it their vital forc
Separated from the head they must of necessity die. "The church
he says cannot be divided into parts by the separation and cuttin
asunder of its members. What is cut from the mother cann
live apart, (ibid). What similarity is there between a dead an
a living body?" For no man ever hated his own flesh, but che
ished it, and nourished it, as also Christ the Church; because w
are members of His Body, of His Flesh, and of His Bones. (Ep
V. 29-30) Another head like unto Christ must be invented, th
is another Christ, if beside the one Church which is His Bod
men wish to set up another. "See what you must be aware of, se
what you must avoid, see what you must dread."

It happens that, as in the human body, some member may b
cut off – a hand, a finger, a foot. Does the soul follow the ampu
tated member? As long as it was in the body, it lived; separate
it forfeited its life. So the Christian is a Catholic as long as h
lives in the body; cut off from it he becomes a heretic; the lif
of the spirit follows not the amputated member. (St. Augustin
Sermo, cclvii-n-4). The Church of Christ, therefore is one an
the same forever; those who leave it depart from the will an
command of God, and Christ the Lord – leaving the path o
salvation, they enter the path of perdition. "Whosoever is sepa
rated from the Church, is united to an adulteress." He has cu
himself off from the promises of the Church, and he who leave
it, (the Church) cannot arrive at the rewards of Christ. He wh
observes not this unity observes not the law of God, holds no

he faith of the Father, and the Son, clings not to life and salvation. (St. Cyprian De Cath. Ecclesia Unitate).

"The one Church possesses unity of Faith"

Now He, Who founded this one single Church, also made it one in such a way that all who belong to it must be united by the closest bonds, so as to form one society, one kingdom, one body; One body and one spirit, as you are called in in one hope of your calling (Eph. Iv-4). Jesus Christ, when His death was nigh at hand, declared His will in this matter, and solemnly consecrated it, thus addressing His Father "Not for them only do I pray, but for them also who through their world shall believe in Me" (John 17-20-21-23).

Indeed, He commanded that this unity should be so closely knit and so perfect among His followers that it might, in some measure, imitate the union between Himself and His Father; "I pray that they may be one as Thou Father in Me and I in Thee" (ibid) 21.

Agreement and union of minds is the necessary foundation of so perfect concord amongst men, from which concord there naturally results a concurrence of wills and similarity of actions. Wherefore, in His divine wisdom, Christ ordained in His Church, unity of Faith, a virtue which is the first of those bonds which unite men to God, and whence we receive the name of the faithful, "one Lord, one Faith, one baptism" (Eph. 4-5).

That is, as there is one Lord, and one baptism, so should all Christians without exception have but one Faith. And so the Apostle Paul not merely begs, he entreats and implores Christians to be all of the same mind, and to avoid differences of opinions. "I beseech you brethren by the name of our Lord Jesus Christ, that you all speak the same thing, and that there be no schisms amongst you, and that you be perfect in the same mind, and in the same judgment" (1st. Cor. 1-10).

Such passages certainly need no interpretation; they speak for

themselves. Besides, all who profess Christianity allow that the
should be but one Faith. It is positively of the greatest importan
and indeed of absolute necessity, as to which, many are deceive
that the nature and character of this unity of Faith should
recognized.

And as We have already stated, this is not to be ascertain
by conjecture, but by the certain knowledge of what was actual
done; that is by seeking for and ascertaining what kind of uni
in Faith has been commanded by Jesus Christ.

The heavenly doctrine of Christ, altho in great part committ
to writing by Divine inspiration, could not unite the minds
men if left to the human intellect alone; for it would then
subject to many and contradictory interpretations. This is n
only because of the nature of the doctrine itself, and of t
mysteries it involves, but also because of the divergencies
human minds and of the elements of conflicting passions. Fro
a variety of interpretations, a variety of beliefs is necessarily b
gotten; hence come controversies, dissensions, and wranglin
such as have arisen in the past ages of the Church. Iraneus writ
of heretics as follows: "Accepting the Sacred Scriptures the
distort the interpretation thereof," and Augustine, "heresies hav
arisen, and certain perverse views ensnaring souls and precipit
ting them into the abyss, only when the scriptures, good in then
selves, are not properly understood." (Evang. Joan, tract XVII
Cap 5-n-1.)

In addition to holy writ then, to insure this union of men
minds, and to effect and preserve unity of ideas, it is absolute
necessary that there should be another principle. This, the wisdo
of God requires for He could not have willed that the Fait
should be one if He did not provide means sufficient for th
preservation of this unity; and this means Holy Writ clearly se
forth, as We shall presently point out. Assuredly the Infini
power of God is not bound to any individual means; All thing

obey Him as so many passive instruments. In regard to this external principle, therefore, we must inquire which one of all the means in His power Christ did actually adopt. For this purpose it is necessary to turn our minds to the institution of Christianity.

The teaching authority of Christ.

What We are now about to say is witnessed to by Holy Writ, and is otherwise well known. Christ proved His own Divinity and the Divine origin of His mission by His miracles. He taught the multitudes by doctrine and He absolutely commanded that the assent of Faith should be given His teaching and promised rewards eternal to those who believe, and eternal punishment to those who do not; "If I do not the works of My Father, Believe Me not (John X37). If I had not done among them the works that no other man had done, they would have sin, (ibid Xv-24). But if I do the works, though you do not believe Me, believe the works."

Whatsoever He commanded He commanded by the same authority. He required the assent of the mind to all things without exception. It was thus the duty of all who heard Jesus Christ, if they wished to attain eternal salvation, not merely to accept His doctrine in general, but to assent with their entire mind to all and every point of it, for it would be wrong to withhold Faith from God even in regard to one single point.

The teaching authority of the Apostles.

When about to ascend into heaven, He sent His Apostles in virtue of the same power by which He had been sent by the Father; and He charged them to spread abroad and propagate His teaching. "Go therefore, and teach all nations; teach them to observe all things whatsoever I have commanded you" (Matthew XXVIII-18-20). So that those who obeyed the Apostles would be saved, but those who disobeyed would perish; "He tha believeth and is baptized shall be saved, but he that believeth nc shall be condemned" (Mark 16-16). But because it is obviousl most in harmony with God's Providence that no one shoul have confided to him a great and important mission unless h is furnished with the means of properly carrying it out, fo this reason Christ promised that He would send the Spirit o Truth to His disciples to remain with them forever. "But if go I will send Him (the Paraclete) to you . . . But when He the Spirit of Truth is come, He will teach you all truth" (Joh XV-7-13). "And I will ask the Father, and He shall give yo another Paraclete, that He may abide with you forever, th Spirit of Truth. He shall give testimony of Me, and you shal give testimony (ibid 15-17). Hence He commanded that th teaching of the Apostles should be religiously accepted an piously kept as His own. "He who hears you—hears Me" an he who despises you, despises Me. (Luke 6-16). Wherefor the Apostles were Ambassadors of Christ, as was Christ th Ambassador of the Father; as the Father has sent Me, I als send you (John XX-21).

Hence, as the Apostles and disciples were bound to hear Christ so also those whom the Apostles taught were by God's com mand bound to believe them. And, therefore, it was no mor allowable to repudiate one iota of the Apostles teachings tha it was to reject any point of the doctrine of Christ Himself.

Truly the voice of the Apostles, when the Holy Ghost ha come down upon them, resounded throughout the world. Wher ever they went they proclaimed themselves the Ambassadors o Christ, by Whom we have received grace and Apostleship fo obedience to the Faith in all nations for His name" (Roman I-5).

And God made known this Divine mission by numerou miracles; but they, going forth preached everywhere, the Lor working withal, and confirming the word with signs that followed (Mark XVI-20). But what was this "word"? It comprehended all the things which they had learned from their Master, because they openly and publicly declared that they could not help speaking of what they had seen and heard.

But, as We have already said, the Apostles' mission was not destined to die with the Apostles, or to come to an end in the course of time, since it was intended for the people at large, and instituted for the salvation of the human race. For Christ commanded His Apostles to "preach the gospel to every creature, to carry His Name to nations and Kings, and to be witnesses to Him to the ends of the earth." He further promised them to be with them in the fullfillment of their high mission, and that, not for a few centuries only, but for all time, unto the consummation of the world. Upon which, St. Jerome says: "He who promises to retain with His disciples to the end of the world means they will be forever victorious, and that He will never depart from those who believe in him."

But how could this be realized in the Apostles alone, placed as they were under the universal law of dissolution by death? It was therefore provided by God that the Majesterium instituted by Jesus Christ should not end with the life of the Apostles, but that it should remain in perpetuity. We see it in truth propagated, and as it were, passed on from hand to hand. For the Apostles consecrated bishops, and each one appointed those who were to succeed them immediately in the ministry of the Word. Nay more; they likewise required their successors to choose fitting men to endow them with like authority and to confide to them the office and mission of teaching. "Thou, therefore, my son, be strong in the grace which is in Christ Jesus: and the things which thou hast heard of Me by many witnesses, the same commend to faithful men, who shall be fit to teach others also" (2 Tim. II-1-2). Wherefore, as Christ was sent by

God, so the bishops and those who succeeded them were sent by the Apostles.

The Apostles were appointed by Christ to preach the Gospel to us, Jesus Christ was sent by God. Christ is therefore from God, and the Apostles from Christ, and both according to the will of God.

Preaching therefore the word through the centuries, throughout the countries and cities, when they have proved in the Spirit the first-fruit of their teaching, they appointed bishops and deacons for the faithful. They appointed them and ordained them, so that when they had passed away, other tried and competent men should carry on their ministry. (St. Clement of Rome, Epist. I ad Corinth capp. 42-44).

On the one hand then, it is necessary that the mission of teaching all things Christ had taught should remain perpetual and immutable, and on the other hand that the duty of accepting and professing all their doctrines should likewise be perpetual and immutable. This is aptly commented on by St. Cyprian as follows; "Our Lord Jesus Christ, when in His gospel He testifies that those who are not with Him are His real enemies, does not designate any particular form of heresy, but declares that all heretics who are not with Him, do not gather with Him, but scattereth His flock, are His adversaries; "he that is not with Me, is against Me, and he that scattereth, gathereth not with Me."

The Church has always claimed teaching authority.

The Church, founded on these principles and mindful of her office, has in nothing displayed greater zeal and endeavour than in guarding the integrity of the Faith. Hence she has regarded as rebels men who have held beliefs on any point of doctrine different from her own. She has expelled them from the ranks of her children. The Arians, the Montanists the Novations, the Quartodecimans, the Eutychians, certainly did not reject all Catholic doctrine; they abandoned only a certain portion of it.

Still, who does not know that they were declared heretics, and were banished from the bosom of the Church? In like manner were condemned all those authors of heretical tenets who followed them in subsequent ages. "There can be nothing more dangerous than those heretics who admit every cycle of doctrine, and yet with one word, as with a drop of poison, infect the real and simple faith taught by our Lord, and handed down by Apostolic tradition. (Auctor, tract, de fide orthodoxia Arianos)

The practice of the Church has always been the same, as is shown by the unanimous teaching of the Fathers, who were wont to hold as outside Catholic communion, and alien to the Church, whosoever receded in the least degree from any point of doctrine proposed by her authoritative Majesterium. Epiphanius, Augustine, Theodoret, drew up a long list of the heresies of their times. St. Augustine notes that other heresies may spring up, and should a person give assent to anyone of these, he would be by the very fact cut off from Catholic unity. "No one who merely disbelieves in all these (enumerated heresies) can for that reason regard himself as a Catholic, or call himself one. For there may be, or may arise some other heresies, which do not set in this work of Ours, and if any should hold to any one of these he would not be a Catholic Christian." (St. Augustine, de Heresibus n. 88.)

Illustrations of this fact.

The need of this divinely instituted means for the preservation of unity (of faith) about which We speak is urged by St. Paul in his Epistle to the Ephesians. In this he first admonishes them to preserve with every care concord of minds; "Solicitous to keep the unity of the Spirit in the horn of peace." And as souls cannot be perfectly united in charity unless minds agree in faith, he says that all are to hold the same Faith. and this is to be so perfectly one as to prevent all danger of errors; that henceforth we be no more children tossed to and fro, and carried about with every wind of doctrine by the wickedness of men, by cunning craftiness, by which they lie in wait to deceive. (Eph. IV-14). Again, this he teaches is to be observed, not for a time only, but "until we meet in the unity of Faith, unto the measure of the age of the fullness of Christ."

But, in what has Christ placed the primary principle, and the means of preserving this unity? In the fact that He gave some Apostles and the other some Pastors and Doctors, for the perfecting of the saints, for the working of the ministry, for the edifying of the Body of Christ (V-11-12). Wherefore, from the very earliest times, the Fathers and Doctors of the Church have been accustomed to follow and, with one accord, to defend this rule. Origen writes: "As often as the heretics allege the possession of the canonical scriptures, to which all Christians assent, they seem to say: "Behold the world of truth is in the houses." But we should believe them not, and abandon not the primary and ecclesiastical tradition. We should not believe otherwise than has been handed down to us by the succession of the Church of God. (Vetus interpretatio commentarionem in Matthew, n-40). Irenaeus, too, says: "The true knowledge is the doctrine of the Apostles, which is known to us through the Episcopal succession: which has been most fully handed down to our age by the faithful guardianship of the scriptures (contra heresies, lib. IV-cap. 33-n8). And Tertullian: "It is therefore clear that all doctrine that agrees with that of the Apostolic Churches, the matrices and original centres of the Faith, must be looked upon as the truth, holding without hesitation that the Church has received it from the Apostles, the Apostles from Christ, and Christ from God." We are in communication with the Apostolic Churches, which do not differ with one another in doctrine, and in this, we have a testimony of the truth. So also Hilary: "Christ teaching from the ship signifies that those who are outside the Church, can never grasp the Divine teaching, for the ship typifies the Church where the word of life is deposited and preached. Those who are outside are like sterile and worthless sand, and cannot understand. (Comment. Matthew XXIII-1). Again, Rufinus praises Gregory of Nazianum and Basil, because they "studied the texts of Holy Scripture alone, and took the interpretation of its meaning, not from their own inner Consciousness, but from the writings and on the authority of the ancients, who in their turn, as it is clear, took their rule for understanding the meaning from the Apostolic succession. (Hist. Eccl. cap. 9 lib. 11).

The Evil of Heresy.

Wherefore, as appears from what has been said, Christ instituted in the Church a living authoritative and permanent Majesterium, which He, by His own power strengthened, taught by the Spirit of Truth, and confirmed by miracles. He willed and ordered, under the gravest penalties, that its teachings should be received as His own. As often, therefore, as it is declared on the authority of this teaching that this or that is contained in the deposit of Divine Revelation, it must be believed by everyone as true. If it could in any way be false, an evident impossibility would follow for God Himself would be the Author of error in man. "Lord, if we be in error, we have been deceived by Thee." (Richard of St. Victor De Trin. lib 1 cap 2). All cause for doubting being thus removed, can anyone rightfully reject one of those truths, without by the very fact falling into open heresy, separating himself from the Church, and without repudiating in one sweeping act the whole Christian teaching? For such is the nature of things (faith) that nothing can be more absurd than to accept some things and reject others.

Faith, as the Church teaches is that "supernatural virtue by which, with the help and assistance of Divine grace, we believe the things He had revealed to be true, not because of their instrinsic truth perceived by the natural light of reason, but because of the authority of God Himself "the Revealer" who can neither deceive, or be deceived. (Vat. Council) If then it be certain that something is revealed by God, and yet it is not believed, then nothing whatever is believed by Divine Faith; for what the Apostle James judges to be the effect of a moral delinquency, the same is to be said of an erroneous opinion in the matter of faith; Whosoever shall offend in one point, is become guilty of all. (James 11-10).

Nay, it appears to apply with greater force to an erroneous opinion. For it is said less properly that every law is violated by one who commits a single sin, only inasmuch as he has virtually despised the Laws of God the Legislator. But he who dissents even in one point from Faith Divinely revealed absolutely rejects all faith, since he thereby refuses to honor God as the Supreme Truth, and the formal motive of Faith. "In many things they are with Me, in a few things against Me, but in those few things in which they are against Me, the many things in which they are with Me do not profit them." (St. Augustine in Psalm IV. n. 19)

And this indeed most deservedly, for they who take from Christian doctrine what they please, lean on their own judgement, not on Faith; and not "bringing into captivity every understanding into the obedience of Christ: (2 Cor X-5) they more truly obey themselves than God; You who believe what you will of the Gospels and believe not what you will, believe yourselves rather than the Gospel". (St. Augustine, contra Faustrum Manichean lib XVII-cap 3)

The Function of the Church as a Teacher.

For this reason, the Fathers of the Church, (the Vatican Council) laid down nothing new, but followed Divine Revelation and the acknowledged and invariable teaching of the Church, and the very nature of Faith when they decreed as follows: "All those things that are to be believed by Divine and Catholic Faith which are contained in the written or the unwritten word of God, and which are proposed by the Church as Divinely revealed, either by a solemn definition or in the exercise of its ordinary and universal Majesterium (Sess. III- cap 3). Hence, as it is clear that God wills absolutely that there should be unity in the Church, and as it is evident what kind of unity He wills, and by means of what principles He has ordained that this unity is to be maintained, we may address the following words of St. Augustine to all who have not closed their minds to the truth:

"When we see such great help of God, such manifold progress and such abundant fruit, shall we hesitate to take refuge in the bosom of that Church, which as is evident to all possesses the Supreme Authority of the Apostolic See through the Episcopal succession? In vain do heretic peoples rage around it, they are condemned partly by the judgement of the peoples themselves, partly by the right and weight of Councils, partly by the splendid evidence of miracles. To refuse to this Church the primacy is either the height of impiety, or above measure arrogant. And, if any study, no matter how easy and common it may be, requires a teacher or a master in order to be fully understood; what can be greater evidence of pride and weakness, and rashness, than to be unwilling to learn about the books of the Divine mysteries from the proper interpreters, and to wish to condemn the unknown?" (De Utilitate Crendi. cap XVII-n. 35)

Other Functions of the Church.

It is then, the office of the Church to guard Christian doctrine, and to propagate it in its integrity and purity. But that is not all: the right of the Church, and the object for which the Church has been instituted is not wholly attained by the performance of this duty. For, since Jesus Christ delivered Himself up for the salvation of the human race, and to this end directed all His teachings and commands so He ordered the Church to strive by the truth of its doctrine to sanctify and save mankind. But Faith alone cannot compass so great, and important an end. There must needs be also the fitting and devout worship of God which is to be found chiefly in the Divine Sacrifice and in the dispensation of the Sacraments as well as salutary laws and discipline. All these must be found in the Church, since it continues the mission of the Lord and Saviour forever. The Church alone offers to the human race that religion, that state of absolute perfection, which He wished as it were to be incorporated in it And the Church alone supplies those means of salvation which accord with the ordinary counsels of Providence.

The Institution of Church Authority.

But as this heavenly doctrine was never left to the arbitrary judgement of private individuals, but delivered in the beginning by Jesus Christ, and afterwards committed by Him "Exclusively to the Majesterium already named, so also the power of performing and administering the Divine mysteries, together with the authority of ruling and governing, was not by God on all Christians indiscriminately, but on certain chosen persons. For to the Apostles and their legitimate successors alone these words have reference: "Going into the whole world, preach the Gospel . . . baptize them . . . . Do this in commemoration of Me . . . Whose sins you shall forgive, they are forgiven them". . . And in like manner He ordered the Apostles only and those who would succeed them to feed, that is to rule, govern with authority all Christian souls. Whence it also follows that it is necessarily the duty of Christians to be subject and to obey. And these duties of the Apostolic Office are, in general, all included in the words of St. Paul; "Let a man so account of us as of the ministers of Christ, and the dispensors of the mysteries of God." (I Cor. IV-10)

Church Authority in Scripture.

Wherefore Jesus Christ bade all men, present and future, to follow Him as their Leader and Saviour, and this, not merely as individuals, but as forming a society, organized and united in mind, so that a duly constituted society should exist formed out of the multitude, one in Faith, one in object, one in the participation of the means adapted to the attainment of the end, and one subject to one and the same authority. To this end He established in the Church all those natural principles which spontaneously lead men to form societies in order that they may attain the perfection proper to them. That is to say, in it, (the church) all who wish to be the sons of God, by adoption may attain to the perfection demanded by their high calling, and may obtain salvation. The Church therefore, as We have said, is man's guide to heaven. And the Office appointed to it by God is that it may watch over and may order all that concerns religion, and may, without let or hindrance, exercise, according to its judgement its charge over Christianity.

Wherefore, they who pretend that the Church has any wish to interfere in civil matters, or to infringe upon the rights of the State, either know it not, or wickedly calumniate it. God, indeed, even made the Church a society far more excellent than any other. For this end for which the Church exists is as much higher than the end of other societies as Divine grace is above nature, or as immortal blessings are above the transitory things of earth.

Therefore, the Church is a society Divine in its origin, supernatural in its end and in the means proximating to the attainment of that end; but it is a human community in the sense that it is composed of men. For this reason we find it called in Holy Writ by names indicating a perfect society. It is spoken of as the "House of God, the city placed upon the mountains" to which all nations must come. But it is also the "fold" presided over by one shepherd, and into which all Christ's sheep must betake themselves. Yea, it is called the "kingdom which God has raised up and which will stand forever."

Finally, it is the "Body of Christ", that is, of course, His mystical Body, but still, a living body duly organized and composed of many members; members indeed which have not all the same functions, but which, united one to the other, are kept bound together by the guidance and authority of the head.

Now, no true and perfect human society can be conceived which is not governed by some supreme authority. Christ therefore must have given to His Church some supreme authority to which all Christians must render obedience. For this reason, just as unity of Faith is of necessity required for the unity of the Church, inasmuch as it is the body of the faithful, so also for the unity of the Church regarded as a divinely constituted society, calls for unity of government "jure divine," which effects and embraces unity of communion.

The unity of the Church is manifested in two ways; in the mutual connection or communication of its members, and likewise in the relation of all the members of the Church to one Head. (St. Thomas, Summa Theo. IIa-IIae-QXXXIX-Art-I)

From this it is easy to see men can fall away from the unity of the Church, by schism, as well as heresy. We consider that this difference exists between heresy and schism (writes St. Jerome), heresy has some perverse, dogmatic teaching, while schism, through some Episcopal dissension, separates from the Church (Comment, in Epistle ad Titum, III, V, II) in which judgement St. Chrysostom concurs; "I say and protest he writes, that it is as wrong to divide the Church, as to fall into heresy. Wherefore, if no heresy can ever be justifiable, so in like manner there can be no justification for schism. There is nothing more grievous than the sacrilege of schism . . . there can be no just necessity for destroying the unity of the Church." (St. Augustine, Contra Epis. Parmenian Lib II)

The promised appointment of Peter.

Now what this supreme authority is, and of what kind which all Christians are bound to obey, can be ascertained only by finding out what was the positive will of Christ. Certainly Christ is a king forever. And though invisible, He continues unto the end of time to govern and guard His Church from Heaven. But since He willed that His Kingdom should be visible, He was obliged, when He ascended into Heaven, to designate a Vice-regent on earth. "Should anyone say that Christ is the one Head and the one Shepherd, the one Spouse of the one Church, he does not give an adequate reply. It is clear indeed, that Christ is the Author of grace in the sacraments of the Church, it is Christ Himself Who baptizes, it is He Who is the true priest who offered Himself on the cross, and by His power His Body is daily consecrated on the altar; but nevertheless, because He was not to be always visibly present to all the faithful, He has chosen ministers through whom He may dispense the aforesaid things to the faithful, as said above. For the reason therefore, because He was to withdraw His visible presence from the Church, it behooved Him to appoint someone in His place to have charge of the universal Church.

Hence, before His ascension, He said to Peter, "feed My sheep" Jesus Christ therefore appointed Peter to be the supreme ruler of the Church; and He also determined that the authority instituted for the salvation of all in perpetuity should be inherited by his successors, in whom the same permanent authority of Peter himself should continue. And so He made that remarkable promise to Peter, and to no one else; "Thou art Peter, and upon this rock I will build My Church, and the gates of hell shall not prevail against it." (Matt. XVI. 18)

Without any prelude He mentions Peter's name and that of Peter's father (blessed art thou Simon, son of Jona), and He does not wish him to be called any longer, Simon, claiming him for Himself according to His Divine authority. He aptly names him Peter from Petra, the Rock since upon him He was to found His Church.

From this text it is clear that by the will and command of God the Church rests upon St. Peter, as a building rests on its foundation. Now the proper spirit and the proper nature of a foundation, is to be a principle of cohesion for the various parts of the building. It must be in a necessary condition of stability and strength. Remove it and the whole building falls. It is consequently the office of St. Peter to support the Church, and to guard it in all its strength and indestructible unity. How could he fulfill the office without the power of commanding, forbidding, and judging, which is properly called jurisdiction? It is only by this power of jurisdiction that nations and commonwealths are held together. A primary of honor and the shadowy right of giving advice and admonition, which is called "direction" could never secure to any society of men unity or strength. The words "and the gates of hell shall not prevail against it," proclaim and establish the authority of which We speak.

What is meant by the "IT" asks Origen. Is it the Rock upon which Christ builds the Church? The expression is indeed ambiguous, as if the Rock and the Church were one and the same. I indeed think that this is and that neither against the Rock upon which Christ builds His Church, nor against the Church shall the gates of hell prevail". (Origen, in Matthew, Tim. XII-n. II)

The meaning of this utterance is that, notwithstanding the

power of seen or unseen foes, and the cunning which they may bring to bear, it can never be that the Church committed to the care of Peter, shall ever succumb or in any way fail. For the Church, as the edifice of Christ, Who has wisely built His house upon a Rock, cannot be conquered by the gates of hell; these may prevail against any man who may be outside the Rock, and outside the Church, but they shall be powerless against the Church itself.

God confided His Church to Peter so that he might safely guard it with His unconquerable power. He invested Peter, therefore with the needful authority; for the right to rule is absolutely required by him who has to guard human society really and effectively. This, furthermore Christ added; "To thee I give the keys of the kingdom of heaven". And He is clearly still speaking of the Church, which a short time before He had called His own, and which He declared He wished to build on Peter as a foundation.

The Church is typified not alone as an edifice, but as a kingdom, and every one knows that the keys constitute the usual sign of governing authority. Wherefore when Christ promised to give Peter the keys of the kingdom of heaven, He promised to give him power and authority over the Church.

The Son committed to Peter the office of spreading the knowledge of Himself and Father over the whole world. He Who has extended over the earth, and has shown it stronger than the heavens, gave to a mortal man all power in heaven, when He handed to him the keys. (St. John Chrysostom Hom. LIV in Matthew V-2)

Again Christ says; "Whatsoever thou shalt bind upon earth, it shall be bound also in heaven, and whatsoever thou shalt loose upon earth, it shall be loosed also in heaven." This metaphysical expression of binding and loosing indicates the power of making laws, of judging, and of punishing, and the power is said to be of such amplitude and force that God will ratify whatever is decreed by it.

Thus it is supreme and absolutely independent, so that, having no other power on earth as its superior, it embraces the whole Church and all things committed to the Church.

The Fullment of the Promise.

This promise is carried out when Christ the Lord after His resurrection, having thrice asked Peter whether he loved Him more than the rest do, lays on him the injunction; "Feed My lambs, feed My sheep". That is He confides to Peter, without exception all those who are to belong to His fold. "The Lord does not doubt. He interrogates, not to learn, but to teach". When He was about to ascend to heaven He left us as it were, a vice-regency of His love; and so, because Peter of all others professed most loudly his love, he is preferred above all others, that being the most perfect, he should govern the more perfect. (St. Ambrose, exposit in evang. secundum Lucam, lib x-mm-176-176.)

Now these are the duties of a shepherd; to place himself as leader at the head of his flock, to provide proper food for it, to ward off all dangers, to guard against insidious foes, to defend it against violence; in a word, to rule and govern it. Since therefore, Peter was placed as shepherd of the Christian flock, he received the power of governing all men for whose salvation Jesus Christ shed His Blood. "Why has He shed His Blood? To buy the sheep which He handed over to Peter and his successors." (St. John Chrysostom de sacerdoto, lib-II).

Peter confirms his Brethren.

And since all Christians must be closely united together in the communion of one immutable faith, Christ the Lord, in virtue of His prayers, obtained for Peter in the fulfillment of his office he should never fall away from the Faith; "But I have prayed for thee that thy Faith fail thee not," (St. Luke, XXII-2) and He further commanded him to impart spiritual light and strength to his brethren as often as the need should arise; "Confirm thy brethren" (ibid). He willed then, that he to whom He had designated as the foundation of His Church should be the support of its Faith.

Was not Christ, Who confided to Peter the Kingdom by His own power and authority, able to strengthen the faith of one whom He designated as the Rock, to show the foundation of His Church? For this reason Jesus Christ "willed that Peter should share in certain name symbols of great things which properly belong to Himself alone, in order that identity of titles should show identity of power".

Thus He Who is Himself "the chief corner stone" in Whom all the building being framed together, groweth up in a holy temple in the Lord, likened Peter also to a stone, upon which the Church was to be supported. When Peter heard "thou art a Rock" he was ennobled by the announcement. Although Peter is a Rock, he is not so as Christ the Rock, but as Peter the Rock. Christ is essentially the Unshaken Rock; Peter only through this Rock. For Christ imparts indeed His gifts, but He is not impoverished. He is a Priest, and makes priests. He is a Rock, and constitutes a Rock.

Again, He Who is the King of His Church, Who hath the key of David Who openeth and no man shutteth, Who shutteth, and no man openeth, by delivering the keys to Peter, declared him to be the Prince of the Christian Commonwealth. So, too, He, the Great Shepherd, Who calls Himself the Good Shepherd, constituted Peter the good shepherd of His lambs and sheep. Wherefore Chrysostom says: "He was preeminent among the Apostles; the mouthpiece of the Apostles, and the head of the

Apostolic College. At the same time showing him that hence forth he ought to have confidence, and as it were blottin out his denial, He commits to him the government of hi brethren . . . "He saith to him; if thou lovest Me, be over th brethren." Finally, "He Who confirms in every good work an word," commands Peter,—"Confirm thy brethren".

Rightly, therefore, does St. Leo the Great say: "From the worl over, Peter alone is chosen to be placed over the calling of al the nations, to be over all the Apostles, and all the Fathers o the Church. So that, although in the people of God there ar many priests and many pastors, nevertheless Peter properl rules them all, whilst Christ Himself is the principal Ruler.' And so St. Gregory the Great, writing to the Emperor Maurice Augustus says: "It is evident to all who know the Gospel tha the charge of the whole Church was committed to Peter, the Apostle and Prince of the Apostles, by the word of the Lord". . . "Behold, he has received the keys of the heavenly kingdom, the power of binding and loosing is conferred on him; the care of the whole government of the Church is confided to him". (Epis. lib. V-Epis. Xv.)

The permanency of the Petrine Primacy.

But a supreme government of this kind, inasmuch as it belongs to the constitution and formation of the Church as one of its chief elements, that is, as its principle of unity and the foundation of its lasting stability could not possibly come to an end with St. Peter, but must be passed on to his successors from one to another; "there remains, therefore the ordinance of truth, and St. Peter, persevering in the strength of the Rock which he received, has not been abandoned, nor the government of the Church confided to him". (St. Leo the Great, sermo III)

For this reason the Pontiffs who succeeded Peter in the Roman

Episcopate, receive the supreme power in the Church, jure divino, (by divine right). "We define that the Apostolic See and the Roman Pontiff holds the Primacy throughout the whole world, and the said Roman Pontiff is the successor of St. Peter, the Prince of the Apostles, and the true Vicar of Jesus Christ, the Head of the whole Church, and the Father and teacher of all Christians; and that full power was given to him in Blessed Peter, by our Lord Jesus Christ, to feed, to rule, and to govern the universal Church, as is contained in the oecumenical councils and in the sacred canons, "Council of Florence".

Similarly the fourth Council of the Lateran declares; "that, the Roman Church, as the mother and mistress of all the faithful, by the will of Christ, obtains Primacy of ordinary power over all the Churches." These declarations were preceded by the consent of antiquity, which ever recognized and honored without the slightest doubt or hesitation the Bishops of Rome as the legitimate successors of St. Peter.

Who is unaware of the many and evident testimonies of the Holy Fathers which exist to this effect? Most remarkable is that of St. Irenaeus, who referring to the Roman Church says; "With this Church on account of its pre-eminent authority, it should be known, that every Church should be in concord", and St. Cyprian says of the Roman Church, that, "it is the root and mother of the Catholic Church, the chair of Peter, and the principal Church, whence sacerdotal unity has its source". He, (St. Cyprian) calls it the "chair of St. Peter", because it is filled by the successor of Peter; he calls it the "principal Church", on account of its principality conferred on Peter himself, and his legitimate successors, and the "source of unity", because the Roman Church is the efficient cause of unity in the Christian Commonwealth.

For this reason St. Jerome addresses Demasus thus; "My words are addressed to the successor of the Fisherman, to the disciples of the Cross. . . I communicate with Your Blessedness, that is, with the Chair of Peter; for this I know is the Rock on which the Church is built".

Union with the Roman See of Peter is to him always the public criterion of a Catholic. And for a like reason St. Augustine publicly attests that "the principality of the Apostolic chair has always flourished in the Roman Church, and he denies that anyone who dissents from the Roman faith, can be a Catholic. "You are not to be looked upon as holding the true Catholic Faith if you do not teach that the faith of Rome is to be held." So too St. Cyprian, "to be in communion with Cornelius is to be in communion with the Catholic Church". In the same way, Maximus the Abbot teaches that obedience to the Roman Pontiff is the proof of the true Faith and of legitimate communion; therefore, if a man does not want to be, or to be called a heretic, let him not strive to please this or that man, but let him hasten before all things to satisfy the Roman See". If he be in communion with it he will be acknowledged by all everywhere as faithful and orthodox".

"He speaks in vain who tries to persuade me of the orthodoxy of those, who, like himself refuse obedience to the most Pope of the most Holy Church of Rome, that is the Apostolic See." The reason and motive of this he states to be, that, "from the Incarnate Word Himself, and according to the holy Synods, sacred canons and decrees, the Apostolic See has received and does possess the supreme rule, authority, and power of binding and loosing in all things and through all things, in respect of all the holy Churches of God throughout the world." For when this Apostolic See binds and looses the "Word in Heaven Who rules the heavenly powers, also binds and looses" there.

Again, the Christian belief in this matter, which just one nation, or one age held, but all ages, and the East together with the West was accustomed to acknowledge and observe, was thus set forth by Philip the priest, the Pontifical legate, at the Council of Ephesus, no voice being raised in protest.

No one can doubt, indeed, it is known unto all ages, that St. Peter the Prince and Head of the Apostles, the pillar of the Faith and the foundation of the Catholic Church, received the keys of the kingdom from our Lord Jesus Christ, the Saviour and Redeemer of the human race".

The pronouncement of the Council of Chalcedon on the same matter is well known to all; Peter has spoken through Leo, (Actio iii) to which the voice of the 3rd Council of Constantinople responding as an echo; "The chief Prince of the Apostles was fighting on our side; for we had as our ally his followers, the successors of St. Peter to his See. The paper and ink were seen, and Peter spoke through Agatho." (Actio XVIII)

In the formula of Catholic Faith, drawn up and proposed by Hormisdas, which was subscribed at the beginning of the 6th century, by the Emperior Justinian, and by the Patriarchs, by Epiphanius, John and Menna, the following is declared with great weight and solemnity; The solemn pronouncement of our Lord Jesus Christ saying: "Thou are Peter, and upon this Rock I will build My Church" cannot be passed over. These sayings are proved by the results, for the Catholic Faith has always been preserved without stain in the Apostolic See". (Post Epistolem XXVI)

We have no wish to quote every available declaration; but it is well to recall the formula of Faith which Michael Paelologus professed in the second Council of Lyons; "the same holy Roman Church possesses the sovereign and plenary primacy and principality over the whole Catholic Church, which truly and humbly, it acknowledges to have received with the plentitude of power from the Lord Himself, in the person of St. Peter the Prince and Head of the Apostles, of whom the Roman Pontiff is the successor. And as it is bound to defend the truth of Faith beyond all others, so also if any question should arise concerning the Faith, it must be determined by its judgement". (Actio N)

But through the authority of Peter and his successors, though it is plenary and supreme, it is not to be regarded as the sole authority. For He Who made Peter the foundation of the Church, also chose twelve, whom He called Apostles; and just as it is necessary that the authority of Peter should be perpetuated in the Roman Pontiff, so by the fact that the bishops succeed the Apostles, they inherit their ordinary power and thus the Episcopal order necessarily belongs to the constitution of the Church. Although they do not receive plenary, universal or supreme authority, bishops are not to be looked upon as vicars of the Roman Pontiffs, for they exercise a power really their own and are most called the ordinary pastors of the people over whom they rule.

But since the successor of Peter is one, and those of the Apostles are many, it is well for us to examine into the relations which exist between him and them according to the Divine constitution of the Church. And in the first place, the necessity of union between the bishops and successors of Peter is clear and undeniable. This bond once broken the Christians would be scattered and separated and could in no wise form one body and one flock. "The safety of the Church depends on the dignity of the chief priest, to whom if an understanding, extraordinary and supreme power is not given, there are so many schisms to be expected as there are priests". (Jerome, dialogue contra Luciferium n. 9.)

For our present purpose, it is important to bear in mind that nothing was conferred on the Apostles, apart from St. Peter, but that several things were conferred on Peter, apart from the Apostles. St. John Chrysostom, in explaining the words of Christ in John XXI-15 asks: "Why, passing over the others, does

Christ speak to Peter about these things?" and he replies unhesitantly, "because Peter was pre-eminent among the Apostles, the mouthpiece of the Apostles, and the Head of the College."

Peter was alone designated as the foundation of the Church. To him Christ gave the power of binding and loosing: to Peter alone was given the power of feeding. On the other hand, whatever power, whatever office, whatever authority, the Apostles received, they received in conjunction with Peter. If the Divine Benignity willed anything to be common among them, and between Peter and the other princes, whatever He have He gave through Peter, and only him. (St. Leothe Great, sermo IV, cap 2). So that, whereas Peter alone received many things, He conferred nothing on any of the rest, without Peter participating in it.

From this it can be clearly understood that bishops who deliberately secede from Peter and his successors lose their right and power of ruling, because of their secession they are separated from the foundation on which the whole edifice must rest. They are therefore outside the edifice itself; and for same reason they are separated from the fold, whose leader is the Chief Pastor; they are exiled from the kingdom the keys of which were given by Christ to Peter.

These things again reveal to us the heavenly description and the Divine idea in the constitution of the Christian commonwealth. For in as much as the Divine Founder had decreed that the Church should be one in Faith, in government and communion, He chose Peter and his successors as the principal and center so to speak of this unity. Wherefore, Saint Cyprian says: "There is a short and easy proof of the Faith. The Lord saith to Peter: 'I say to thee thou art Peter'. Upon one alone He built His Church, and although after His Resurrection, He gives a similar power to all the Apostles and says; 'All Power is given to Me; as the Father has sent Me, so do I send you:' still in order to manifest authority and unity, by His own authority he lays down that unity as beginning from Onward."

And Optatus of Milevis says: "You cannot deny that you know that in the city of Rome the Episcopal chair was first conferred on Peter. In this Peter, the head of all the Apostles was to sit and in this one chair unity was to be preserved by all, lest any of the other Apostles should claim anything as exclusively his own. So he who would place another chair against that one, would be a schismatic and a sinner". . . Hence the teaching of Cyprian, that heresy and schism arise and are begotten from the fact that due obedience is refused to the supreme authority.

Heresies and schisms have no other origin than that obedience is refused to the priest of God, and that man lose sight of the fact that there is one priest in the Church at a time, and one Judge in the place of Christ".

No one therefore, unless in communion with Peter, can share in authority, for it is bound to be judged as absurd to imagine that he who is outside the Church can command inside the Church. Wherefore Optatus of Milevis blamed the Donatists in the following words; "Against these gates we read that Peter is our Prince to whom it was given—the power by Christ; 'To thee will I give the keys of heaven, and the gates of hell shall not conquer them', whence it is, that you claim for yourselves the use of the keys of the kingdom of heaven—you who fight against the chair of Peter."

The supreme Authority of Peter.

But the Episcopal order is judged to be rightly in communion with Peter in the way that Christ commanded when it is subject to and obeys Peter; otherwise it necessarily becomes a confused and disturbed multitude. It is not sufficient for the due presentation and preservation of unity of Faith and communion that the Head should merely be charged with a primacy of honor, or should have been solely invested with the power of direction. But it is absolutely necessary that he should have received true and supreme authority, which the whole community is bound to obey. For what did the Son of Man mean when He promised the keys of the kingdom to Peter alone? Biblical teaching and usage, and the concordant teaching of the Fathers make it impossible to doubt that supreme authority is designated in the passage of the word "keys". Nor would it be right to interpret otherwise those things which were given to Peter alone, or else were given to the Apostles conjointly with him".

If the power or binding, loosening and feeding confers upon the bishops as the successors of the Apostles, a real authority to rule the people committed severally to them, certainly the same power must have the same nature in the case of him to whom the duty of feeding the lambs and sheep has been signed by God: Christ constituted Peter not only pastor, but pastor of pastors; Peter therefore feeds the lambs and sheep, feeds the children, and feeds the mothers, rules the subjects, and rules the prelates, because the lambs and sheep form the whole of the Church".

(St. Bruno Episcopi segmiensis, comment in Joan, part III, cap 25-n. 55)

Hence those remarkable expressions of the ancients concerning Peter, which clearly set forth the fact that he was placed in the highest degree of dignity and authority. They frequently call him the "Prince of the College of Disciples, Prince of the Holy Apostles, leader of the Choir, the mouthpiece of all the Apostles, the head of that family, the ruler of the whole world, the first of the Apostles, the pillar of the Church".

All these things St. Bernard sums up as follows when writing to Pope Eugenius; "Who art thou? the great priest—the Supreme

Pontiff.—Thou art the Prince of Bishops and the heir of the Apostles. It is to thee that the keys were given, and the sheep entrusted. There are it is true, other gatekeepers of heaven, and other shepherds of the flocks, but thou art so much the more glorious as thou hast inherited a different and more glorious name than all the rest". They have flocks assigned to them, one to each, to thee all the flocks are confided as one flock, to one shepherd and not alone the sheep, but the shepherd also, for thou art the shepherd of all.

"You ask how I prove this? from the words of the Lord. To which one I do not say of the bishops, but even of the Apostles have all the sheep been so absolutely and unreservedly committed? 'If thou lovest Me Peter, feed My sheep.' Which sheep? of this or that city, of that people, of this or that country, or kingdom?—My sheep says Christ; to whom then is it not evident that He does not designate some, but assigns all. Nothing is excepted where no distinction is made."

The Popes superior to bishops collectively.

But it is opposed to the truth, and is evidently a contradiction with the Divine institution of the Church, to hold that while each bishop is individually bound to obey the authority of the Roman Pontiff, taken *collectively,* the bishops are not so bound. For it is the nature and object of a foundation to secure the unity and stability of the edifice as a whole, rather than of each component part; and in the present case there is much more applicable, since it was by the strength of the foundation that Christ willed to insure that the gates of hell should not prevail against the Church.

All are agreed that this Divine promise must be understood of the Church, as a whole, and not of any particular portions of it. These can indeed be overcome by the assaults of the powers of hell, as in point of fact has befallen some of them . . . Moreover, he that is set over the whole flock must have authority, not only over the sheep dispersed throughout the Church, but also when that are assembled together. Do the sheep when they are all assembled together rule and guide the Shepherd? Do the successors of the Apostles assembled together constitute the foundation on which the successor of St. Peter rests in order to derive therefrom his strength and stability? Surely, to him in whose power have been placed the keys of the kingdom of heaven has been given power and authority not only in all promises taken singly, but in all taken collectively.

And as the bishops, each in his own right in his district command with real power, not only individuals, but the community as a whole, so also the Roman Pontiffs, whose jurisdiction extends to the whole Christian commonwealth, have all its parts, even taken collectively subject and obedient to their authority. Christ the Lord, as We have quite sufficiently shown, made Peter and his successors His Vicar, to exercise forever in the Church the same power He exercised during His mortal life. Could the Apostolic college be said to have been above its Master in authority?

This power over the Episcopal college to which we refer, and which is so clearly set forth in Holy Writ, has ever been acknowledged and attested by the Church, as is clear from the teachings of the general Councils; We read that the Roman Pontiffs have pronounced judgement on the prelates of the world Churches; we do not read that anybody has pronounced judgement on them. (Hadrian II, in allocutione iii. ad Synodium Romanum, A.D. 869, of Acts VII. Council Constantinopolitani IV.)

The reason for which is thus stated; "There is no authority greater than that of the Apostolic See". It is evident that the judgement of the Apostolic See, than which there is no greater authority, may be rejected by no one, nor is it lawful for anyone to pass judgement on its judgement. Wherefore, Gelasius on the decrees of Councils says: "Just as that which the first See has not approved of cannot stand, so what it has thought well to decree has been received by the whole Church". It has ever been unquestionably the office of the Roman Pontiffs to ratify or reject the decrees of Councils.

Leo the Great rescinded the acts of the Conciliabulum of Ephesus, Damasus rejected those of Rimini, and Hadrian I, those of Constantinople. The 28th canon of the Council of Chalcedon, by the very fact that it lacks the assent and approval of the Apostolic See is admitted by all to have collapsed. Rightly therefore, did Leo X lay down in the Fifth Council of Lateran, that the Roman Pontiff alone, as having authority over all Councils, has full authority and jurisdiction, and power to summon, to transfer, to dissolve Councils, as is clear from Holy Writ, from the teaching of the Fathers, and from the decrees of the Roman Pontiffs and the sacred canons, but also from the teaching of the Councils themselves. Indeed Holy Writ attests that the keys of the kingdom of heaven were given the Apostles, together with Peter; but there is nothing to show that the Apostles received supreme power without Peter, or against Peter. Such power they certainly did not receive from Jesus Christ. Wherefore, the decrees of the Vatican Council as to the nature and authority of the primacy of the Roman Pontiff, no newly conceived opinion is set forth, but the venerable and constant belief.

The Popes and Episcopal Rights.

Nor does it beget any confusion in the administration that Christians are bound to obey a two-fold authority. We are prohibited in the first place by Divine Wisdom from any such thought, since this form of government was constituted by the Counsel of God Himself. In the second place, we must note that due order of things and their mutual relations would be disurbed if there was a two-fold magistracy of the same rank set ver a people, neither of which was amenable to the other. But he authority of the Roman Pontiff is supreme, universal, inde- endent; that of course must be. It is not congruous that two uperiors with equal rank should be placed over the same flock; ut that two, one of whom is higher, should be placed over the ame people is not incongruous. Thus the parish priest, the ishop, and the Pope, are placed immediately over the same eople. (St. Thomas Aquinas, in II Sent. dist. XVII, a, 4, adq. ad3)

So the Roman Pontiffs, mindful of their duty, wish above all hings that the Divine Constitution of the Church should be in all hings preserved. Therefore, as they defend with all necessary are and diligence their own authority, so they have always abored, and will continue to labor, that the authority of the ishops may be upheld. Indeed they look upon whatever honour r obedience is given to the bishops as paid to themselves: "My onor is the honour of the Universal Church. My honour is the trength and stability of my brethren. Then am I honoured when ue honour is given to everyone." (St. Gregory the Great, Episo- arium, lib, VII-cp XXX ad elogium.)

Appeal to sheep not of Fold.

In what has been said, We have faithfully described the xemplar and form of the Church as Divinely constituted. We ave treated at length of its unity; We have explained suffi- iently the nature of this unity, and pointed out the way in which he Divine Founder of the Church willed that it should be pre- erved.

There is no reason to doubt that all those who, by Divine race and mercy, have had the happiness to have been born, as : were, in the bosom of the Catholic Church, and to have lived n it, will listen to Our Apostolic Voice; "My sheep hear My voice" (John X-27) and that they will derive from Our words fuller instruction and a more perfect disposition to keep united with their respective pastors, and through them with the Supreme Pastor, so that they may remain more securely within the one fold, and may derive therefrom a greater abundance of salutary fruit."

But We, who notwithstanding Our infitness for this great Office, govern by virtue of the vicarious authority conferred on Us by Jesus Christ, looking on Jesus, the author, and finisher of Our faith (Hebrew XII-2), We feel Our heart fired by His charity. What Christ said of Himself, We truly repeat of Ourselves: "Other sheep I have that are not of this fold, them also I must bring, and they shall hear My voice." Let all those therefore, who despise and detest the wide irreligion of our times, and acknowledge and confess Jesus Christ to be the Son of God and the Saviour of the human race, but who wandered from the Spouse, listen to Our voice: let them not refuse to submit to Our paternal love and charity.

Those who acknowledge Christ must acknowledge Him wholly and entirely. "Christ whole and entire consists of the head and body. The Head is the only begotten Son of God, the Body is His Church; the bridegroom and the bride, two in one flesh."

All who dissent from the scriptures concerning the Head, although they may be found in all places in which the Church is found, are not themselves in the Church. And again, all those who agree with the scriptures concerning the Head, but do not communicate in the unity of the Church are not in the Church. (St. Augustine, contra Donatistas Epistol., sive de unit. eccl. cap Iv-n7.)

And with the same learning Our soul goes out to those whom the foul breath of irreligion has not completely corrupted, and who at least seek to have the true God, the Creator of heaven and earth, as their Father. Let such as these take counsel with themselves, and realize they can in no wise be counted among the children of God, unless they take Christ as their brother at the same time they take the Church as their Mother. We most lovingly address these words of St. Augustine to all; St. Augustine observes; "Let us love the Lord our God; let us love His Church; the Lord as our Father, the Church as our mother. Let no one say I go indeed to idols, I consult fortune tellers and soothsayers; but still I leave not the Church of God; I am a Catholic. Clinging to thy mother, thou offend thy Father; another too says; far be it from me; I do not consult fortune-telling, I seek not soothsaying, I seek not the profane divinations, I go not to the workshop of devils, I serve not stones; but I am on the side of Donatus."

What doth it profit thee not to offend the Father, Who avenges an offense against the Mother? What doth it profit to confess the Lord, to honor God, to preach Him, to acknowledge His Son, and to confess that He sits on the right hand of the Father, if you blaspheme His Church? If you had a beneficent friend, whom you honored daily and even once you calumniated his spouse, would you enter his house? Hold fast, therefore dearly beloved, hold fast together to God as your Father, and to the Church as your Mother." (Enmaratio in Psalm LXXXVIII-sermo II-n-14.)

Above all things, trusting in the mercy of God, Who is able to move the hearts of men and to incline them as and when He pleases. We most earnestly commend to His care and loving kindness all those of whom We have spoken. As a pledge of Divine grace, and as a token of Our affection We most lovingly impart to you in the Lord, venerable brethren, to your clergy and people, Our Apostolic Blessing."

Given at St. Peter's, Rome, the 29th day of June in the year 1896, and in the 19th year of Our Pontificate.

Leo XIII, Pope.

Chapter Fifteen

Encyclical Letter of Pope Pius XI,
"Mortalium Animos"
On fostering true religious unity.

Prompted by the Conference of Christian Churches,
at Lausanne, January 6, 1928.

"Pope Pius XI to his Venerable Brethren gives Greeting and
Apostolic Blessing."

Never perhaps in the past have the minds of men been so en-
grossed as they are today with the desire to strengthen, an
extend for the common good of mankind that tie of brotherhoo
—the result of our common good and origin and nature, whic
binds us all so closely together. The world as yet does not enjo
the fruits of peace; on the contrary, dissensions old and new i
various lands issue in rebellion and conflict. Such disputes, affecting the tranquil prosperity of nations, can never be settled with
out the combined and active good-will of those who are respon
sible for their government, and hence it is easy to understand -
especially now — that the unity of mankind is no longer calle
into question; the widespread desire that all nations, in view c

is universal kinship, should daily find closer union with one
nother.

It is with a similar motive that efforts are being made by
me, in connection with the new law promulgated by Christ our
ord. Assured that there exists few men who are entirely devoid
the religious sense, they seem to ground on this belief a hope
at all nations, while differing indeed in religious matters, may
t without great difficulty be brought to fraternal agreement
certain points of doctrine, which will form a common basis
r spiritual life.

With this object congresses, meetings, and addresses are
ranged, attended by a large concourse of hearers, where all
ithout distinction, unbelievers of every kind, of all Christians,
ven those who unhappily rejected Christ and denied His Divine
ature or mission, are invited to join in the discussion. Now,
ich effort can meet with no kind of approval of Catholics. They
ppose the erroneous view that all religions are more or less
ood and praiseworthy, inasmuch as all give expression under
rious forms, to that innate sense which leads men to God and
the obedient acknowledgment of His rule. Those who hold
ich a view are not only in error, they distort the true idea of
ligion, and thus reject it, falling gradually into naturalism and
theism. To form this opinion therefore, and to encourage such
ndertakings is tantamount to abandoning the religion revealed
y God.

Nevertheless, when there is a question of fostering unity
mong Christians, it is easy for man to be misled by the very
xcellence of the object to be achieved. Is it not right they ask,
it not the obvious duty of all who invoke the name of Christ,
nd yet not strive with all his might to accomplish the desire of
Iim Who asked His Father that His disciples might be one?
John XVIII-21.) Did not Christ will that mutual charity
hould be the distinguishing characteristic of His disciples? "By

this shall all men know you are My disciples, if you love c
another," (John XIII-35).

If all Christians were "one" it is contended that they mi
do so much more to drive out the pest of irreligion which w
its insidious and far reaching advance is threatening to sap
strength of the Gospel. These and similar arguments with a
plification are constantly on the lips of the pan-christians w
so far from being a few isolated beings, have formed an ent
class and grouped themselves into societies of extensive memb
ship, under the direction of non-Catholics who also disagree
matters of faith. The energy with which scheme is being p
moted has won for it many adherents, and even many Catho
are attracted by it, since it holds out the hope of a union app
ently consonant with the wishes of Holy Mother Church, wh
chief desire is to recall her erring children and to bring th
back to her bosom. In reality however, these fair and allur
words cloak a most grave error subversive of the foundations
the Catholic Faith.

Conscious, therefore of Our Apostolic office, which warns
not to allow the flock of Christ to be led astray by harm
fallacies, We invoke your zeal, Venerable Brethren, to avert t
evil. We feel confident that each of you, by written and spok
word, will explain clearly to the people the principles and ar
ments that We are about to set forth, so that Catholics may kn
what view and what course of action they should adopt regardi
schemes for the promiscuous union into one body of all who c
themselves Christians.

God, the Creator of all things, made us that we might kn
Him, and serve Him; to our service therefore He has full rig
He might indeed have been contented to prescribe for ma
government the natural law alone, that is, the law which
creation. He has written upon man's heart, and had regulat
the progress of that law by His ordinary Providence.

He willed however, to make positive laws which we should bey, and progressively from the beginnings of the human race, ntil the coming and preaching of Jesus Christ, He Himself aught mankind the duties which a rational creature owes to his Creator. "God Who at sundry times and in divers manners spoke n the past to the Fathers by the prophets last of all in these ays hath spoken to us by His Son." (Heb. I-Iseq.)

Evidently, therefore, no religion can be true save that which ests upon the revelation of God, a revelation begun from the ery first, continued under the old Law, and brought to completion by Jesus Christ Himself under the new Law. Now, if God as spoken — and it is historically certain that He has spoken — hen it is clearly man's duty to implicitly believe His revelation nd to obey His commands. That we might rightly do both, for he glory of God, and forever our own salvation; the only Son of God founded the Church — His Church, on earth. None, We hink, of those who claim to be Christians will deny that a Church, and one sole Church was founded by Jesus Christ.

On the further question however, as to what in the intention of its Founder was to be the precise nature of that Church, there s not the same agreement. Many of them, for example, deny that he Church of Christ was intended to be visible and manifest, at ny rate in the sense that it was to be visibly the one body of the aithful, agreeing in one and the same doctrine under one teaching and growing authority. They conceive the visible Church as nothing more than a portion — a federation of various Christian communities, even though these may hold different and mutually exclusive doctrines. The truth is that Christ founded His Church as a perfect society, of its nature external and perceptible to the enses, which in the future should carry on the work of the alvation of mankind under one head, with a teaching authority, administering the sacraments which are the sources of heavenly grace (John iii-5-vi-48-49). Wherefore He compared His

Church to a kingdom, to a house, to a sheepfold and to a floc
(attested to by various writings by Matthew and John).

The Church thus wondrously instituted could not cease t
exist with the death of its Founder and of the Apostles, th
pioneers of its propagation; for its mission was to lead all me
to salvation, without distinction of time or place; "Going, there
fore, teach ye all nations." Nor could the Church ever lack th
effective strength necessary for the continued accomplishmen
of its task, since Christ Himself is perpetually present with i
according to His promise; "Behold I am with you all days, eve
to the consummation of the world." Hence, not only must th
Church still exist today and continue always to exist, but it mus
ever be the same as it was in the days of the Apostles. Otherwis
we must say — which God forbid — that Christ has failed in Hi
purpose, or that He erred when He asserted of His Church tha
the gates of Hell would not prevail against it. And there it wi
be opportune to expound and reject a certain false opinion whic
lies at the root of this question, and of that complex movemen
by which non-catholics seek to bring about the union of al
Christian Churches. Those who favor this view constantly quot
the words of Christ, "that they may be one . . . and there shal
be one fold and one shepherd (John XVII-21), in the sense tha
Christ thereby merely expressed a desire, or a prayer which as ye
has not been granted. For they hold that the unity of faith an
government which is a note of the one true Church of Christ ha
up to the present time hardly ever existed, and does not exis
today.

They consider that this unity is indeed to be desired, and may
even, by co-operation and good will be actually obtained, bu
that meanwhile it must be regarded as a mere ideal. The Church
they say, is of its nature divided into sections, composed of severa
churches or communities which still remain separate, and although holding in common some doctrine, nevertheless diffe

oncerning the remainder, that all these enjoy the same rights; nd that the Church remained one and undivided at the most nly from the Apostolic age until the first Oecumenical Councils. Hence, they say, controversies and long standing differences, which they still keep, tend to keep asunder the members of the Christian family, must be set aside entirely, and from the residue f doctrines a common form of faith drawn up and proposed for belief, in the profession of which all may not only know but also eel themselves to be brethren. If the various Churches or communities were united in some kind of universal federation they would not then be in a position to oppose resolutely and successfully the progress of irreligion.

Such, venerable brethren, is the common contention. There re indeed some who recognize and affirm that Protestantism has with inconsiderate zeal rejected certain articles of Faith, and xternal ceremony which are in fact useful and attractive, and which the Roman Church still retains. But they immediately go on to say that the Roman Church, too, has erred, and corrupted he primitive religion by adding to it and proposing for belief doctrines not only alien to the Gospel but contrary to its spirit. Chief among these they count that of the primacy of jurisdiction granted to Peter and to his successors in the See of Rome.

There are actually some, though few, who grant to the Roman Pontiff a primacy of honor and even a certain power or jurisdiction; this however they consider to arise not from the Divine Law, but merely from the consent of the faithful. Others again, even go so far as to desire the Pontiff himself to preside over their mixed assemblies.

For the rest, while you may hear many non-Catholics loudly preaching brotherly communion in Jesus Christ, yet not one will you find to whom it ever occurs with devout submission to obey the Vicar of Christ in his capacity of teacher or Ruler. Meanwhile they assert their readiness to treat with the Church of Rome, but

on equal terms, as equals with an equal. But if they could so tre
there seems little doubt that they would do so only on conditi
that no pact into which they might enter should compel the
to retract those opinions which still keep them outside the o
fold of Christ.

The Church cannot compromise on revealed Truth. This bei
so, it is clear that the Apostolic See can by no means take part
these so-called assemblies, not is it in any way lawful for Cath
lics to give to such enterprises their encouragement and suppo
If they did so, they would be giving countenance to a fal
Christianity quite alien to the Church of Christ. Shall we comn
the iniquity of suffering the truth, the truth revealed by God,
be made a subject of compromise? It is indeed a question
defending revealed truth.

Jesus Christ sent His Apostles into the whole world to decla
the faith of the Gospel to every creature, and to every natio
and, to save them from error. He willed that the Holy Gho
should first teach them all truth. Has this doctrine then, disa
peared, or at any time been obscured in the Church of which Go
Himself is the Ruler and Guardian?

Our Redeemer plainly said that the Gospel was intended n
for only the Apostolic age, but for all time. Can the object
faith, in the process of time become so dim and uncertain th
today we must tolerate contradictory opinions? If this were s
then we should admit the coming of the Holy Ghost upon th
Apostles, the perpetual indwelling of the same spirit in th
Church, nay, the very preaching of Jesus Christ, have centuri
ago lost their efficacy and value. To confirm this would b
blasphemy.

The only begotten Son of God not only bade His represent
tives to teach all nations; He also obliged all men to give cr
dence to whatever was taught them by "witnesses preordained c
God." (acts X-41.) Moreover, He enforced His command wit

this sanction: "he that believeth and is baptized shall be saved: he that believeth not shall be condemned."

These two commands, the one to teach, the other to believe for salvation must be obeyed. But they cannot be understood unless the Church proposes an inviolate and clear teaching, and in proposing it is immune from all error. It is also false to say that, although the truth does indeed exist, yet it is to be found only with such labourious efforts, and after such lengthy study and discussion that a man's life is hardly long enough for its discovery and attainment.

This would be equivalent to saying that the most merciful God spoke through the prophets and His only begotten Son merely in order that some few men, and those advanced in years, might learn what He had revealed, and not in order to inculcate a doctrine of faith and morals by which man should be guided throughout the whole of his life.

These pan-christians who strive for the unity of the Churches would appear to pursue the noblest of ideals in promoting charity among all Christians. But how charity tends to the detriment of Faith? Every one knows that John himself the Apostle of love, who seems in his Gospel to have revealed the secrets of the sacred Heart of Jesus, and who never ceased to impress upon the memory of His disciples the new commandment to "Love one another," nevertheless strictly forbade any intercourse with those who professed a mutilated and corrupt form of Christ's teaching; "If any man come to you, and bring not this doctrine, receive him not into the house, nor say to him, 'God speed you.' " (John 2.)

Therefore, since the foundation of charity is faith pure and inviolate, it is chiefly by the bond of one faith that the disciples of Christ are to be united. A federation of Christians then, is inconceivable in which each member retains his own opinions and private judgments in matters of Faith, even though they differ from the opinions of all the rest. How can men with different convictions belong to one and the same federation of the faithful? those who accept sacred tradition as a source of revelation and those who reject it; those who recognize as divinely constituted the Hierarchy of Bishops, priests, and ministers in the Church, and those who regard it as gradually introduced to suit the conditions of the times; those who adore Christ really present in the Holy Eucharist through the wonderful conversion of the Bread and Wine, transubstantiation, and those who assert that the Body of Christ, is only there by Faith, or the signification and virtue of the sacrament; those who in the Eucharist recognize both sacrifice and sacrament, and those who say IT is nothing more than a memorial of the Lord's Supper: those who think it right and useful to pray to the saints reigning with God, and who venerate their images, and those who refuse such veneration as derogatory to the honor due Jesus Christ, the one "mediator of God and man" (ch.-Tim. III-5.)

How so great variety of opinions can clear the way for the unity of the Church, We know not. That unity can arise from one teaching authority, one law of belief and one faith of Christians. But we do know that from such a state of affairs it is but an easy step to the neglect of religion or indifferentism, and the errors of the modernists, who hold that dogmatic truth is not absolute but relative, that is, that it changes according to the varying necessities of time and place, and the varying tendencies of the mind; that it is not contained in an immutable tradition, but can be altered to suit the needs of human life.

The supernatural virtue of Faith has as its formal motive the authority of God revealing, and this allows of no such distinction. All true followers of Christ, therefore will believe the dogma of the Immaculate Conception of the Mother of God with the same faith as they believe the mystery of the August Trinity, the infallibility of the Roman Pontiff, in the sense defined by the

Oecumenical Vatican Council, with the same Faith as they believe the "Incarnation of our Lord."

That these truths have been solemnly sanctioned and defined by the Church at various times, some of them quite recently, makes no difference to their certainty, nor to our obligation of believing them. Has not God revealed them all?

The teaching authority of the Church in the Divine Wisdom was constituted on earth in order that the revealed doctrines might remain forever intact and might be brought with ease and security to the knowledge of men. This authority is indeed daily exercised through the Roman Pontiff, and the bishops who are in communion with him; but it has the further office of defining some truth with solemn decree whenever it is opportune, and whenever this is necessary either to oppose the errors or the attacks of heretics, or again to impress the minds of the faithful with a clearer and more detailed explanation of the articles of sacred doctrine.

But in the use of this extraordinary teaching authority no fresh invention is introduced, nothing new is ever added to the numbers of those truths which are at least perceptibly and implicitly contained within the deposit of revelation divinely committed to the Church; but truths which to some perhaps may still seem obscure are rendered clear, or a truth which some may have called into question is declared to be of Faith.

"All should return to one Church."

Thus, Venerable Brethren, it is clear why this Apostolic See has never allowed its subjects to take part in the Assemblies of non-catholic denominations. There is but one way in which the unity of Christians may be fostered, and that is by furthering the return to the one true Church of Christ to those who are separated from it; from that one true Church they have in the past fallen away. The one Church of Christ is visible to all, and will remain according to the will of its Author, exactly the same as He instituted it, The Mystical Spouse of Christ, has never in the course of centuries been contaminated, nor in the future can she ever be, as Cyprian bears witness; "The bride of Christ cannot become false to her Spouse; she is inviolate and pure: she knows but one dwelling, and chastely and modestly she guards the sanctity of the nuptial chamber." (De Catholica Eccleaia Unitate.)

The same holy martyrs marveled that any one could believe that "this unity of the Church built upon a Divine foundation, knit together by heavenly sacraments, could ever be rent asunder by the conflict of wills for since the Mystical Body of Christ, like His physical Body is composed as one, and compactly and fitly joined together (Eph. IV-15) it were foolish to say that the Mystical Body is composed of disjointed and scattered members. Whosoever therefore, is not united with the Body is no member thereof, neither is he in communion with Christ, its Head."

Furthermore, in this one Church of Christ no man can be or remain who does not accept, recognize, and obey the authority and supremacy of Peter and his legitimate successors.

Did not the ancestors of those who are now entangled in the errors of Photius and of the Reformers, obey the Bishop of Rome, the Chief Shepherd of souls? Their children alas, have left the home of their Fathers: but that house did not fall to the ground or perish forever, for it was supported by God. Let them, then, return to their Father, Who, forgetting the insults heaped upon the Apostolic See, will accord them a most loving welcome, If, as they constantly say, they long to be united with Us and Ours, why do they not hasten to enter the Church, "the mother and mistress of all Christ's faithful?" (Council Lateran IV-c-5). Let them heed the words of Lactantius: "The Catholic Church is alone in keeping the true worship. This is the fount of truth, this the house of Faith, this the temple of God: if any man enter not here, or if any man go forth from it, he is a stranger to the hope of life and salvation. Let none delude himself with obstinate wrangling; for life and salvation are here concerned, and will be lost forever unless their interests be carefully and assiduously kept in mind." (Divini Instituti, VI-30-12.)

Let our separated brethren and children therefore, draw nigh to the Apostolic See, set up in the city from which Peter and Paul, Princes of the Apostles, consecrated by their blood; to the See which is the "root and womb whence issues the Church of God" (Cyprian E. 48 Cornelius) and let them come, not with any intention or hope that the Church of the living God, the pillar and the ground of the truth, will cast aside the integrity of the Faith, and tolerate their errors, but to submit themselves to its teaching and government. Would that the happy lot, denied to so many of Our predecessors might at least be Ours to embrace with Fatherly affection those children whose unhappy separation from Us, We now deplore. Would that God our Saviour "Who will have all men to be saved and come to the knowledge of the truth" might hear Our humble prayer and vouchsafe to recall to the unity of the Church all that are gone astray.

To this all important end, We implore, and We desire that others should implore, the intercession of the Blessed Virgin Mary, Mother of Divine grace, help of Christians, victorious over all heresies, that she may entreat for us the speedy coming of that day when all men shall hear the voice of her Divine Son and shall be careful to keep the unity of the Spirit in the bond of peace. (Eph. Iv-3.)

You, Venerable Brethren, know how dear to Our heart is this desire, and We wish that Our children also should know, not only those belonging to the Catholic fold, but also separated from Us. If these will humbly beg light from heaven, there is no doubt but that they will recognize the true Church of Christ, and entering therein, will at last be united with Us in perfect charity. In the hope of this fulfillment, and as a pledge of Our Fatherly love and good will, Venerable Brethren, We impart most lovingly to you and your clergy and people the Apostolic Blessing. Given at St. Peter's, Rome, on the 6th day of January, the Feast of the Epiphany of our Lord Jesus Christ, in the year 1928, the sixth of Our Pontificate. Pius P. P. XI.

Chapter Sixteen

Official Papal Condemnation of Anglican Orders.
Bull of Pope Leo XIII (Apostolicae Curae)
September 18, 1896.

I

Leo, Bishop,

Servant of the servants of God, in perpetual remembrance.

We have dedicated to the welfare of the noble English nation no small portion of the Apostolic care and charity, by which, helped by His grace We endeavor to fulfill the Office and follow in the footsteps of "The Great Shepherd of the sheep, our Lord Jesus Christ," (Heb. XIII-20).

The Letter, which last year We sent to the "English seeking the Kingdom of Christ in the unity of the Faith," is a special witness of Our good will towards England. In it We recalled the memory of the ancient union of the people with Mother Church, and We strove to hasten the day of a happy reconciliation by stirring up man's hearts to offer diligent prayer to God. And, again, more recently, when it seemed good to Us to treat more fully the unity of the Church in a General Letter, England had both the last place in Our mind, in the hope that Our teaching might both strengthen Catholics and bring them the saving light to those who were divided from Us.

It is pleasing to acknowledge the generous and kindly way in which Our zeal and plainness of speech, inspired by no human motives, have been received by the English people; and this testifies not less to their courtesy than to the solicitude of many for their eternal salvation.

"Reasons for re-opening the question."

With the same mind and intention We have now determined to turn Our consideration to a matter of no less importance, which is closely connected with the same subject and with Our desires. For already the belief confirmed more than once by the action and constant practice of the Church, maintained that when in England, shortly after it was rent from the centre of Christian unity, a new "Rite" for conferring Holy Orders was publicly introduced under Edward VI, the true Sacrament of Orders as instituted by Christ, lapsed, and with it the Apostolic Succession. For some time, however, and in these last years especially, a controversy has sprung up as to whether the sacred Orders conferred to the Edwardine Ordinal possessed the nature and effect of a Sacrament; those in favor of the absolute validity, or of a doubtful validity, being not only certain Anglican writers, but some few Catholics, chiefly non English.

The consideration of the excellency of the Christian priesthood, moved Anglican writers in this matter, desirous as they were that their own people should not lack the two-fold power over the Body of Christ, Catholic writers were impelled by a wish to smooth the way for a return of Anglicans to holy unity. Both, indeed, thought that in view of studies brought up to the level of recent research, and of new documents rescued from oblivion, it was most opportune for the question to be re-examined by Our authority. And We, not disregarding such desires and opinions, and, above all, obeying the dictates of Apostolic charity, have considered that nothing should be left undone that might in any way tend to preserve souls from injury, or procure their advantage.

It has, therefore, pleased Us graciously to permit the cause to be re-examined, so that the extreme care taken in the new examination, all doubt, or even a shadow of doubt, should be removed for the future. To this end We commissioned a certain number of men noted for their learning and ability, whose opinions in this matter were known to be divergent, to state the grounds of their judgments in writing.

We then, having summoned them to Our person, directed them to interchange writing and further, to investigate and discuss all that was necessary for a full knowledge of the matter. We were careful also that they should be able to re-examine all documents bearing on the question which were known to exist in the Vatican archives, to search for new ones, and even to have the acts relating to this subject which were preserved by the Holy Office, at their disposal; and to consider whatever had up to this time been adduced by learned men on both sides. We ordered them, when prepared in this way to meet together in Special Session.

These sessions, to the number of twelve under the Presidency of one of the Cardinals of the Holy Roman Church, appointed by Ourselves, and all were invited to free discussion. Finally, We directed that the acts of these meetings, together with all other documents, should be submitted to Our Venerable Brethren, the Cardinals of the same council, so that, when all had studied the subject, and discussed it in Our presence each might give his opinion.

"Previous decisions — Julius and Paul IV."

This order for discussing the matter having been determined upon, it was only right that, in order to form a true estimate of the real state of the question, careful study and inquiry should first be made, as to how the matter stood according to the prescription and settled policy of the Apostolic See, the origin and force of which custom it was of great importance to determine.

For this reason, in the first place, the principal documents in which Our Predecessors, at the request of Queen Mary, exercised their special care for the reconciliation of the English Church, were considered. Thus, Julius III sent Cardinal Reginald Pole, an Englishman, and illustrious in many ways, to be his "Legate a latere" for the purpose, "as his angel of peace and love," and gave him extraordinary and unusual mandates or faculties and directions for his guidance. These Paul IV confirmed and explained.

And here, to interpret rightly these documents, it is necessary to lay it down as a fundamental principle that they certainly were not intended to deal with an abstract state of things, but with a specific and concrete issue. For since the faculties given by these Pontiffs to the Apostolic Legate had reference to England only, and to the state of religion therein, and since the rules of action were laid down by them at the request of the said Legate, they could have been mere directions for determining the necessary conditions for the validity of ordinations in general, but they must have dealt directly with the subject of Holy Orders in the said kingdom, in view of the condition of the circumstances and times as set forth. This, besides being clear from the nature and form of the said documents, is also obvious from the fact that it would have been altogether irrelevant to instruct the Legate—one whose learning had been conspicuous in the Council of Trent — as to the condition necessary for the bestowal of the Sacrament of Orders.

To all rightfully considering the matters it will not be difficult to understand why, in the Letters of Julius III issued to the Apostolic Legate on March 8, 1554, there is a distinct mention, first of those who, "rightly and lawfully promoted" were to be retained in their Orders and then of others who, "not promoted to Sacred Orders, might be promoted if they were found to be worthy and fitting subjects."

For it is clearly and definitely noted, as was indeed the case, that there were two classes of men; the first, those who had really received Sacred Orders, either before the secession of Henry VIII, or, if after it, and by ministers infected by error and schism, still according to the accustomed Catholic Rite; second, those who were initiated according to the Edwardine Ordinal, who on that account could not be promoted, since they had received an ordination which was null.

And that the mind of the Pope was this and nothing else is confirmed by the Letter of the same Legate (January 29, 1555) sub-delegating his faculties to the Bishop of Norwich. Moreover, what the Letters of Julius III themselves say about freely using the Pontifical faculties even in behalf of those who had received their consecration "minus rite and not according to the accustomed form of the Church" is to be especially noted. By this expression those only could be meant who had been consecrated by the Edwardine Rite, since beside it and the Catholic form there was then no other in England.

This becomes even still clearer when we consider the legation which, on the advice of Cardinal Pole, the Sovereign Princess Mary, and Philip, sent to the Pope in Rome in the month of February 1555. The royal agents, Ambassadors, (three men) "most illustrious, and endowed with every virtue" of whom one was Thomas Thirlby, Bishop of Ely — were charged to inform the Pope more fully as to the religious conditions of the Country and especially to beg that he would ratify and confirm what the Legate had been at pains to effect, and had succeeded in effecting, towards the reconciliation of the kingdom with the Church.

For this purpose all the necessary evidence, (written) and the pertinent parts of the new Ordinal were submitted to the Pope. The Legation having been splendidly received, and their evidence having been "diligently discussed by several of the Cardinals" after due deliberation, Paul IV issued his Bull "Praeclara Carissimi" on June 20 of that same year. In this, whilst giving force, and approbation to what Cardinal Pole had done, it is ordered in the matter of the ordination as follows: "Those who have been promoted to ecclesiastical Orders, by anyone but by a bishop validly and lawfully ordained are bound to receive those Orders again."

But who those bishops were who were "not validly and lawfully ordained" had been made sufficiently clear by the foregoing documents and the faculties used in the said matter by the Legate; those, namely, who had been promoted to the Episcopate, as others to other Orders, "not according to the accustomed form of the Church, or as the Legate himself wrote to the Bishop of Norwich the form and intention of the Church" not having been observed.

These were certainly those promoted according to the new form of "Rite," to the examination of which the Cardinals especially deputed had given their careful attention. Neither should the much to the point in the same Pontifical Letter be overlooked where, together with others needing dispensation, are enumerated those "who had obtained as well Orders as benefices nulliter et de facto." For to obtain Orders nulliter means the same as by an act null and void, that is, *invalid,* as the very meaning of the word and as common parlance require.

This is especially clear when the word is used in the same way about Orders as about "ecclesiastical benefices," which, by the teaching of the sacred Canons, were clearly null if given with any vitiating defect. Moreover, when some doubted as to who, according to the mind of the Pontiff, could be called and considered "validly and lawfully ordained," the same Pope shortly after, on October 30, issued a further Letter in the form of a brief and said: "We, wishing to remove the doubt and to provide opportunity for the peace of conscience of those who during the schism were promoted to Orders, by expressing more clearly the mind and intention which We had in the aforesaid Letter, declare, that only those bishops and archbishops, who were not ordained and consecrated in the form of the Church cannot be said to have been validly and lawfully ordained."

Unless this declaration had applied to the actual case in England — that is to say, to the Edwardine Ordinal — the Pope would certainly have nothing by this last Letter for the removal of doubt and the restoration of peace of conscience. Further, it was in this sense that the Legate understood the documents and commands of the Apostolic See and duly and conscientiously obeyed them; and the same was done by Queen Mary and by all the others who helped her restore religion and Catholic institutions to their former estate.

"Invariable practice of the Holy See."

The authority of Julius III and of Paul IV, which We have quoted, clearly shows the origin of that practice which has been observed without interruption for more than three hundred years, that ordinations conferred according to the Edwardine Ordinal should be considered null and void. This practice is fully proved by the numerous cases of absolute re-ordination according to the Catholic Rite even in Rome. In the observance of this practice we have a proof directly affecting the matter in hand. For if by any chance doubt should remain as to the true sense in which these Pontifical documents are to be understood, the principle holds good that "the custom is the best interpreter of law." Since in the Church it has ever been a constant and established rule that it is sacrilegious to repeat the Sacrament of Orders, it seems it never could come to pass that the Apostolic See should have silently acquiesced and tolerated a system or custom. But not only did the Apostolic See tolerate this practice, it approved and sanctioned it as often as any particular case arose which called for its judgment in the matter.

We adduce two facts of this kind out of many which have from time to time been submitted to the Supreme Council of the Holy Office. The first was (in 1684) of a certain French Calvinist, and the other (in 1704) of John Clement Gordon; both of whom had received their Orders according to the Edwardine Ordinal. In the first case, after a searching investigation, the consulters, not a few in number, gave in writing their answers, or, as they call it, their vota — and the rest unanimously agreed with their conclusion for the *invalidity of Ordination,* and only on account of reasons of opportuneness, did the Cardinals deem it well to answer by a dilata (not to formulate the conclusion at the moment).

The same documents were called into use and considered again at the examination of the second case, and additional written statements of opinion were obtained from consultors, and the most eminent Doctors of the Sorbonne and of Douai were likewise asked for their opinion. No safe-guard which wisdom and prudence could suggest to ensure the thorough sifting of the question was neglected.

"Decree of Clement XII and its Importance."

And here it is important to observe that although Gordon himself, whose case it was, and some of the consultors had adduced, amongst the reasons which went to prove the invalidity, the Ordination of Parker, according to the account then current, in the delivery of the decision, was altogether set aside, as documents of incontestable authenticity prove. Nor, in announcing the decision, was weight given to any other reason other than the defect of form and intention; and in order that the judgment concerning this form might be more certain and complete, precaution was taken that a copy of the Anglican Ordinal should be submitted to examination, and that with it should be collated the Ordination forms gathered together from the various Eastern and Western Rites. Then Clement XI himself, with the unanimous vote of the Cardinals concerned, on the Feria V, April 17 1704, decreed; "John Clement Gordon shall be ordained from the beginning, and unconditionally to all the Orders, even sacred Orders, and chiefly of Priesthood, and in case he has not been confirmed, he shall first receive the sacrament of Confirmation."

It is important to bear in mind that this judgment was not based merely on the omission of the "tradition of the Instruments," for in such a case, according to the established custom, the direction would have been to repeat the Ordination conditionally; and still more important it is to note that the judgment of the Pontiff applies to all Anglican Ordinations, universally, because, although it refers to a particular case, it is not based upon any reason special to that case, but upon the defect of *Form* which defect equally affects all these ordinations; so much so, that when similar cases subsequently came up for decision the same decree of Clement XI was quoted as the norm.

"The Question already definitely Settled."

Hence, it must be clear to everyone that the controversy lately revived had been already definitely settled by the Apostolic See, and that it is to the insufficient knowledge of these documents that we must perhaps attribute the fact that any Catholic writer should have considered it still an open question. But, as We stated at the beginning, there is nothing We so deeply and ardently desire as to be of help to men of good will by showing them the greatest consideration and charity. Wherefore, We ordered that the Anglican Ordinal, which is the essential point of the whole matter, should be once more carefully examined.

"The Anglican Ordinal."

In the examination of any Rite for the effecting and administering of a sacrament, distinction is rightly made between the part which is "ceremonial" and that which is "essential," commonly called the "matter and form." All know what the sacraments of the New Law, as sensible and efficient signs of invisible grace, ought both to signify the grace which they effect, and effect the grace they signify.

Although the signification ought to be found in the whole essential Rite — that is to say, in the matter and form, it still pertains to the form chiefly; since the matter is a part which is not determined by itself, but which is determined by the form. And this appears still more clearly in the sacrament of Orders, the matter of which, in so far as We have to consider in this case, is the imposition of hands, which indeed by itself signifies nothing definite, and is equally used for several Orders and for Confirmation.

But the words which until recently were commonly held by Anglicans to constitute the proper form of priestly Ordination — namely — "Receive the Holy Ghost" certainly do not in the least express definitely the sacred Order of Priesthood, or its graces and power, which is chiefly the power of "consecrating and of offering the true Body and Blood of the Lord" (Council of Trent, Sess. XXIII, de Sacra. Ord. Can. I) in that sacrifice which is "no bare commemoration of the sacrifice offered on the Cross" (ibid, Sess. XXII — de sacrif. Missae. Can. 3).

This form had indeed afterward added to it the words "for the work and office of a priest" (1662) but this rather shows that the Anglicans themselves perceived that the first form was defective and inadequate. But even if this addition could give to the form its due signification, it was introduced too late, as a century had already elapsed since the adoption of the Edwardine Ordinal; for as the Hierarchy had become extinct there remained no power of ordaining. In vain has help been recently sought for the plea of the validity of Orders from the other prayers of the Ordinal. For, to put aside other reasons which show them to be insufficient for the purpose in the Anglican Rite, let this argument suffice for all: from them has been deliberately removed whatever sets forth the dignity and duties of the priesthood in the Catholic Rite. That form consequently cannot be considered apt or sufficient for the sacrament which omits what it precisely ought to signify.

The same holds good of Episcopal Consecration. For to the formula "Receive the Holy Ghost" not only were the words "for the Office and work of a Bishop" added at a later period (1662) but even these, as We shall presently state, cannot be regarded in the same way as if they were in a Catholic Rite. Nor is there anything gained by quoting the prayer of the preface, "Almighty God," since it in like manner has been stripped of the words which denote the "Summum Sacerdotium." It is not here relevant to examine whether the Episcopate be a completion of the Priesthood or an Order distinct from it, or whether when bestowed, as they say, "per saltem," on one who is not a priest, it has or has not its effect.

But the Episcopate undoubtedly by the institution of Christ most truly belongs to the sacrament of Orders, and constitutes the Sacerdotium in the highest degree, namely, that which by the teaching of the Holy Fathers and our liturgical customs is called the "Summum Sacerdotium, Sacri Ministeri Summa." So it comes to pass that, as the sacrament of Orders, and the true sacerdotium of Christ were utterly eliminated from the Anglican Rite, and hence the sacerdotium is in no wise conferred truly and validly by it; and this the more so because among the first duties of the Episcopate is that of ordaining ministers for the Holy Eucharist and sacrifice.

"The mind and aim of those who composed the Edwardine Ordinal."

For the full and accurate understanding of the Anglican Ordinal, besides what We have noted as to some of its parts, there is nothing so pertinent than to examine carefully the circumstances under which it was composed and publicly authorized. It would be tedious to enter into details, nor is it necessary to do so, as the history of that time is sufficiently eloquent as the animus of the authors of the Ordinal against the Catholic Church, as to the abettors whom they associated with themselves from the heterodox sects, and as to the end they had in mind. Being fully cognizant of the necessary connection between Faith and worship, between the "law of believing and the law of praying," they corrupted the liturgical order in many ways to suit the errors of the reformers, under the pretext of restoring it to its primitive form.

Thus in the whole Ordinal there is not a clear mention of the sacrifice, of consecration, of the sacerdotium, and of the powers of consecration and offering sacrifice, but, as We have just noted, every trace of these things, which had been in such prayers of the Catholic Rite as they had not entirely rejected, was deliberately removed and struck out.

In this way the native character — or spirit, as it is called — of the Ordinal clearly manifests itself. Now, if, vitiated in its origin, it was wholly insufficient to confer Orders, it was impossible that in the course of time it could become sufficient, seeing that it remained essentially the same.

Vainly did those who, from the time of Charles I onwards, endeavored to hold some kind of sacrifice or of priesthood, make some addition to the Ordinal; vainly also have a small section of the Anglican body, in recent times, contended that the said Ordinal can be understood and interpreted in a sound and Orthodox sense. Such efforts, We affirm, have been and are all made in vain, and for this further reason, that any words in the

Anglican Ordinal, as it now is, which lends themselves to ambiguity, cannot have the same sense they possess in a Catholic Rite. For once a new Rite has been initiated, as we have seen, the sacrament of Orders is adulterated or denied, and from which all idea of consecration and sacrifice has been rejected, the formula "Receive the Holy Ghost" no longer holds good, because the Spirit is infused into the soul with the grace of the sacrament; and the words "for the work and office of a priest or bishop" and the like no longer hold good, but remain as words without the reality which Christ instituted.

Several of the more shrewd Anglican interpreters of the Ordinal have perceived the force of this argument and they openly urge it against those who take the Ordinal in a new sense and vainly attach to the Orders conferred thereby, a value and efficacy they do not possess. Moreover, by this same argument is refuted the contention of those who think that the prayer "Almighty God, Giver of all good things," which is found at the beginning of the ritual action, may suffice as a legitimate form of Orders, although possibly it might be regarded as sufficient in a Catholic Rite approved by the Church.

"Catholic Doctrine of *Intention.*"

With this inherent "defect of form" is joined the "defect of intention," which is equally essential to the sacrament. The Church does not judge about the mind or intention in so far as it is something by its nature internal; but in so far as it is manifested externally she is bound to judge concerning it.

When anyone has rightly and seriously made use of the due form and the matter required for effecting or conferring the sacrament, he is considered by the very fact to do what the Church does. On this principle the doctrine that a sacrament is truly conferred by the ministry of one who is a heretic or unbaptized, provided, the Catholic Rite be employed. On the other hand, if the Rite be changed, with the manifest intention of introducing another Rite not approved by the Church, and rejecting what the Church does, and what by the institution of Christ belongs to the nature of the sacrament, then it is clear that, not only is the necessary intention wanting to the sacrament, but that the intention is adverse to and destructive of the sacrament.

"Decision of the Holy Office, and the Pope's Final Decree."

All these matters have been long and carefully considered by Ourselves and Our Venerable Brethren, the Judges of the Supreme Council, of whom it has pleased Us to call a special meeting upon the Feria V, the 16th day of July last, upon the solemnity of Our Lady of Mt. Carmel. They, with one accord agreed that the question laid before them had already been adjudicated upon with full knowledge of the Holy See, and that this renewed discussion and examination of the issues had only served to bring out more clearly the wisdom and accuracy with which that decision had been made.

Nevertheless, We deemed it well to postpone a decision in order to afford time, both to consider whether it would be fitting or expedient that We should make a fresh authoritative declaration upon the matter, and humbly to pray for a full measure of Divine guidance. Then, considering that this matter of discipline, although already decided, had been by certain parties, for whatever reason, recalled into discussion, and that thence it might follow that a pernicious error would be fostered in the minds of many who might suppose that they possessed the sacrament and effects of Orders, where these are nowhere, and nowise to be found, it has seemed good to Us in the Lord to pronounce Our judgment.

Wherefore, strictly adhering in this matter to the decrees of the Pontiffs, Our predecessors, and confirming them most fully, and as it were, reviewing them by Our authority, of Our own motion and certain knowledge, We pronounce and declare that

Ordinations carried out according to the Anglican Rite, have been and are absolutely null and utterly void.

It remains for Us to say that even as We have entered upon the elucidation of this grave question in the name and in the love of the Great Shepherd, in the same We appeal to those who desire and seek with a sincere heart the possession of a Hierarchy and of Orders. Perhaps until now, aiming at the greater perfection of Christian virtue, and searching very devoutly the Divine Scriptures, and redoubling the fervor of their prayers, they have, nevertheless, hesitated in doubt and anxiety to follow the voice of Christ, which so long has interiorly admonished them. Now they see clearly whither He in His goodness invites them and wills them to come.

In returning to His one only fold, they will obtain the blessings which they seek, and the consequent helps to salvation of which He has made the Church the dispenser, and as it were, the constant guardian and promoter of His Redemption amongst the nations. Then indeed "they shall draw waters in joy from the fountain of the Saviour" (Isa. XII-3).

His wondrous sacraments, whereby His faithful souls have their sins truly remitted and are restored to the friendship of God, are nourished and strengthened by the Heavenly Bread, and abound with the most powerful aids for their eternal salvation. May the Father, and God of peace, the God of all consolation, in His Infinite tenderness enrich and fill with all these blessings those who truly yearn for them.

We wish to direct Our exhortation and Our desires in a special way to those who are ministers of religion in their respective communities. They are men who from their very office take precedence in learning and authority, and who have at heart the glory of God and the salvation of souls. Let them be the first in joyfully submitting to the Divine call, and obey it and furnish a glorious example to others. Assuredly with an exceeding great joy their Mother the Church will welcome them, and will cherish with all her love those whom the strength of their generous souls has amidst many trials and difficulties led back to her bosom.

Nor could words express the recognition which this devoted courage will win for them from the assemblies of the brethren throughout the Catholic world, or what hope or confidence it will merit for them before Christ as their Judge, or what reward it will obtain from Him in the Heavenly Kingdom.

And We Ourselves, in every lawful way shall continue to promote their reconciliation with the Church in which individuals and masses, as We ardently desire, may find so much their imitation. In the meantime, by the tender mercies of the Lord Our God, We ask and beseech all to strive faithfully to follow in the open path to Divine grace and truth.

We decree that these Letters and all things contained therein shall not be liable at any time to be impugned or objected to by reason of fault or any other defect whatsoever of subreption or obreption of Our intentions, but are and shall be always valid and in force, and shall be inviolably observed both juridically and otherwise, by all of whatsoever degree and pre-eminence; declaring null and void anything which in these matters may happen to be contrariwise attempted, whether wittingly or unwittingly, by any person whatsover, by whatsover authority or pretext, all things to the contrary notwithstanding.

We will that there shall be given to copies of these Letters, even printed, provided that they be signed by a Notary and sealed by a person constituted in ecclesiastical dignity, the same credence given that would be given to the expression of Our will by the showing of these presents.

Given at Rome, at St. Peter's in the year of the Incarnation of our Lord, one thousand eight hundred and ninety-six, on the Ides of September, in the nineteenth year of Our Pontificate.

A. Card. Bianchi, Pro-Datarius. C. Card. DeFuggiero.
Visa-Official of Despatch De Curia, J. Dell'Aquila Visconti.
In place of cross the seal, registered in the secretariate of briefs.
I. Cugnomi.

Letter of Pope Leo XIII to Cardinal Richard, Archbishop of Paris (on the Authority of the Bull, Apostolicae Curae) Nov. 5, 1896.

To Our beloved son, Francis Mary, Cardinal Richard, Archbishop of Paris:

Beloved Son:

Health, and the Apostolic Benediction.

Providing for religion and for the eternal salvation of souls among the English, in accordance with Our office, We lately published, as you know a Constitution "Apostolicae Curae." It was Our intention in this to judge absolutely and to settle finally (absolute judicare penitusque dirimere) that most grave question of Anglican Orders and Ordinations, which had indeed been rightly settled by Our predecessors long ago, but which nevertheless by Our indulgence was completely reconsidered.

And this We have done with such weight of reasoning and with such clearness and authority of language that no prudent or rightly minded person may call Our decision into question, but all Catholics ought to embrace it with complete submission, as forever settled, determined and irrevocable; (perpetuo, firmam, ratam, irrevocababilem).

But We are obliged to say that some Catholics have not so responded to it, a matter which has caused Us no little sorrow. It has pleased Us beloved son, to communicate this to you, because it especially concerns the journal "Revue Anglo-

Romaine" which is published in your city. For there are some among its writers who do not defend and explain the force of this Constitution as they ought, but rather weaken it by excusing it and arguing about it. Wherefore you must see that nothing appears in this journal which is not in full harmony with Our statement, and it is certainly better that it should cease and be silent rather than bring up difficulties against the said statements and decision.

Similarly, at a time when certain Englishmen who seem to be inquiring from Us the truth concerning their Ordinations with a sincere mind, have nevertheless received the truth declared by Us before God in a very different spirit, it obviously behooves those Catholics of whom We spoke and amongst them a certain religious, to recognize what their duty is. For now it is no longer right or fitting to join in or assist the plans of those people in any way, for this may be no small hindrance to the desired spread of religion.

We confidently entrust these things, which are of great moment, to your tried prudence and wisdom, beloved son, and most beloved people, and impart to you the Apostolic benediction, as Our gift, and in token of Our special benevolence.

Given at Rome, on the 5th day of November, in the year 1896 – nineteenth year of Our Pontificate.

Leo XIII. Pope.

Chapter Seventeen

Answer to the Apostolic Letter

"Apostolicae Curae" of Pope Leo XIII
condemning "Anglican Orders" as invalid
by the
Anglican Archbishop of York and Canterbury England
dated Friday, February 19, 1897
(addressed to the whole body of Bishops of the Catholic Church)

"To the whole body of Bishops of the Catholic Church,
from the Archbishops of England"

Greetings:

It is the fortune of our office that often when we would fain write about the common salvation, an occasion arises for debating some controverted question which cannot be postponed to another time. This certainly was recently the case when in the month of September last (1896) there suddenly arrived in this country from Rome a letter already printed and published, which aimed at overthrowing our whole position as a Church. It was upon this "Letter" that our minds were engaged with the attention it demanded when our beloved brother Edward at that time Archbishop of Canterbury, Primate of all England and Metropolitan, was in God's Providence taken from us by sudden death. In his last written words he bequeathed to us the treatment of the question which he doubtless was about to treat with the greatest learning and theological grace. It has therefore seemed good to us the Archbishops and Primates of England that this answer should be written in order that the truth on this matter might be made known both to our Venerable brother Pope Leo XIII in whose name the Letter from Rome was issued, and also to all the Bishops of the Christian Churches settled throughout the world.

II

The duty indeed is a serious one: one which cannot be discharged without a certain deep and strong emotion. But since we firmly believe that we have been truly ordained by the "Chief Shepherd" to bear a part of His tremendous office in the Catholic church, we are not at all disturbed by the opinion expressed in that "Letter." So we approach the task which is of necessity laid upon us "in the spirit of meekness" and we deem it of greater importance to make plain for all time our doctrine about holy "Orders," and other matters pertaining to them, than to win a victory in controversy over a sister "Church of Christ."

Still, it is necessary that our answer be cast in a controversial form lest it be said by anyone that we have shrunk from the force of the arguments put forward on the other side.

III

There was an old controversy, but not a bitter one, with respect to the form and matter of "Holy Orders," which has arisen from the nature of the case, inasmuch as it is impossible to find any tradition on the subject coming from Our Lord or His apostles except the well known example of prayer with laying on of hands.

But little is to be found bearing on this matter in the decrees of "Provincial Councils," and nothing certain or decisive in "Ecumenical and General Assemblies."

Nor indeed does the "Council of Trent" in which our Fathers took no part, touch the subject directly. Its passing remark about the laying on of hands (session XIV – on Extreme Unction, chapter III) and its more decided utterance on the force of the words "Receive the Holy Ghost" which it seems to consider the form of Order (session XXIII – on the Sacrament of Order, canon 4) are satisfactory enough to us, and certainly are in no way repugnant to us or our feelings.

There has been a more recent and a more bitter controversy on the validity of Anglican Ordinations, into which theologians on the Roman side have thrown themselves with eagerness, and in so doing have, for the most part, imputed to us various crimes and defects. There are others, and those not the least wise among them, who, with a nobler feeling, have undertaken our defense. But no decision of the Roman Pontiffs has ever appeared nor has it been possible for us, while we knew that the practice of reordaining our priests clearly prevailed (though this practice has not been without exception) to learn on what grounds of defect they were reordained. We know of the unworthy struggles about Formosus, and the long vacillations about heretical, schismatic and simoniacal ordinations. We had access to the "Letter" of Innocent III on the necessity of supplying unction, and the decree of Eugenius IV for the Armenians; we had the historical documents of the 16th century, though of these many are unknown even to the present day (1897); we had various decisions of later Popes, Clement XI and Benedict XIV, but those of Clement were couched in general terms and therefore uncertain.

We had also the Roman Pontifical as reformed from time to time, but, as it now exists, so confusedly arranged as to puzzle rather than enlighten the minds of inquirers. For if any one considers the rite "Of the ordination of a Presbyter," he sees that the proper laying on of hands stands apart from the uttering of the form. He also cannot tell whether the man, who in rubrics is called "ordained" has really been ordained, or whether the power, which is given at the end of the office by the words "Receive the Holy Ghost: whose sins thou shalt remit they are remitted unto them, and whose sins thou shalt retain they are retained," with the laying on of Pontifical hands, is a necessary part of the priesthood (as the Council of Trent seems to teach are not necessary).

In like manner if anyone reads through the rite "Of the Consecration of an elect as Bishop," he will nowhere find that he is called Bishop in the prayer and benediction referring to the man to be consecrated, or that Episcopate is spoken of in them in regard to him. As far as the prayers are concerned the term "Episcopate" occurs for the first time in the mass during the Consecration.

From these documents, therefore, so obviously discordant and indefinite, no one, however wise, could extract with certainty what was considered by the Roman Pontiffs to be truly essential and necessary for Holy Orders.

IV

Thus our most venerable brother Pope Leo XIII in his letter dated September 13, 1896, which begins with the words "Apostolicae Curae," has approached the question after a manner hitherto unexampled, although the arguments urged by him are sufficiently old.

Nor do we desire to deny that in entering upon this controversy he has consulted the interests of the Church and of truth in thinking over the very vain opinion about the necessity of the delivery of the "instruments" which nevertheless was widely accepted by scholastic theologians from the time of St. Thomas Aquinas up to that of Benedict XIV, and even up to the present day. At the same time he has done well in neglecting other errors and fallacies, which for our part we shall neglect in this reply, and in regard to which we hope that theologians on the Roman side will follow his example and neglect them for the future.

V

His whole judgment (Leo 13) therefore hinges on two points, namely, one the practice of the "Court of Rome" and the form of the Anglican rite to which is attached a third question, not easy to separate from the second, on the intention of our Church. We will answer at once about the former, though it is, in our opinion, of less importance.

VI

As regards the practice of the Roman Court and Legate in the 16th century, although the Pope writes at great length, we believe that he is as uncertain as ourselves. We see that he has nothing to add to the documents which are already well known, and that he quotes and argues from an imperfect copy of the "Letter" of Paul IV, "Praelara Carissimi." Where, for example, are the faculties granted to Pole after August 5, 1553, and before March 8, 1554 which Julius confirms in his "Letter" of the later date to be "freely used" in respect to orders received with any irregularity or failure in the accustomed form, but does not detail and define? Without these faculties the "rules of action" to be followed and observed by Pole are imperfectly known. For the distinction made in the "letters" of both dates between men "promoted" and "not promoted," to which the Pope refers does not touch the position of the Edwardian clergy, but the case of those who held benefices without any pretence of ordination, as was then often done. Who in fact knows thoroughly either what was done in this matter or on what grounds it was done? We know part: of part we are ignorant. It can be proved however on our side that the work of reconciliation under Queen Mary

(July 6, '53 to Nov. 17, 1558) was in very great measure finished under royal and Episcopal authority, before the arrival of Pole.

In the conduct of such business there is evidence of much inconsistency and unevenness. Yet while many Edwardian priests are found to have been deprived for various reasons, none are so found, as far as we know, on account of defect of "Order." Many were particularly on account of entering into wedlock. Some were voluntarily reordained. Some received anointing as a supplement to their previous ordinations, a ceremony to which some of our Bishops attached great importance. Some, and perhaps the majority, remained in their benefices without reordaining, nay, were promoted in some cases to new cures.

Pole did not return to England after his exile until November 1554, and brought the reconciliation to a conclusion in the fifteen (15) months that followed. The principle of his work appears to have been to recognize the state of things which he found in existence on his arrival, and to direct all his powers towards the restoration of papal supremacy as easily as possible. In this period one man and perhaps a second (for more than one had not yet been discovered) received new orders under Pole, in the years 1554 and 1557; but it is uncertain in what year each of them began the process of being reordained. At any rate very few were reordained after Pole's arrival. Others perhaps received some kind of supplement or other to their Orders; a record of which is not to be found in our register.

But if a large number had been reordained under Pole, as Papal Legate, it would not have been at all surprising, inasmuch as in his twelve "Legatine Constitutions," he added as an appendix to the second, the Decree of Eugenius IV for the Armenians, saying that he did so "inasmuch as great errors have been committed here in England with respect to the doctrine concerning the Head of the Church and the Sacraments." And this he did not as our Archbishop, but as Papal Legate. For these Constitutions were promulgated at the beginning of the year 1556. But Pole was only ordained Presbyter on the 20th of March of the same year, and said Mass for the first time on the following day, being the day on which our lawful Archbishop Cranmer was burned alive at the stake, and on the 22nd day of March he was consecrated Archbishop.

We quote there the decree of Eugenius IV as reissued by Pole, because it shows how weak and slippery the judgment of the Church of Rome has been in the matter. Further, when Pope Leo extols the learning of Pole on this point and writes that it would have been quite irrelevant for the Pope to instruct Pole (Legate) as to the conditions necessary for the bestowal of the Sacrament of Orders, he seems wholly to forget Eugenius' Decree, which he has silently thrown over in another part of his letter, (Chp.¶3 and ¶5). The sixth sacrament is that of "Order," the matter of which is the thing by the delivery of which the Order is conferred: as for instance the order of the presbyteriate is conferred by the correction of the chalice with wine, and the paten with bread; the diaconate by the giving of the "Book of Gospels"; the subdiaconate by the delivery of the empty chalice with the empty paten on it; and in like manner as regards other orders by the assignment of the things pertaining to their ministries. The form of the priesthood is as follows: Receive the power of sacrifice in the church for the living and the dead, in the name of the Father and of the Son and of the Holy Ghost. And so as regards the forms of the other orders as is contained at length in the Roman Pontifical.

The ordinary minister of this Sacrament is the Bishop: the effect, an increase of grace, so that a man may be a fit minister. Here the laying on of hands, and the invocation of the Holy Spirit upon the candidates for Orders, are not referred to even by a single word, yet Eugenius, as is clear by his explanations of other Sacraments, is not speaking of things to be supplied by the Armenians (as writers on the Roman side are sometimes fond of saying) but is teaching the Church, as if it were the master in careful adherence to Aquinas, about what is absolutely necessary to the administration of the Sacraments. So also he writes in the earlier part of his Decree. All these Sacraments have three requisites for their performance, things as their "matter," words as their "form," and the person who celebrates the Sacrament with the intention of doing what the Church does; and if any of these be absent, the Sacrament is not performed. (conc. XIV p. 1738).

Now in our Church from March 1550 to Nov 1, 1552, though the delivery of the instruments still remained in some degree (i.e. of the chalice with bread in the case of Presbyters, and of the pastoral staff in that of Bishops, and of the Bible in both), yet the forms attached to them had already been changed very nearly into those which are now in use. In the year 1552 the delivery of the chalice and the staff were dropped, and that of the bible alone remained. King Edward died on the 6th day, July 1553.

According to this Decree, then, all these Presbyters ought to have been reordained. But Pole's opinion scarcely agreed with his practice. Nor does Paul IV himself in his brief "Regimini Universalis" make any demands as to the form in which Presbyters are ordained though careful about properly and rightfully ordained Bishops.

The second, but scarcely stronger foundation of the Papal opinion about the practice of his court, appears to be the judgment of Clement XI, in the case of John Gordon, formerly Bishop of Galloway, delivered on Thursday, April 17, 1704 in the general Congregation of the Inquisition, or as it is usually called, the "Holy Office."

We here make a short answer on this case, inasmuch as it cannot be clearly treated on account of the darkness in which the Holy Office is enveloped, a darkness insufficiently dispersed by

Pope Leo's Letter. The fuller treatment of this has been relegated to the appendix.

There are, however, four reasons in particular for considering his case as a weak and unstable foundation for his judgment.

In the first place, inasmuch as Gordon himself petitioned to be reordained according to the Roman rite, the case was not heard on the other side. Secondly, his petition had as its basis, the old "Tavern Fable" and was vitiated by falsehoods concerning our rite. Thirdly, the new documents of "incontestable authenticity" cited by the Pope are still involved in obscurity and he argues about them as if he were himself uncertain as to their tenor and meaning. Fourthly, the decree of the Congregation of the Holy Office, if it is to be considered to agree with Pope Leo's judgment, can scarcely be reconciled with the reply of the consultors of the Holy Office on "Anglican ordinations," said to have been given about a week before and often published as authoritative by Roman theologians up to 1893. Therefore all those documents ought to be made public if the matter is to be put on a fair footing for judgment.

Finally, it must be noted, that Gordon never went beyond minor orders in the Roman Church. That is to say he only did enough to receive a pension for his support from certain benefices.

VIII

The Pope has done well not to rest upon such weak conclusions, and to determine to reopen the question and to treat it afresh; altho this would seem to have been done in appearance rather than reality. For inasmuch as the case was submitted by him to the Holy Office, it is clear that it, being bound by its traditions, could hardly express dissent from his judgment, however ill founded, which was passed in the case of Gordon.

Further, when he touches upon the matter itself and follows the steps of the Council of Trent, our opinion does not greatly differ from the main basis of his judgment. He rightly calls laying on of hands, the "matter" of ordination. His judgment on the "form" is not so clearly expressed; but we suppose him to intend to say that the "form" is prayer or benediction appropriate to the ministry to be conferred, which is also our opinion. Nor do we part company with the Pope when he suggests that it is right to investigate the intention of a Church in conferring Holy Orders in so far as it is manifested externally.

For whereas it is scarcely possible for any man to arrive at a knowledge of the inner mind of a Priest, so that it cannot be right to make the validity of a Sacrament depend upon it, the will of the Church can both be ascertained more easily, and ought to be both true and sufficient. Which intention our Church shews generally, requiring a promise from one who is to be ordained that he will rightly minister the Doctrine, Sacraments, and discipline of Christ, and teaches that he who is unfaithful to this promise, may be justly punished. And in our Liturgy we regularly pray for "all Bishops and Curates, that they may both by their life and doctrine set forth God's true and lively word, and rightly and duly administer the holy Sacraments.

But the intention of the Church must be ascertained "insofar as it is manifested externally" that is to say from its public formularies and definite pronouncements which direct the main point of the question, not from its omissions and reforms, made as opportunity occurs, in accordance with the liberty which belongs to every Province and Nation, unless it may be that something is omitted which has been ordered in the Word of God, or the known and certain statutes of the universal Church.

For if a man assumes the customs of the middle ages and of more recent centuries as the standard, consider, brethren, how clearly he is acting against the liberty of the Gospel and the true character of Christendom. And if we follow this method of judging the validity of Sacraments, we must throw doubt upon all of them, except Baptism alone, which seems according to the judgment of the Universal Church to have its "matter" and "form" ordained by the Lord.

IX

We acknowledge therefore with the Pope that laying on of hands is the "matter" of ordination; we acknowledge that the "form" is prayer or blessing appropriate to the ministry to be conferred; we acknowledge that the intention of the Church, as far as it is externally manifested, is to be ascertained, so that we may discover if it agrees with the mind of the Lord and His Apostles and with the statutes of the Universal Church. We do not, however, give so much weight to the Doctrine so often descanted upon by the "Schoolmen" since the time of Auxere (A.D. 1215), that each of the Sacraments of the Church ought to have a single "form and matter" exactly defined. Nor do we suppose that this is a matter of Faith with the Romans, for it introduces a very great danger of error, supposing any Pope or Doctor, who may have great influence over men of his time, should persuade people to acknowledge this or that "form or matter" which has not been defined either in the word of God or by the Catholic Fathers or Councils.

For as we have said, Baptism alone stands as a Sacrament in being quite certain both in its "form" and its "matter." And this is the entrance into the Church for all men, and can be administered by all Christians, if there be a passing need, the conditions of a valid Baptism ought to be known to all. As regards the Eucharist (if you set aside, as of less importance, questions of or about unleavened bread, and salt, about water and the rest,) it has a sufficiently certain "matter"; but up to the present day a debate is going on as to its full and essential "form."

But the matter of Confirmation is not so entirely certain; and we at any rate do not at all think that Christians who have different views on the subject should be condemned by one another. The form of Confirmation again is uncertain and quite general, prayer, that is to say, or benediction, more or less suitable, such as is used in each of our Churches. And so with respect to others.

X

But this topic of Confirmation requires to be treated rather more at large; for it throws much light on the question proposed by the Pope. He writes truly that laying on of hands is a "matter" which is equally used for Confirmation. The matter therefore of Confirmation seems in his judgment, to be laying on of hands as we too hold in accordance with Apostolic tradition. But the Roman Church for many centuries has, by a corrupt custom, substituted a stretching out of hands over a crowd of children or simply towards those who are to be confirmed in the place of laying on of hands to be conferred on each individual.

The Orientals (with Eugenius IV) teach that the "matter" is chrism, and use no laying on of hands in this rite. If therefore the doctrine about a fixed "matter and form" in the Sacraments were to be admitted, the Romans have ministered Confirmation imperfectly for many centuries past, and the Greeks have none. And not a few of the former practically confess the corruption introduced by their Fathers having joined laying on of hands to the anointing, as we have learned in many places, while a rubric on the point has been added in some Pontificals. And is it fair to ask whether Orientals who are converts to the Roman Communion require a second Confirmation? Or do the Romans admit that they, who have changed its "matter" have had as good a right to do as themselves who have corrupted it?

XI

We enquire therefore what authority the Pope has for discovering a definite form in the bestowal of Holy Orders? We have seen no evidence produced by him except two passages from the determinations of the Council of Trent (Session XXII on the Sacrifice of the Mass, Canon II and Session XXIII on the Sacrament of Order) which were promulgated after our Ordinal was composed, from which he infers that the principal grace and power of the Christian priesthood is the consecration and oblation of the Body and Blood of the Lord. The authority of that Council has certainly never been admitted in our Country, and we find that by it many truths were mixed with falsehoods, much that is uncertain, with what is certain. But we answer as regards the passages quoted by the Pope, that we make provision with the greatest reverence for the consecration of the Holy Eucharist and commit it only to properly ordained priests and to no other ministers of the Church. Further we truly teach the doctrine of Eucharistic sacrifice and do not believe it to be a "nude commemoration" of the Sacrifice of the Cross, an opinion which seems to be attributed to us by the quotation from that Council. But we think it sufficient in the Liturgy which we use in celebrating the Holy Eucharist, while lifting up our hearts to the Lord, and when now consecrating the gifts already offered that they may become to us the Body and Blood of our Lord, Jesus Christ, to signify the sacrifice which is offered at that point of the service in such terms as these.

We continue a perpetual memory of the precious death of Christ, who is our Advocate with the Father and the propitiation for our sins, according to this precept until His coming again. For first we offer the sacrifice of praise and thanksgiving; then next we plead and represent before the Father the sacrifice of the cross, and by it we confidently entreat remission of sins and all other benefits of the Lord's Passion for all the whole Church; and lastly we offer the sacrifice of ourselves to the Creator of all things which we have already signified by the oblations of His creatures. This whole action, in which the people has necessarily to take its part with the priest, we are accustomed to call the "Eucharistic Sacrifice."

Further, since the Pope reminds us somewhat severely of the necessary connection between faith and workshop, between the "law of believing and the law of praying" it seems fair to ask and call closer attention, both on your part and ours, to the Roman Liturgy.

And when we have looked carefully into the "Canon of the Mass," what do we see clearly exhibited there as to the idea of sacrifice? It agrees sufficiently with our formularies (Eucharistic), but scarcely at all with the determinations of the Council of Trent. Or rather it should be said that two methods of explaining the "Sacrifice" are put forth at the same time by that Council, one which agrees with liturgical science and Christian wisdom, the other which is under the influence of dangerous popular theology on the subject of Eucharistic propitiation.

Now in the "Canon" of the Mass the sacrifice which is offered is described in four ways. First it is a "sacrifice of praise" which idea runs through the whole action and so to say supports it and makes it of a piece. Secondly, it is the offering made by God's servants and His whole family, about which offering request is made that it may become to us the Body and Blood of His Son our Lord. Thirdly, it is an offering to His Majesty of His "own gifts and boons" (that is, as Innocent III, rightfully explains it, of the fruits of the fields and trees, although the words of the Lord have already been said over them by the priest,) which we call the holy Bread of Life (eternal) and the chalice of everlasting salvation. Fourthly, and lastly (in the prayer "Supra quae propitio) the sacrifice already offered in three ways, and according to Roman opinion now fully consecrated, is compared with the sacrifices of our Patriarch's Abel and Abraham, and with that of Melchisedech. This last, being called "holy sacrifice, unblemished Victim," shews that the comparison is not only in respect to the offerer, but also to the things offered. Then the Church prays that they may be carried up by the hands of the holy Angel to the altar of God on high. Lastly, after the second series of names of Saints, there occurs the piece of a prayer (per quem haec omnia) which appears rather suitable to a benediction of fruits of the earth, than to the Eucharistic sacrifice.

It is clear therefore from what has been already said that the law of believing, set forth by the Council of Trent, has gone some distance beyond the boundaries of the law of praying. The matter is indeed one of mystery and fitted to draw onwards the minds of men by strong feelings of love and piety to high and deep thoughts. But, inasmuch as it ought to be treated with the highest reverence and to be considered a bond of charity rather than occasion of subtle disputation too precise definitions of the manner of the sacrifice, or of the relations which unites the sacrifice of the Eternal Priest, and the sacrifice of the Church, which in some way are one, ought in our opinion to be avoided rather than pressed into prominence.

XII

What therefore is the reason for impugning our form and intent in ordaining Presbyters and Bishops?

The Pope writes, if We omit things of less importance, "that the Order of priesthood or its graces and powers, which is especially the power of consecrating and offering the true Body of the Lord in that sacrifice which is no nude commemoration of this sacrifice offered on the Cross," must be expressed in the ordering of a Presbyter. What he desires in the form of consecration of a Bishop is not so clear; but it seems that, in his opinion, in some way or other, "high priesthood" ought to be attributed to him.

Both of these opinions are strange, however, inasmuch as in the most Ancient Roman formulary used, as it seems, at the beginning of the third century after Christ (seeing that exactly the same form is used for a Bishop and a Presbyter except the name) nothing whatever is said about "high priesthood" or "priesthood," nor about the sacrifice of the Body and Blood of Christ. "The prayers and oblations which he will offer (to God) by day and by night" are alone mentioned, and the power of remitting sin is touched upon.

Again in the old "Roman Sacramentary" which may perhaps be assigned to the 6th Century only three prayers are employed for the ordination of a Presbyter. Two are short collects, namely "Oremus delectissimi," and "Exaudi nos" and a third longer, like a Eucharistic preface, which is the real Benediction, and was in former times attached to the laying on of hands, which begins "Domine Sancte pater omnipotens aeterne Deus, honorium omnium," etc. These prayers later made up the whole rite of ordaining a Presbyter in the Church of Rome, with no other ceremonies whatever. These prayers, scarcely altered, are retained in the Roman Pontifical, and forms as it were the nucleus of the service of ordaining of a Presbyter, although the laying on of hands which used to be attached to the longer form has passed to the commencement of the office and is given again at the end of the Mass. But in the Benediction "priesthood" is not attributed to Presbyters, and in none of that series of prayers is anything said of the power of sacrificing or of the remission of sins. "Priestly grace" too which is prayed for in the second Collect in most of the Pontificals is simply "spiritual grace" in some other uses both English and foreign. Yet this form is undoubtedly valid.

Similar things may be said about the form for the consecration of a Bishop. The collects and the benedictions remain in the Roman Pontifical only slightly changed. They begin "Exaudi Domine supplicum preces (now Adesto) propitiare Domine," and "Deu honorum omnium." The second of these mentions "the horn of priestly grace," the third the "high priesthood," but nothing else which can be alleged as supporting the Pope's position. All the rest of the matter in the Pontifical is derived from the usage of later times, and especially from Gallican rites.

And this also may be said as to the power of remitting sins, which is mentioned by the Council of Trent (see chap. III-n-1) together with a "certain power of consecrating and offering," and with equal emphasis. It appears nowhere up to the XIth century in the ordination of a Presbyter; nowhere in the old Roman form for the consecration of a Bishop. It appears only in the long Gallican interpolation in the blessing of a Bishop: "Sint speciosi munere tuo pedes eius" up to "ut fructum de profectu omnium consequator."

But the Pope who appeals to the Council of Trent must submit to be judged by it. Either then these Roman formulas were valueless because of their defect in the matter of sacrifice and remitting sins, or else the authority of that Council is of value in settling this question about the necessary form of Order.

We may here quote another ancient form of consecrating a Bishop which was used both in England and elsewhere during the XIth century and displays the same simplicity. It begins "Pater Sancte omnipotens Deu per Dominum," and prays for those about to be consecrated that they may be enabled to celebrate the mysteries of the Sacraments which have been ordained of old. "May they be consecrated by Thee to the high priesthood to which they are called," but it says not a word about sacrifice nor about the power to forgive sin.

XIII

On the subject of the title of Bishops our simple and immediate reply is that the name of "high priest" is in no way necessary to decide this office in the form of consecration. The African Church openly forbade even her Primates to use this title; the words "pontifical glory" which sometimes appears in Sacramentals, denote a secular or Jewish distinction rather than a rank in the Church. We are not content with the name of Bishop to describe the office of those who when they were left, after the removal of the Apostles, to be chief Pastor in the Church exercised the right of ordaining and confirming, and ruled, together with a body of Presbyters, over a single "parochia" or diocese, as it is now called.

And to this order the Pope, in the beginning of his "Letter," following the sound custom of antiquity, reckons himself to belong.

Bishops are undoubtedly priests, just as presbyters are priests, and in early ages they enjoyed this title more largely than presbyters did, nay, it was not till the fourth or fifth century that presbyters, in the Latin church at any rate, came to be called priests in their own right.

But it does not follow therefore that Bishops nowadays ought to be called "high priests" in the form of consecration. The question of the priesthood of Bishops was perhaps different in early times, certainly up to the IXth and possibly to the XIth century, when a simple deacon was made (often) Bishop "per saltum," i.e. without passing through the presbyterate.

In those days it was fitting, if indeed not necessary, to apply to the Bishop the term priest as e.g. is done in the prayer still used in the "Pontifical," which speaks of the "horn of priestly grace." But inasmuch as this custom of consecrating "per saltum" has long since died out (though perhaps not expressly forbidden by statute), and every Bishop has already been a priest, it is no longer necessary to confer the priesthood afresh, nor, if we give our candid opinion, is it a particularly good and regular proceeding. Nor ought the Romans to require it, inasmuch as the Council of Trent calls preaching of the Gospel "the chief duty of Bishops," (Session V on reform, chap. II and session XXIV on reform, chap. IV). It is not therefore necessary that either high priesthood or any other fresh priesthood should be attributed to Bishops.

But although in our Ordinal we say nothing about high priest and pontiffs we do not avoid using the terms in other public documents. Examples may be taken from the Latin edition of the "Book of Common Prayer," A.D. 1560, from the letter written by twelve (12) Bishops on behalf of Archbishop of Grindall, A.D. 1580, and from Archbishop Whitgifts commission to his suffragan, the Bishop of Dover, A.D. 1580.

XIV

Two of the arguments advanced against our form which especially commend themselves to the Pope shall receive a somewhat larger answer. The first of these is, that about a century after the Ordinal was published, (in 1662) we added to the words "Receive the Holy Ghost" other words intended to define the office and work of a priest or Bishop (cp. chap. 15 notes 1-2). The Pope suggests that these words of our Lord without the subsequent addition are in themselves insufficient, imperfect, and inappropriate.

But in the "Roman Pontifical" when a Bishop is consecrated by the laying on of hands of the consecrating Bishop and assisting Bishops, the only form is "Receive the Holy Ghost." In our later Pontificals, on the other hand, the Holy Spirit was invoked by the hymn "Come, Holy Ghost," with the exception of the Exeter book in which the Roman form is added. Then came the prayer about the "horn of plenty" and priestly grace. As we have already said, the words "Bishop" or "Episcopate" do not appear in any prayer of the "Pontifical" until after the consecration; so that if, according to the Pope's suggestion, our Fathers of the year 1550 and after, went wrong in the form by omitting the name of "Bishop," they must have gone wrong in company with the modern Roman Church. At that time too there immediately followed in our Ordinal those words of St. Paul which were believed to refer to the consecration of St. Timothy to be Bishop of Ephesus, and were clearly used in this sense: – "And remember that thou stir up the grace of God which is in thee by imposition of hands, for God hath not given us the spirit of fear, but of power, and love, and of soberness (2nd Im. 1-6-7).

You may remember, brethren, that these are the only words quoted by the Council of Trent to prove that "Order" confers grace (session XXIII on the Sacrament of Order, C.III). This form, then, whether contained in one sentence as in the Roman Church, or in two as in ours, is amply sufficient to create a Bishop, if the true intention be openly declared, which is done in the other prayers and suffrages (which clearly refer to the office, work and ministry of a Bishop), in the examination and in other ways.

We say that the words "Receive the Holy Ghost" are sufficient, not that they are essential. For they do not occur in the more ancient "Pontificals" whether "Roman" or "English," nor in any "Eastern" book of any date. But we gladly agree with the "Council of Trent" that the words are not vainly uttered by Bishops either in consecrating a Bishop or in ordaining a Presbyter, since they are words spoken by our Lord to His "disciples" from whom all our offices and powers are derived, and are fit and appropriate for so sacred an occasion. They are not equally appropriate in the case of the "diaconate" and are accordingly not used by us in admitting to that office.

XV

The form of ordering a "Presbyter" employed among us in 1550 and afterwards was equally appropriate. For after the "Eucharistic" prayer which recalls our minds to the institution of our Lord, there followed the laying on of hands by the Bishop with the "assistant Priests," to which is joined the "imperative" form taken from the "Pontifical" but at the same time fuller and more solemn. For after the words "Receive the Holy Ghost" there immediately followed, as in the modern "Roman Pontifical" (though the Pope strangely omits to mention it) "Whose sins thou dost forgive they are forgiven; and whose sins thou dost retain, they are retained," and then the words from the Gospel (St. Luke XII-12 and St. Paul 1 Cor-IV-1) which were very rightly added by our "Fathers," "and be thou a faithful dispenser of the Word of God and of His holy Sacraments, in the name of the Father, and of the Son, and of the Holy Ghost."

This form is suitable to no other ministry of the church but that of a priest, who has what is called the "power of the keys," and who alone with full right dispenses the word and mysteries of God to the people whether he remains a presbyter or be advanced to a Bishop. Then there followed, as there still follows, the ceremony of conferring the power to preach and to minister the Sacraments in the sphere where a man has been appointed to that ministry, together with the delivery of the "Holy Bible" which is in our opinion the chief instruments of the sacred ministry and includes in itself all its other parts, according to the particular "Order" to which the man is ordained. And in view of Gordon's case it may not perhaps be idle to explain that these forms are not only verbally but really different. The former "Receive the Holy Ghost" with what follows, together with laying on of hands, confers the general faculties and powers of priesthood, and as is generally said, imprints the character. The second, together with the delivery of the Bible, gives a man the right to offer public service to God and to exercise authority over the Christian people who are to be entrusted to his charge in his own parish or cure. The two commissions taken together include everything essential to the Christian priesthood, and, in our opinion, exhibit it more clearly than is done in the "Sacramentaries and Pontificals." Nor indeed do we avoid the term

"Sacerdos" and its correlatives either in the Latin edition of the "Book of Common Prayer," or of the Ministry of the Sacraments as administered in the Church, published in 1560 in the reign of Queen Elizabeth, nor in other public documents written in Latin.

That this was not done without intention appears from the fact that in translation of the Bible published in the XVI century, the word "iepeus" is rendered by the priest (the word which is always used in the "Anglican Ordinal," and very often in the "Communion Office" elsewhere) while "mpeopurepoc" is translated "Elder."

When therefore in 1662 the addition of "for the work and office of a Bishop or Priest" was made, it would not seem to have been done in view of the Roman controversy, but in order to enlighten the minds of the "Presbyterians" who were trying to find a ground for their opinions in our prayer book. Historians are well aware that at this period, when the King had been killed, his son driven into exile, and the Church government upset, the "Church of England's" dispute and debate with the "Presbyterians" and other innovators was much more severe than it was with the "Romans." These words then were not added to give "liturgical completeness" to the form. For the changes made drew us farther away from the "Pontificals," instead of bringing us nearer. The object of the addition therefore was to declare the difference in the "Orders." And at this period other similar additions were made by way of protest against the innovators, as for example the suffrages in the Litany against rebellion and schism, the prayer for the "High Court of Parliament," and for the establishment of religion and peace at home, and the "Ember Weeks Collects."

That these facts should escape the Pope's notice is perhaps not strange; they prove only the difficulty in interpreting our "Prayer Book" that has arisen from the separation of our nationalities and churches.

But the XVI century form was not only sufficient in itself, but more than sufficient. For the collect "Almighty God, giver of all good things" which beseeches God on behalf of those called "to the office of Priesthood, that they may faithfully serve Him in that office" was at that time part of the "form" and used to be said by the Bishop immediately before the examination. Now, however, since the new words clearly express the same sense, it has been moved elsewhere and takes the place of the "Collect" for the day.

That the Pope should also have been unaware of this change is no matter of wonder; but the fact is worthy of your attention. For we note that he shows some hesitation in this part of his "Letter," when he suggests that the form of 1662 ought perhaps to be considered sufficient if it had only been a century older. He also seems to adopt the opinion of those theologians who believe that the "form" does not consist of one prayer or benediction, whether "precative" as they call it, or "imperative," but in the whole series of formulas which are bound together by a moral union. For he goes on to argue about the help which has been quite recently (as he believes) sought for our case from the other prayers of the same "Ordinal"; although this appeal on our part is by no means recent, but was made in the XVIth century, when first the argument on the Roman side was brought to our notice. Nor do we suppose that the Pope disagrees with Cardinal John Lugo in his teaching that the whole ordination service is a single action, and that it makes no difference if the "matter and form" are separated from one another (as is the case in the "Pontifical") if what intervenes makes up a moral whole.

XVI

The argument, however, which the Pope appears to consider of chief importance and stability is not that which concerns the addition of any words to our "form," but that which lays to our change, the removal of certain acts and prayers from the rest of the rite. His "Letter" says (¶7) "For, to put aside other reasons which show these (prayers) to be insufficient for the purpose in the Anglican rite, let this argument suffice for all; from them has been deliberately removed whatever sets forth the dignity and offices of the priesthood in the Catholic rite. That form consequently cannot be considered apt or sufficient for the Sacrament which omits what it ought essentially to signify." And a little later he adds words, which in one way are untrue, and in another very likely to mislead the reader, and are unfair to our Fathers and ourselves. "In the whole Ordinal not only is there no clear mention of the Sacrifice, of consecration, of the Sacerdotium, and of the powers of consecrating and offering sacrifice, but every trace of these things was deliberately removed and struck out (¶8)." In another passage he speaks (with great ignorance of the facts, we regret to say) of that "small section" of the Anglican body, formed in recent times, whose contention is that the said Ordinal can be understood and interpreted in a sound and orthodox sense.

Next he declares that we deny the Sacrament of Order, or corrupt it, that we reject (viz., in the Ordinal) all idea of consecration and sacrifice, until at last the offices of presbyter and Bishop are left, mere names without the reality Christ instituted.

The answer to these harsh and inconsiderate words has already been partly made when we gave the warning that he who interprets the acts of our Church by mere conjecture and takes it upon himself to issue a new decree as to what is necessary in the form of Order, condemning our lawful Bishops in their government of the Church in the XVIth century, by a standard which they never knew, is entering upon a slippery and dangerous path. The liberty of National Churches to reform their own rites may not thus be removed at the pleasure of Rome. For, as we shall show in part later, there is certainly no one "Catholic rite," but even the forms approved by the Roman Church vary much from one another. The Pope says nothing, however, of the well known intention of our Church set forth in the preface to the Ordinal, and nothing of the "Principles" which our Fathers always set before themselves and which explains their acts without any adverse interpretations.

XVII

Now the intention of our Church, not merely of a newly formed part in it, is quite clearly set forth in the title and preface of the "Ordinal." The title in 1552 ran, "The fourme and manner of making and consecrating Bishoppes, Priests and Deacons."

The preface immediately following begins thus, "It is evident unto all men, diligently reading holy scripture and ancient authorities, that from the Apostles' time, there hath been these "Orders" of ministers in "Christ's Church": Bishops, Priests and Deacons; which offices were evermore had in such reverent estimation, that no man by his private authority might presume to execute any of them, except he were first called, tried, examined, and known to have such qualities as were requisite for the same; and also, by public prayer and imposition of hands approved and admitted thereunto. And therefore, to the extent that these "Orders" should be continued, and reverently used and esteemed, in this Church of England; it is requisite that no man (not being at this present, Bishop, Priest or Deacon) shall execute any of them, except he be called, tried, and examined, according to the form hereafter following."

Further on it is stated incidentally that "every man which is to be consecrated a Bishop shall be fully thirty years of age." And in the rite itself the "consecration" of a Bishop is repeatedly mentioned. The succession and continuance of these "Offices" from the Lord to the Apostles and the other ministers of the primitive Church is also clearly implied in the "Eucharistical" prayers which precede the words "Receive the Holy Ghost."

Thus the intention of our Fathers was to keep and continue these Offices which come down from the earliest times and "reverently to use and esteem them" in the sense, of course, in which they were received from the Apostles and had been up to that time in use. This is a point on which the Pope is unduly silent.

XVIII

But all this and other things of the same kind are called by Pope Leo "names without the reality instituted by Christ." But, on the contrary our Fathers' fundamental principle was to refer everything to the authority of the Lord revealed in the Scriptures. It was for this that they rescinded ceremonies composed and added by men, even including that best known one, common to the modern Latin and Eastern churches, though unknown to the ancient Roman Church, of holding a copy of the Gospels over the head of one about to be ordained Bishop during the utterance of the blessing and the laying on of hands.

Thus then, our Fathers have one matter in imprinting the character, viz., the laying on of hands, one matter in the commission to minister publicly and exercise powers over the flock entrusted to each, viz., the delivery of the Bible or Gospels. This last they probably borrowed from the office of inaugurating a new Bishop and similar rites; thus in the "Pontifical" the Gospels are still delivered to the Bishop after the ring is given.

Other ceremonies of somewhat later date, and imported into the ancient "Roman Ordinal" from sources for the most foreign and especially Gallican, such as the delivery of the instruments and ornaments, the blessing and unction of hands and head, with the accompanying prayers they cut out, as they had a right to do.

The correction of the instruments came, as is well known, from the formularies of minor orders, and was unknown to any

"Pontifical" before the XIth century, which appears to be the earliest of its mention in writing.

When it was reformed, the new formula, "Receive the power of offering sacrifice to God and of celebrating mass, (or as in the Roman Pontifical, masses) on behalf of both the quick and dead," are likewise dropped. The prayer for the blessing of the hands could be said or omitted at the discretion of the Bishop before the XVIth century. The anointing is a Gallican and British custom not Roman at all. Not only is it absent from the Leonine and Galesian Sacramentaries, but also from Mabillon's VIIIth and IXth centuries Ordines, and those of St. Amand which apparently represent the custom of the VIIIth and IXth centuries.

Furthermore we find Pope Nicholas I writing in the IXth century (874) to Rudolph of Burgest that in the Roman Church the hands neither of priests nor deacons, are anointed with chrism. The first writer who mentions anything of the kind is Gildas, the Briton. The same may be said of the anointing of the head which clearly came, in company with much else, from an imitation of the consecration of Avon, and makes its first appearance in the IXth and Xth centuries outside Rome, as may be gathered from Amarlarius (on the offices of the Church 11-14) and our own Pontificals.

There remains to be mentioned the Gallican benediction "Deus sanctificationem omnium auctor," which was added superfluously to the Roman benediction (cap. XII) and was rejected like the rest by our Fathers. This prayer which is manifestly corrupted by interpolation as it stands in the Roman Pontifical, seemed to favour the doctrine of "Transubstantiation," rejected by us, and is in itself scarcely intelligible, so that it was singularly inappropriate to a liturgy to be said in the vulgar tongue for the edification of our own people. And yet this very prayer, whatever it may imply teaches nothing about the power to sacrifice.

XIX

What wonder then if our Fathers, wishing to return to the simplicity of the Gospel, eliminated those prayers from a liturgy which was to be read publicly in a modern language? And herein they followed a course which was certainly opposed to that pursued by the Romans. For the Romans, starting from an almost Gospel simplicity, have relieved the austerity of their rites with Gallican embellishments, and have gradually as time went on added ceremonies borrowed from the old "Testament" in order to emphasize the distinction between people and priests more and more. That these ceremonies are "contemptible and harmful," or that they are useless at their proper place and time, we do by no means assert, we declare only that they are not necessary.

Thus in the XVIth century when our Fathers drew up a liturgy at once for the use of the people and the clergy they went back almost to the Roman starting point. For both sides alike, their holy Fathers, and ours, when they call innovators, followed the same most sure leaders, the Lord and His Apostles. Now, however, the example of the modern Church of Rome, which is entirely taken up with the offering of sacrifice, is held up to us as the only model for our imitation. And this is done so eagerly by the Pope that he does not hesitate to write that "whatever sets forth the dignity and offices of the priesthood has been 'deliberately removed' from the prayers of our Ordinal."

But we confidently assert that our Ordinal, particularly in this last point, is superior to the "Roman Pontifical" in various ways, inasmuch as it appears to express more clearly and faithfully those things which by Christ's institution belong to the nature of the priesthood (¶9) and the effect of the Catholic rites used in the Universal Church. And this, in our opinion, can be shown by a comparison of the Pontifical and Ordinal.

The Roman formulary begins with a presentation made by the

Archdeacon and a double address by the Bishop, first to the clergy and people, and then to the candidates for ordination, for there is no public examination in the ordination of a presbyter. Then follows the laying on of the Bishop's hands, and then those of the assistant presbyters, performed without any words: in regard to which obscure rite we have quoted the opinion of Cardinal De-Lugo (chapter XV). Then the three ancient prayers are said, the two short collects, and the larger benediction, which is now said by the Bishop "with his hands extended in front of his breast". This prayer which is called the consecration in ancient books is considered by weighty authorities since the time of Morimus, to be the true "form" of Roman ordination, and doubtless was in old days joined with laying on of hands. Now, however, "extension of hands" is substituted for laying on of hands, as is the case in Confirmation, while even that gesture is not considered necessary. At any rate, if the old Roman ordinations are valid directly because this prayer has been said the ordinations of presbyters are complete in that Church even at the present day. For any "form" which has once sufficed for any Sacrament, and is retained still unaltered and complete, must be considered to be retained with the same intent as before; nor can it be asserted without a sort of sacrilege that it has lost its virtue, because other things have been silently added after it.

In any case the intention of the more recent part of the Roman formulary cannot have been to empty the more ancient part of its proper force; but its object may not improperly be supposed to have been as follows: first, that the priests already ordained should be prepared by various rites and ceremonies for the offering of the "Sacrifice", secondly, that they should begin to exercise the right of the priesthood in the celebration of the Mass, lastly, that they should publicly be invested with another priestly power, that of remitting sins. Which opinion is confirmed by the language of the old "Pontificals", as for example in the "Sarum Pontifical" we read "bless and sanctify these hands of our priests". All therefore that follows after that ancient "form" just like our words added in 1662, is simply not necessary. For these powers above specified can be conveyed either implicitly and by usage as was the method in ancient times, or at once and explicitly; but the method of conveyance has no relation to the efficacy of ordination.

Our Fathers then, having partly conceived these points, and seeing that the scholastic doctrine concerning the transubstantiation of the Bread and Wine and the more recent doctrine of the repetition (as was believed) of the "sacrifice of the Cross" in the Mass, were connected by popular feeling with certain of the ceremonies and prayer that followed, asking themselves in what way the whole rite of ordination might not only be brought to greater solidity and purity, but might become more perfect and more noble. And inasmuch as at that time there was nothing known for certain as to the antiquity of the first prayers, but the opinions of learned men assigned all efficacy to the "imperative forms", they turned their attention to the latter rather than to the former.

With this object therefore in view they first aimed at simplicity, and consecrated the parts of the whole rite as it were on one prominent point, so that no one could doubt at what moment the grace and power of the priesthood was given. For such is the force of simplicity that it lifts men's minds towards divine things more than a longer series of ceremonies united by however good a meaning.

Therefore having placed in the forefront the prayers which declared both the office of the priesthood and its succession from the ministry of the Apostles, they joined the laying on of hands with our Lord's own words. And in this matter they intentionally followed the example of the "Apostolic Church" which first "fell to prayer" and then "laid on" hands and sent forth its ministers, not that of the "Roman Church" which was laying on of hands before the prayers. Secondly, when they considered in their own minds the various offices of the priesthood they saw that the "Pontifical" in common use was defective in two particulars. For whereas the following office were recounted in the Bishop address: "It is the duty of a priest to offer, to bless, to provide, to teach and baptize" and the like, and mention was made in the old "form" for the "presbyterate" of the account which they are to give of the stewardship entrusted to them, nevertheless and in the other "forms" nothing was said except about offering sacrifice and remitting sin, and the "forms" conveying those powers were separated some distance from one another. Again too, they saw that the duties of the pastoral office had but little place in the "Pontifical", although the Gospel speaks out fully upon them. For this reason then they especially set before our priests the pastoral office, which is particularly that of watchman, messenger, and steward of the Lord, in the noble address which the Bishop has to deliver, and in the very serious examination which follows, in words which must be read and weighed and compared with the holy Scriptures, or it is impossible really to know the worth of our Ordinal. On the other hand, as regards the Sacraments, in their revision of the "imperative forms", they gave the first place to our Lord's own words, not merely out of reverence, but because those were then commonly believed to be the necessary "form". Then they entrusted to our priests all the Sacraments anciently instituted (to use the words of our old "Sacramentary", see chap. 12-14) and did not exalt one aspect of one of them and neglect the others. Lastly, they placed in juxtaposition the "form" which imprints the character, and the "form'" which confers jurisdiction.

And in these and similar matters, which it would take too long to recount, they followed without doubt the example of our Lord and His Apostles. For the Lord is not only recorded to have said "Do this in commemoration of Me" and "Go therefore and teach all nations, baptizing them," in order to teach the due ministry of the Sacraments but many things and those most worthy of attention about the pastoral office, both His own, as the "Good Shepherd", and that of His Disciples, who instructed by His example ought to lay down their lives for all brethren (St. John X 13-18-19 1 Eph. III-16).

Many things too did he deliver in the Gospel about the preaching of the Word, the stewardship entrusted to His chosen servants, the mission of His Apostles and His Disciples in His stead, the conversion of sinners and remission of offenses in the Church, mutual service to one another and much else of the same kind.

This then was the manner in which it behooved the Divine Wisdom especially to instruct His messengers, watchmen and stewards, in order that they might bear witness to the world after His departure and duly prepare a holy people until He should come again. And as the Lord had done, so had the Apostles. St. Peter was a witness to this, when as a fellow Elder he exhorts the Elders, that is the Bishops and presbyters to "feed the flock of God, which is among you" and promises them that "when the chief Shepherd shall appear, ye shall receive a crown of glory, that fadeth not away." (I Peter V-I-V)

St. Paul is a witness when he admonishes the presbyters and Bishops of Ephesus with his own lips (Acts XX-18-25) and instructs them in an epistle of extraordinary spiritual power (Eph. IV-II). A witness too is St. Gregory to whom the whole English race now scattered over the face of the earth owes so much, who in his book "On the pastoral care" has so much to say on these matters, and on the personal life of pastors, but is almost or entirely silent on the offering of sacrifice. His book too was held in such high honor that it was delivered to Bishops in the IXth century, together with the book of the "canons" at the same time of the ordination, when they were further exhorted to frame their lives according to its teaching.

St. Peter also himself, who commends the pastoral office so

urgently to the presbyters, exhorts the whole people, in the earlier part of the same epistle, about offering, as a holy priesthood, spiritual sacrifices to God. This shews that the former office is more peculiar to presbyters, seeing that it represents the attitude of God towards men, while the latter (Psalms XXIII, XXIV, Isaiah XI-10-11, Jeremiah XXIII-1-4, Ezek XXXIV-11) is shared in some manner with the people.

For the priest, to whom the dispensing of the sacraments, and especially the consecration of the Eucharist is entrusted, must always do the service of the Altar with the people standing by and sharing it with him. Thus the prophecy of Malachai (1-11) is fulfilled, and the name of God is great among the Gentiles through the pure offering of the Church.

We therefore, taking our stand on holy Scripture, make reply that in the "ordering of priests" we do duly lay down and set forth the stewardship and ministry of the Word and Sacraments, the power of remitting and retaining sins, and other functions of the pastoral office, and that in these we do sum up and rehearse all functions. Indeed the Pope himself is a witness to this who especially derives the honor of the Pontifical tiara from Christ's triple commendation of his flock to the penitent St. Peter. Why does he then suppose that, which he holds so honorable in his own case, to contribute nothing to the dignity and office of the priesthood in the case of Anglican priests.

Finally, we would have our reverend brother in Christ beware lest in expressing this judgement he do injustice not only to us, but to other Christians also, and among them to his own predecessors, who surely enjoyed in equal measure with himself the gift of the Holy Spirit.

For he seems to condemn the "Orientals" in company with ourselves, on account of defective intention, who in the "Orthodox Confession" issued about 1640 name only two functions of a sacramental priesthood, that is to say, that of absolving sins and preaching; who in the "Longer Russian Catechism" (Moscow 1839) teach nothing about the sacrificing of the Body and Blood of Christ, and mention among the offices which pertain to "Order" only those of ministering the Sacraments and preaching, and feeding the flock.

Further it thus speaks of the three "Orders"—"The Deacon serves at the Sacraments; the priest hallows the Sacraments, in dependence on the Bishop; the Bishop not only hallows the Sacraments himself, but has the power also to impart to others by the laying on of his hands the gift and grace to hallow them." The Eastern Church is assuredly at one with us in teaching that the ministry of more than one mystery describes the character of the priesthood better than the offering of a single sacrifice.

This indeed appears in the "form" used in the "Greek Church" today in the prayer beginning "O God who art great in power, fill this man, whom Thou hast chosen to attain the rank of presbyter, with the gift of Thy Holy Spirit, that he may be worthy blamelessly to assist at Thy Sanctuary, to preach the Gospel of Thy Kingdom, to minister the World of Thy Truth, to offer Thee Spiritual gifts and sacrifices, to renew Thy people with the laver of regeneration" (Hobart, Green Pontifical, p. 314 ed. 1643).

But let the Romans consider now not once or twice what judgement they will pronounce upon their Fathers, whose ordinations we have described above. For if the Pope shall by a new decree declare our Father of two hundred and fifty years ago wrongly ordained, there is nothing to hinder the inevitable sentence that by the same law all who have been similarly ordained have received no "orders." And if our Fathers, who used in 1550 and 1552 "forms" which as he says are null were altogether unable to reform them in 1662, his own Fathers come under the same law. And if Hippolytus and Victor and Leo and Gelasius and Gregory have said too little in their rites about the priesthood and the high priesthood, and nothing about the power of offering the sacrifice of the Body and Blood of Christ, the Church of Rome herself has an invalid priesthood, and the reformers of the Sacramentaries, no matter what their names, could do nothing to remedy her rites. "For as the Hierarchy" (to use the Pope's words) had become extinct on account of the nullity of "form," there remained no power of ordaining. And if the Ordinal "was wholly insufficient to confer 'Orders' it was impossible that in the course of time it could become sufficient since no change had taken place."

In vain those who from the VIth and XIth centuries have attempted to hold some kind of sacrifice or of priesthood, (and power of remitting and retaining sin) have made some additions to the "Ordinal."

Thus in overthrowing our "Orders," he overthrows his own, and pronounces sentence on his own Church.

Eugenius IVth indeed brought his Church into great peril of nullity when he taught a new "matter" and a new "form" of "Order" and left the real issue with a word. For no one knows how many ordinations may have been made, according to his teaching, without any laying on of hands or appropriate "form." Pope Leo 13th demands a "form" unknown to previous Bishops of Rome, and an intention which is defective in the catechisms of the "Oriental Church."

To conclude, since all this has been laid before us in the name of peace and unity, we wish it to be known to all men that we are at least equally zealous in our devotion to peace and unity in the Church. We acknowledge that the things which our brother Pope Leo 13th has written from time to time in other "Letters" are sometimes very true and always written with a good will.

For the differences and debate between us and him arises from a diverse interpretation of the self-same Gospel, which we all believe and honour as the only true one. We also gladly declare that there is much in his own person that is worthy of love and reverence. But that error, which is inveterate in the "Roman Communion," of substituting the visible head for the invisible Christ, will rob his good works of any fruit of peace. Join with us then, we entreat you, most reverend brethren, in weighing patiently what Christ intended when He established the ministry of His Church and His Gospel. When this has been done, more will follow as God wills it in His own good time. God grant even from this controversy may grow fuller knowledge of the truth, greater patience and a broader desire for peace in the Church of Christ, the Saviour of the world.

F. Cantaur
Willelm EBOR.

Dated Friday 19th

February A.D. 1897 (Published by Longman's Green and Co., London England)

Letter of Pope Leo XIII to the Archbishops of Canterbury and York, England (acknowledging receipt of their "Reply" to his Encyclical "Apostolicae Curae")

June 20, 1879

Most Illustrious and Right Reverend Lords

We have received, together with your Letter, the pamphlet which you have written in reply to the Constitution which We published last year concerning Ordinations carried out according to the "Anglican rite."

We do not propose to go through the points you raise. Everyone must realize that We could not have settled the question otherwise than by the rules of Catholic doctrine (ex praescriptis catholici dogmatis), and it is plain that in what you yourselves say about the said ordinations, the priesthood (sacerdotium), the Eucharist, and the Sacrifice, you are far removed from what is laid down by the Catholic and Roman Church.

We could not possibly swerve from the duty incumbent upon Us towards God and the souls redeemed by the Blood of Christ, which arise out of the custody of the Faith and the Sacraments committed to Us, though unworthily and hence, having reflected repeatedly and for a long time on the matter, We decided that We could no longer delay to pronounce that ordinations carried out according to your rite are altogether null and void.

Although, while We were carrying out the duty of Our office, We entertained hopes that there would be some who would regard Our decision in a just and fair light, and would accept it, at the same time, We were saddened by the thought that this, Our decision would be badly received by many who, thinking as they do differently from us, in good faith could not easily be brought to accept the truth.

For prejudiced opinions, one sided studies, the training of the mind from childhood and lastly the very love of the institutions of one's country, which seems to receive added dignity from the greatness of the race itself, exercise a very great influence upon men's minds, and thus it was easy to foresee that those who had hitherto entertained no doubts upon the matter in question would recieve Our adverse judgment somewhat badly.

We indeed allow that those who are separated from Catholic unity, and have been imbued with other doctrines from their youth up, may be sincere, and in good faith, so long as the truth is not suitably or sufficiently clear set before them. The one Judge of the secrets of hearts is God.

Moreover We are greatly affected by the consoling thought that religious zeal is very flourishing throughout Britain, and that not only amongst those who observe Anglican rites, but also amongst many others who are separated equally from the communion of Catholics and of Anglicans. Our beloved son, the Archbishop of Westminster, has often confirmed this belief of Ours, and has told Us many things about your sincerity and zeal in promoting religion, and about the special efforts made in your country for the preservation of religion among the people, the repressing of intemperance, the defense of chastity, and the equitable recompense of the working classes.

When We consider in Our mind these splendid qualities, moral virtues, and Catholic traditions, which still flourish among you, and have been received from former ages, We burn with desire that your race should once more seek for that unity of the Church of Christ to which it held fast during so many centuries, to its benefit and lasting peace and praise. But if these Our efforts, which We have made solely for the love of Christ and of the eternal salvation of souls, are not yet to have the desired result, at any rate We can exhort all urgently and earnestly to constant prayer, than which nothing is more necessary for the attainment of unity. For "no man cometh to Christ unless the Father draw him."

Not long ago We wrote a letter to all Catholics concerning prayer to the Holy Spirit, especially that the same Spirit, to whom it belongs to teach all truth and to spread forth the love of God in the hearts of mankind, may join together all nations, and particularly those who are called by the Christian name, in the same bond of faith and charity. Will not those amongst you who sincerely love to obey the Divine Will, also accept Our invitation?

We ourselves very gladly take advantage of the occasion presented by the receipt of your letter to assure you once more, and all those who care for religious unity of Our most benevolent will. Our heart is still open wide to you, impelled as We are by that love which the Roman Pontiffs have ever cherished for your nation, and which We ourselves will transmit to the Pontiffs who will succeed Us as a most sweet inheritance.

In the meantime, invoking the most benign Mary, Mother of Christ, Peter the Prince of the Apostles, Gregory and Augustine, by whose labours the light of the Gospel was carried to your country, We earnestly beg of Almighty God to pour out upon you abundantly the richness of His goodness.

Pope Leo XIII
The Vatican, June 20, 1879

(From Rome and Reunion—Edited by Rev. Dr. E. J. Messinger, pages 128, 132, 620. 1897.)

Chapter Eighteen

The title of the Pope of Rome,—"The Vicar of Christ" is Challenged by Rt. Rev. and Rt. Hon. Cyril F. Garbett, D.D. Archbishop of York, England. (Anglican)

On Sunday April 2nd, 1944, Rt. Rev. Cyril F. Garbett, Anglican Archbishop of York, England, in an address delivered at Washington, D. C. asserted that the Pope of Rome had no rightful claim to the title of "Vicar of Christ on Earth." In this assault upon the Holy Father, he was supported by the newly enthroned Patriarch Sergi of Moscow, Russia, Metropolitan of the Russian Orthodox Church, (deceased).

In this address challenging the Pope's title of "Christ's Vicar," the Archbishop quoted the words of Christ, to wit: "I am with you always even unto the consummation of the world." The Archbishop contended that, by these words Christ meant the entire Christian Church without distinction; that all Christian bishops being the lawful successors of the Apostles have an equal right to the eminence of the title, "Vicar of Christ on earth."

It is inconceivable that the Archbishop of York is unaware of the words of Jesus Christ concerning the establishment of His Church. The Gospels of St. Matthew, St. Mark, St. Luke, recite the facts of the establishment of the Church by Christ, varying perhaps in the phraseology, but the subject matter being the same, and it is certain that all three Apostles could not err in the chronicling of so momentous an episode in the life of Jesus Christ, affecting the souls of billions of souls unborn.

Surely, the Archbishop of York did not intend to charge our Divine Lord with being a charlatan, a deceiver, a liar, and the most presumptuous person in the history of the world?—yet what other construction can be placed upon his words, when he questions the Pope's right to the title of the Vicar of Christ on earth. Does the Anglican Archbishop of York doubt history? Does he maintain that Jesus Christ, God, was romancing, playing with words, when He said to Peter "Simon, son of John, thou art Peter, and upon this Rock I will build My Church, and the gates of hell shall not prevail against it; whatsoever thou shalt bind on earth, shall be bound also in heaven; and whatsoever thou shalt loose on earth, shall be loosed in heaven"; and again, in the night He was betrayed by Judas, and Peter drawing his sword to defend Christ was admonished to put up his sword, and Peter was obedient. Turning to Peter, Christ said: "Simon, bar Jonah, Satan hath great desires over thee, but I have prayed for thee, that Satan may not sift thee as wheat, and thou being once converted, confirm thy brethren."

These words were not uttered by a civil magistrate conferring powers upon a public official; these words were the solemn pronouncement of the Infinite God irrevocably placing the mantle of Primacy and Supremacy upon St. Peter, designating him as Vicar of Christ on earth.

St. Peter was the first bishop of Rome and his successors in that See always, and still claim the title of "Vicar of Christ on earth." No other bishop in the world claims it. Down through the ages, in peace, turbulence, or war, the bishop of Rome has been recognized by all Catholic bishops and Catholic Kings as the Supreme visible ruler and administrator of the Catholic Church, and those who rejected that supreme authority were not regarded as Catholics.

The early Fathers of the Church acknowledged the supremacy of the Bishop of Rome; he was the chief Pastor of the "sheep and lambs"—the flock of Christ—the visible source of all spiritual jurisdiction. To disavow this truth was to participate in the destruction of the fabric of the Church. To deny the Pope as the Vice-Regent of Christ on earth, was akin to denying Jesus Christ as the Divine Founder and the Head of the Catholic Church.

One of the earliest great Fathers of the Church, St. Irenaeus, the "Peacemaker" explicitly states: "all Churches and all the faithful of Christ are bound to agree with the Roman Church because of her superior Principality."

It is indeed difficult to believe that the Anglican Archbishop of York, the Rt. Rev. and Rt. Hon. Cyril F. Garbett is unfamiliar with the history of his own See. The records of the See of York must disclose that as early as the year 314 A.D. the bishops of York, London, and Caelon, (now Lincoln), attended the first "Council of Arles" and confessed in the name of all British bishops their acceptance of the Supreme rights and prerogatives of the bishop of Rome. It is of course possible that no records of his See previous to the "Reformation" so called are in existence, as all semblance to anything Catholic was destroyed by Archbishop Cranmer and his successors, in their mad endeavor to destroy the Catholic faith in England.

It is also recorded that the three British bishops participated in the "great Council of Sardica" assembled in the year 347, renewing their confession in the supremacy of the "Bishop of Rome"; in fact, they introduced a Canon to that effect, and were most prominently identified by voice and vote in the promulgation of the Canon.

The "Supremacy of the Bishop of Rome" as the Vicar of Christ on earth was strikingly set forth when England conquered Wales. The bishop of St. David's was commanded to make obeisance to the Archbishop of Canterbury, England. The bishop of St. David's refused to do so, as he recoginzed the Bishop of Rome as his superior in jurisdiction. The Church of Scotland likewise refused to recognize the Archbishop of York as his superior, and this action was approved by Pope Clement III. (Lingrads History).

St. Thomas Aquinas remarks that "the supremacy of the Roman Pontiff was not conferred on him by men, but by God. It is God's provision, God's creation. It was not conferred on the Pontiffs by the Church, it came direct from God. It is inherited directly from St. Peter, to whom it was given by Jesus Christ."

In the "old dispensation" or Mosaic Law, there was only one high priest, and the Jews were scattered over the then known world. It is reasonable then to believe, that under the "New Dispensation" Christ would establish but one supreme administrator of His household on earth, so that it would always be one, as He is one with the Father. The authority of the Roman Pontiffs, successors of St. Peter, is therefore from Christ, under the guidance of Christ, and God the Holy Ghost Who directs all of its spiritual endeavors for Christ. No group, however powerful, can ever annihilate it.

For more than 1000 years the bishops of the Church of England, acknowledged the Bishop of Rome as the Supreme Head of the Church, and the Vicar of Christ on earth. The tenacity of the Catholic people of England to the tenets of their Faith was known throughout the whole Catholic world, earning for that fair land the sobriquet of the "Island of Saints." It was only after the seizure of ecclesiastical authority by King Henry 8th, that the jurisdiction of the Pope as Head of Christ's Church on earth was ever abolished.

At the Vatican Council held in Rome in 1869-70 the Primacy of Peter was solemnly defined, and the infallibility of the Pope was set forth, not as a new invention of the papacy, but authoritatively promulgated as follows:

"The Eternal Pastor and Bishop decided to build a Church so that all the faithful should be included together in the bond of one Faith and charity.

Wherefore, before He was glorified, He prayed to His Father, not only for the Apostles, but also for those who were to believe in Him through their word, that they should all be one as the Son Himself and Father are one (John XXIII-1-20-23 et seq.). Therefore, just as Christ Himself was sent forth by the Father, and the Son sent forth these Apostles whom He had chosen from the world, so also He willed that there should be in his Church pastors and doctors until the end of time.

Further, in order, that the Episcopate itself should be one and not divided, and through the coherence of priests one to another the universal multitude of believers should be kept in the unity of the Faith and communion; He placed Blessed Peter over the other Apostles, and in him instituted the perpetual principal and visible foundation of these two bonds of unity; the temple was to be built, and the Church, the summit of which was to reach the heavens, was to rise upon the firmness of his faith (St. Leo the Great, sermo IV de nateli ipsius c.2.Migne. P.L.150).

And inasmuch as the gates of hell constantly and everywhere rise up in greater hatred against the divinely placed foundation of the Church, We judge it necessary for the custody, safety, and increase of the Catholic flock—the Holy Council approving—to set forth the doctrine concerning the institution, the perpetuity, and the nature of the sacred primacy of the Apostolic See, in which consists the force and solidity of the whole Church, to the faithful for their belief, to be held by them, according to the ancient and constant faith of the universal Church, and also to proscribe and condemn the contrary errors, so dangerous to the Lord's flock.

Chapter I

Concerning the institution of the Apostolic Primacy Blessed Peter.

We therefore teach and declare, in accordance with the testimonies of the Gospels, that a primacy of jurisdiction over the whole Church of God was immeditely and directly promised and also conferred on the Apostle Peter by Christ the Lord. For to the one Simon, to whom He had previously said: "Thou art Peter, thou shalt be called Cephas" (John 1) after he had made his confession saying; "Thou art the Christ, the Son of the Living God," the Lord spoke up these solemn words: "Blessed art thou Simon, son of John, because flesh and blood hath not revealed it to thee, but My Father Who is in heaven, And I say to thee; That thou art Peter; and upon this Rock I will build My Church, and the gates of hell shall not prevail against it; And I will give to thee the keys of the kingdom of heaven; and whatsoever thou shalt bind on earth, shall be bound also in heaven, and whatever thou shalt loose on earth, it shall be loosed also in heaven" (Matthew XVI-18-19).

And also to the same Simon Peter, Jesus gave His Resurrection jurisdiction over His whole flock as its Supreme Pastor and Ruler, saying "Feed My Lambs, feed My sheep" . . . To this very clear teaching of the Holy Scriptures, as always understood by the Catholic Church are openly opposed the evil opinions of those who, perverting the form of government instituted by Christ in His Church, deny that the one Peter was given by Christ a true and proper primacy of jurisdiction over the other Apostles, whether singly or collectively, or also who affirm that the said primacy was not given to Blessed Peter immediately and directly, but to the Church, and the latter was passed on to Peter as the minister of the Church.

Canon:

"If therefore anyone shall say that Blessed Peter the Apostle was not constituted by Christ the Lord to be the Prince of the Apostles, and the visible Head of the Church, (Militant), or that he received directly and immediately from the same Lord Jesus Christ a primacy of honor only, but not true and proper jurisdiction, let him be anathema."

Chapter II

Concerning the perpetuity of the Primacy of Blessed Peter in the Roman Pontiffs.

Now that which the Prince of Pastors, and the Great Shepherd of the sheep, our Lord Jesus Christ, instituted in the blessed Apostle Peter for the perpetual well-being and constant good of the Church, must of necessity by the will of the same Author, endure forever in the Church, which, being founded on a rock, will stand firm until the end of the world. For it is matter of doubt to none, but rather it is known to all ages, that the holy and most blessed Peter, the prince and head of the Apostles, and the pillar of the Faith and the foundation of the Catholic Church received the keys of the kingdom of heaven from Our Lord Jesus Christ, the Saviour and Redeemer of the human race; Who until this very time and constantly lives, presides, and exercises judgement in His successors the Bishops of the Holy Roman See, which was founded by, and consecrated with His sacred Blood. (Council of Ephesus, Act 3.)

Hence, whoever succeeds to Peter in this chair, obtains the primacy of Peter over the whole world (church) according to the institute of Christ Himself. There remains therefore, the arrangements made by the truth, and blessed Peter, perservering in the strength of the Rock which he received, does not give up the government of the Church which he has undertaken (St. Leo the Great, sermo III de natali ipsius, c-3-liv-146).

For this cause, to the Roman Church on account of its more powerful principality, it has become necessary for every Church to come, namely those faithful who are in all places, so that in that See, from which the rights flow out to all may coalesce into the structure of one body as members joined together in their Church. (St. Ambrose Eph. II-n4.P.L.XVI)

Canon:

If therefore anyone shall say that it is not by the institution of Christ the Lord Himself, that is, by Divine right, that blessed Peter should have successors forever in his primacy over the whole Church, or that the Roman Pontiffs are not the successors of blessed Peter in the same primacy, let him be anathema.

Chapter III

"Concerning the nature and extent of the Primacy of the Roman Pontiff."

Wherefore, having Ourselves based Our position upon the manifest testimonies of Holy Writ, and adhering to the open and plain decrees with of Our predecessors the Roman Pontiffs, We renew the definition of the Ecumenical Council of Florence, according to which it must be believed by all the faithful that the Holy Apostolical See, and the Roman Pontiff hold a primacy over the whole world, and that the Roman Pontiff himself is the successor of blessed Peter, the Prince of the Apostles, and the true Vicar of Christ, and the Head of the whole Church, and the Father and teacher of all Christians, and that to Him, in blessed Peter there has been given the plenary power of ruling and governing the whole Church by Our Lord Jesus Christ, as is contained in the decrees of the Ecumenical Councils and in the sacred Canons.

Moreover, We teach and declare that the Roman Church, has by the disposition of the Lord a principality of power over all other churches, and that this power of jurisdiction of the Roman Pontiff, which is truly Episcopal, is immediate, and that to him the pastors and faithful, of whatever Rite or dignity, owe a hierarchal subordination and of true obedience, not only in things concerning Faith and morals, but also in those which pertain to the discipline and government of the Church diffused throughout the world, so that, unity being kept with the Roman Pontiff, both in communion, and in the profession of the same Faith, the Church of Christ is one flock under one supreme pastor. This is the doctrine of Catholic truth, from which there is no one able to deviate without danger to Faith and salvation.

But it is so far from the truth that this power of the supreme Pontiff injures the ordinary and immediate power of Episcopal jurisdiction by which bishops, placed by the Holy Ghost, have succeeded in the place of the Apostles and govern the flocks assigned to them as true pastors, that rather this is asserted, strengthened, and defended by the supreme and universal Pastor, in accordance with the saying of St. Gregory the Great: "My honor is the honor of the universal Church. My honor is the solid strength of My brethren. Then am I truly honored, when to each one the honor due is not denied" (Ep.ad eulog.ex Alexis, lib VIII c-30 P.L. LXXVII-933).

Moreover, from the supreme power of the Roman Pontiff to govern the universal Church, it follows that he has the right freely to communicate with the pastors and flocks of the whole Church, in the exercise of his Office, in order that these may be taught and governed by him in the way of salvation. Wherefore we condemn and reprobate the opinions of those who say that this communion of the supreme head with pastors and flocks may lawfully be prevented, or who say that the same is harmful to the secular power, so that they contend that those things which are laid down by the Apostolic See, or by its authority, for the government of the Church, have no force or value unless confirmed by the approval of the secular power.

Since the Roman Pontiff, by the Divine right of the Apostolic primacy, is over the whole Church, we also teach and declare that he is the supreme judge of the faithful, (Pius VI, brief, "Super Solidatate, Nov. 28, 1786), and that all ecclesiastical causes may be referred to his judgement, but that a judgement of the Apostolic See, than which there is no greater authority, cannot be called into question by anyone, nor is it lawful to anyone to judge its judgements, (Epistle of Nicholas I ad Michael, Imper.) Wherefore, they stray from the right path of truth who affirm that it is lawful to appeal from the judgements of the Roman Pontiffs to an Ecumenical Council, as to an authority superior to that of the Roman Pontiff.

Canon:

If therefore anyone shall say that the Roman Pontiff has the Office only of inspection or direction, but not a plenary and supreme power of jurisdiction over the universal Church, and not only in matters concerning Faith and morals, but also in those which pertain to the discipline and government of the Church, diffused throughout the world, or that he has only the greater part, but not the whole plentitude of this supreme power, or that this, his power is not ordinary and immediate, whether in respect of all or single churches, and all and single pastors and faithful, let him be anathema.

Chapter IV

"Concerning the Infallible teaching Office of the Roman Pontiff."

Now, the Holy See has always held, and the perpetual sense of the Church confirms, and the Ecumenical Councils, especially those in which the East came together with the West in the union of Faith and charity, have declared that in the Apostolic primacy, which the Roman Pontiff as the successor of St. Peter, the Prince of the Apostles, has obtained over the whole Church, there is included also the supreme power of teaching. For the Fathers of the Fourth Council of Constantinople, following in the footsteps of their predecessors gave forth this solemn warning and profession: "The first condition of salvation is to keep the rule of the true Faith. And inasmuch as the sentence of our Lord Jesus Christ cannot be passed over, in which He says: "Thou art Peter, and upon this Rock I will build My Church," these things which have been said have been proved by effects, for in the Apostolic See the Catholic religion has always been kept immaculate, and her well known doctrine kept holy. Therefore, desiring not to be in the least degree separated from the Faith and doctrine of this See, we hope that we may deserve to be in the communion which the Apostolic See preaches, in which See is the entire truth and true solidity of the Christian religion. (From the formula of St. Hormisdas, Pope, set forth by Hadrian II to the Fathers of the Fourth Council of Constantinople, (the Eighth General Council) and subscribed by them.

And, with the approval of the Second Council of Lyons, the Greeks there professed that the Roman Church has obtained the full primacy and principality over the universal Catholic Church, which it truly and humbly acknowledges to have received, with the fullness of power from the Lord Himself in blessed Peter, whose successor the Roman Pontiff is, and as the Apostolic See is bound before all others to defend the truth of Faith, so also, if any questions should arise about Faith, they must be determined by its judgement.

Finally, the Council of Florence defined that, that the Roman Pontiff is the true Vicar of Christ, the Head of the whole Church, and the Father and teacher of all Christians, and that to him in blessed Peter there has been given by Our Lord Jesus Christ the full power of ruling and governing the whole Church of God.

To satisfy this pastoral duty, Our predecessors ever made unwearied efforts that the saving doctrines of Christ should be propagated amongst all the peoples of the earth, and have watched with a like care that where it has received acceptance, it should be conserved genuine and pure. Wherefore, the bishops of the whole world, now singly, now gathered together in Synods, following a long established custom of the Church and the form of the ancient rule, have sent word to the Apostolic See especially of those dangers which sprang up in matters of Faith, that from the place where the Faith cannot experience defect there should come that which would repair the injuries to the Faith. (Cf. St. Bernard ep. cxc. P.L. C1 XXXII-1053).

And the Roman Pontiffs, according to the requirements of the times and the condition of things, sometimes assembling Ecumenical Councils, or examining the mind of the Church throughout the world, sometimes by particular synods, or by other helps which Divine Providence has supplied have defined those things as to be held, which, with the help of God, they have received and have recognized as in agreement with the Holy scriptures and Apostolic traditions.

For the Holy Ghost was not promised to the successors of St. Peter that by His revelation they might make known new doctrines, but that by His assistance they might holily keep and faithfully expound the sacred revelations handed down through the Apostles, that is, the deposit of Faith.

The Apostolic teaching of the successors of St. Peter have been embraced by all the venerable Fathers and venerated by all the Orthodox Doctors, who have most fully recognized that this See of St. Peter remains free from all error, according to the promise of our Lord and Saviour made to the Prince of His disciples. "I have prayed for thee that thy Faith fail thee not, and thou being converted, confirm thy brethren."

Hence, this charisma of never failing truth and Faith was divinely conferred upon Peter and his successors in this chair, in order they might exercise their high Office for the salvation of all, that the universal flock of Christ being turned away by them from the poisonous food of error, might be nourished with the pasture of heavenly doctrine and that, the occasion of schism being taken away, the whole Church should be conserved as one, and resting on its foundation, might stand firm against the gates of hell.

But since in this very age, in which the salutary efficacy of the Apostolic Office is so greatly needed there are not a few who detract from its authority, we deem it altogether necessary to solemnly assert the prerogatives which the only begotten Son of God designed to join together with the supreme pastoral Office.

We therefore, faithfully adhering to the tradition received from the beginning of the Christian Faith and for the glory of God our Saviour the exaltation of the Catholic religion, and the salvation of Christian people, with the approval of the Holy Council, teach and define as a Divinely revealed doctrine, that the Roman Pontiff, when he speaks "ex Cathedra," that is, when fulfilling his Office of the Pastor and Doctor of all Christians, he defines, by his supreme Apostolic authority a doctrine concerning faith or morals, to be held by the whole Church, he is, through Divine assistance promised to him in blessed Peter, endowed with the infallibility which the Divine Redeemer willed His Church should possess in defining doctrines concerning Faith and morals, and that therefore such definitions of the Roman Pontiffs are irreformable of themselves, and not because of the agreement of the Church.

But if anyone shall presume to contradict this, our definition, which God avert, let him be anathema.

Chapter Nineteen

Presentation of various efforts of dissident churches to effect a re-union with the Apostolic See of Peter.

In 1910, at Lambeth Palace, London, England, the Anglican Church, and the Protestant Episcopal Church, through their Hierarchy assembled in convention, passed resolutions seeking the assent of Rome to join a world conference to discuss re-union of the Christian Churches. For ten years preceding, the matter had been discussed, actually agitated, and all churches were approached to join the movement, but it was not able to bring this to a conclusion.

Again in 1919, more than seventy Protestant churches, through delegates gathered at Geneva, Switzerland, for a conference "without controversy" as the basis for deliberation. All participating churches were on an equal level, without regard to Episcopacy, Apostolic succession, validity of Orders or sacraments, or ordinations of ministers or priests. Everybody and anything were invited and accepted; provided, that no church participating claimed for itself the distinction of being "the one true church." This qualification, of course, precluded the attendance of any representative of the Roman Catholic Church, as she is the one true Church of Christ, and had nothing to discuss.

The interesting thing, and the least understandable about this conference was the presence of at least a dozen of the ancient schismatical Eastern churches, including the occupants of the primitive Sees of Jerusalem, Antioch, and Alexandria. These ancient Sees, possessing valid sacraments, true priests and bishops, though not in communion with the See of Peter, and in agreement with the Church of Rome concerning the invalidity of Anglican and Episcopal Orders, nevertheless, by their acceptance of this invitation accepted these Protestant groups on their own level; a renunciation of all the principles that heretofore had governed their action; it afforded definite proof that schism can easily degenerate into heresy.

When the Anglican group went to Rome in 1919 to interest His Holiness Benedict XV to let down the bars and permit the "great Roman Church" to enter into discussion of a common "Creed" for one "universal Church" the Holy Father received them graciously as the Vicar of Christ on earth. But the end was the same—no participation. The Catholic Church had nothing to discuss. She never lost unity in the Body of Christ—and never would, for Christ had promised that the Holy Ghost, God, the Spirit of truth, would protect the Church against the gates of hell, and all error.

The Holy Father did not disapprove nor discourage the efforts of those who were not in communion with the See of Peter, from discussing the matter of re-union with the Roman Church; he gave them his blessing and assured them of his fatherly interest in their endeavors, and also expressed the joy it would give him as Vicar of Christ, to witness their return to the embrace of Holy Mother Church. However, in his capacity as Vicar of Christ he must remind them that "the teaching and practice of the Roman Catholic Church regarding the unity of the visible Church of Christ is well known to everybody." To confirm his position he ordered the group be provided with copies of the Constitution "Apostolicae

Curae" and the Letter of the "Prefect of the Holy Office" dated Nov. 8, 1865 explanatory of the Catholic position. A portion of the Letter issued by Cardinal Patrizi wherein he eloquently and succinctly sets forth the position of the Catholic Church regarding participating in this Conference will suffice to clearly understand the obstacles presented. He stated: . . . "From all which, honoured and very dear Sirs, you will see by this sacred congregation has so carefully provided against the faithful of Christ be permitted to enroll themselves in, or to favor in any way, the society you have lately set on foot to promote, (as you express it) the unity of Christendom.

"You will also see that every effort at reconciliation must needs be in vain unless it be based on these principles on which the Church was first founded by Christ and was thenceforward in every succeeding age propagated, one and the same throughout the world, by their Apostles and their successors clearly expressed in that well known formula of Hosmisdas which was approved beyond all question; may the Holy Ghost vouchsafe to fulfill and perfect without delay what he has begun in you by that good will towards the Church He has imparted to you. And this, in union with the Sacred Congregation, our most Holy Lord, Pius IX desires with all his heart; and earnestly beseeches from the God of mercies and Father of lights that all of you at length, escaping from your severed, disinterested condition into the inheritance of Christ, the true Catholic Church, to which unquestionably your forefathers belonged before the deplorable separation of the 16th century, may happily attain the root of charity, in the bonds of peace and fellowship of Christ."

Impartial analysis of this Letter by Cardinal Patrizi cannot be interpreted other than a final authoritative pronouncement upon a matter of grave import to the Christian Church. It is phrased in simple language conveying a genuine desire to bring all Christians into the Body of Christ; but, conscious of responsibility as the Shepherd of souls of men placed upon the Catholic Church by Christ Himself, the Holy Office cannot unbend; the Holy Father cannot compromise with error. The Church of Christ as represented by His Vicar is the Rock of Christ—constant, immovable, permanent until the end of time, for Jesus Christ, Infinite God, has so ordained.

Many attempts have been made during the present century to bring about Christian unity among the churches not in communion with the Holy See. These efforts were not confined to Protestant churches only, the invitation was extended to the ancient churches, which, while schismatic nevertheless possessed valid sacraments, sacrificing priesthood and true bishops.

Invariably, the Church of England initiated these movements, but the motivating purpose was usually the same—to erect a religious barrier to re-union with the Roman and Apostolic Church; to permanently prevent the submission of these various dissidents to the jurisdiction of the Pope of Rome, as the chief pastor of the universal Church. Prominent among these groups were the "Old Catholics" of Europe in communion with the church of Utrecht, the rebellious "Philippine Independent Church," at present engaged in a bitter schism between two sets of prelates, the National Polish Church of the United States, and the Lutheran Evangelical Church of Sweden, which, while claiming Apostolic succession of their Hierarchy, have not until recently made much of an issue concerning it. There is no doubt that Peter Magnusson was validly consecrated as an Archbishop in the Catholic Church, serving as Archbishop of Upsala, and he is credited with consecrating two bishops, one, Lawrence Petersen, the other Lawrence Pedersen, and at the present time, a resurgence of the claims of Apostolic succession is underway. It is also true that the Latin Mass is offered in the Lutheran Cathedral of Stockholm, and one would have difficulty in determining it was not a genuine Roman Catholic service. However, the Lutheran Evangelical Church is the established State Church of Sweden, and they make no pretensions of possessing an Hierarchy. Their higher clergy are designated as Superintendents, and they assume all the prerogatives of the bishopric.

This was the pattern of church leadership among the dissident churches when the Archbishop of Canterbury called a conference of the Anglican and Protestant Episcopal bishops of the world at Lambeth Palace, England, for the "purpose of discussing a possible re-union of all the Christian churches in a common creed which might be accepted by all denominations, yet reserving to each group its own form and practices including their "distinctive liturgy." This gesture of course was doomed to defeat, as it was impossible to recognize and reconcile the various antagonism, both racially and ecclesiastically. There was no definite authority present, and without authority, there could be no foundation. This was in 1927.

The Anglican church insisted upon Episcopacy and Episcopal ordinations, but were willing to compromise insofar as ministers previously ordained were concerned; they would be recognized, and a form of commission would be issued to them permitting them to continue their ministerial functions; but all subsequent ordinations were to be carried on by laying on of hands by the Anglican bishops. This plan was rejected by the "Committee of the Free Evangelical Churches of England" as a violation of their independence in the choosing and appointing of their ministers, and the Conference resulted in no gainful advance towards reunion or unity in one Creed.

There is a marked distinction in the policy of the Church of England in 1950, as against its stand in 1927. At the Lambeth Conference of that year (1927), insisting upon Episcopal ordination of future ministers and a commission, or license to the ministers of the Free Evangelical Churches already appointed *before expressing willingness to discuss unity* among the Protestant groups. Now, in 1950, all ministers are accepted as *equal to their own,* and no mention made of Episcopacy or Episcopal ordinations . . . In a word, they have surrendered their ages old belief and insistence that bishops are essential to the continuance of the Apostolic succession, and in a mad scramble to save the physical structure of their church, they have compromised and recognized as equals those ministers who threw off the yoke of Elizabeth, and were anathamatized by the Church of England. The repudiation of Episcopal ordinations as essential for a valid ministry is a reversal of the sentiments and official promulgations of Archbishop Cranmer.

Again, on August 22nd, 1948 the first "Assembly of the world Council of Churches" opened. All Christian bodies including the Roman and Greek Orthodox Churches declined to take part in the deliberations on the same general grounds and set of principles; no recognition of Anglican Orders or Episcopacy; no sacrificing priesthood, all schismatical and heretical; therefore was nothing to discuss—no compromise to be made. The Catholic Church, holding deposit of the true Faith, and guided by the Holy Ghost God, the Spirit of Truth could not engage in any discussion where even the suggestion of compromise was introduced.

As recent as May 26, 1950 suggestion were offered for possible unity; the moving spirit in the endeavor was the Methodist bishop the Rt. Rev. Bromley Oxnam of New York. He delivered the ecumenical address to some four thousand delegates attending the convention of the Northern Baptist Convention. Bishop Oxnam is also a President of the world Council of Churches, and his words are carefully weighed by the many divergent groups of non-catholics.

Bishop Oxnam lays down as the yard-stick to measure the efforts his own proposition. His effrontery in assuming the role of an exeget would be ludicrous, in the light of past performances were it not for the serious conditions throughout the world, when nations, and people harassed by war and unbelieveable tragedies are vainly seeking some relief from their material and spiritual adversities. Bishop Oxnam professess to be highly gratified that the Pope at long last has consented to permit Catholics to enter into a discussion and conference with non-catholic groups, and he issues a statement which is a direct challenge to the Holy Father. His statement in part is here presented.

"Antecedent to such a conference, Protestants believe the Pope should enunciate a new doctrine of religious liberty. Let him, as the Head of a great body of Christians, declare 'that the Roman Catholic Church recognizing, will co-operate in protecting the rights of every man to worship God according to the dictates of his own conscience, or in his own way; the rights of parents to rear their children in their faith; the right of churches to educate, to preach, carry on missionary work, and to own property for these purposes.' In a word, let the Holy Father declare that in all matters involving religious liberty, the Roman Catholic Church will do unto others as it would have others do unto the Roman Catholic Church."

Continuing the bishop observes; "Protestants stand ready to confer with their Roman Catholic brethren and await some word from the Hierarchy that such a conference may be held. Protestants call for a clear-cut affirmation from the Pope in which religious liberty is accepted. Protestants are eager to co-operate with all Christians in a world wide endeavor to win the minds and hearts of men for Christ."

Bishop Oxnam states further: "I am certain that the major Protestant denominations would accept, and would appoint representatives to sit with such leaders as Cardinal Mooney of Detroit, Cardinal Spellman of New York, and Archbishop Cushing of Boston with others to confer relative to the world situation, and to take such steps as would be found necessary to bring to mankind a fuller knowledge of the love of God, of the Christian conception of the worth of man, of the kingdom of God on earth would electrify the world." The proposal submitted by Bishop Oxnam is the same age old hackneyed one. The Holy Roman Church, established by Jesus Christ, must veer from its foundations; must throw over the precepts laid down by her Divine Founder, and substitute the plans of those who call Him Beelzebub, and who would banish Him out of the world He Redeemed with His Precious Blood. The overpowering conceit of these so-called, self-appointed, spiritual leaders is constant; no repudiation seems to dull their hated appetite for power, and in their vanity they would consider the virtue of submission to the Vicar of Christ, a banal badge, with the bar sinister across it.

For years Bishop Oxnam has been the spear-head in violent attacks upon the Catholic Church, both in matters of dogma and Hierarchal administration. Even the Holy Father has not been immune from vicious assaults at his hands. Nothing has been too foul for him to allege against the Vicar of Christ; he has plumbed the depths to hold His Holiness up to the scorn of the Christian world; he has been held suspect regarding communistic affiliations; yet he unctuously insists he does so in order to save Christianity and the world from the spiritual enslavement of anti-christ, the Pope of Rome.

If Bishop Oxnam and his associates in the groups comprising the "World Council of Churches" sincerely desire unity in the Body of Christ let each group surrender their ephemeral ambitions and petty quarrels; let them humbly seek the guidance of the Holy Ghost, God, and return to unity with His Holiness Pius XII, the Pope of Rome, now gloriously reigning, thus giving living proof that they willingly accept the plea of Jesus Christ when He prayed to His Father; "that they all may be one as Thou Father art in Me, and I in Thee; that they also may be one in Us that the world may know that Thou hast sent Me; and the glory which Thou gavest Me, I have given to them, that they may be one with Us." (John 23)

Epilogue.

In the August 15th, 1948 issue of the "Living Church" one of the leading weekly publications of the Anglican Church in America, an unusual item of interest to one studying Anglican Orders was reported. The article describes the consecration of an Anglican bishop to the "See of Bedford" once occupied by John Hodgkins, who was consecrated a bishop in the Catholic Church in 1537.

In this article, Hodgkins is referred to as "one of those bishops through whom the Apostolic succession was transmitted to Matthew Parker, the first Elizabethan Anglican bishop." The consecration took place in St. Alban's Abbey, the Archbishop of Canterbury, assisted by two other suffragan bishops, consecrating.

This statement of "transmission of Apostolic succession" is plain unadulterated poppy-cock, and the editors of the "Living Church" should be aware of it. They must likewise know that Barlow, the consecrator of Parker, never was validly consecrated (or invalidly for that matter) a bishop in any church, and that Scory, and Coverdale, his assisting consecrators, were schismatically consecrated under the "Edwardine Ordinal." They possessed no Apostolic succession themselves, therefore, they could not transmit to others.

The editors of the "Living Church" are ordained men—learned men—by virtue of their calling they are respected, and looked upon as leaders in the spiritual world, interested solely in the salvation of souls. No one, even the most bitter partisan will deny them this virtue. Because of this general good will and the confidence placed in their spiritual eminence, it behooves them to make certain that their faith and good works stand upon a firm foundation.

If the clergy of these Protestant churches approached this subject from an historical angle only, they would recognize the incompatibility of their position with the incontrovertible facts of history, so clearly set forth by historians, Catholic and non-catholic.

During this study of Anglican and Protestant Episcopal Orders the following facts were interwoven, and for purpose of emphasis only, are reiterated. Chronologically therefore, the principal events leading to the schism of the Church of England is again presented.

In 1532 the English Catholic bishops in convocation agreed and voted to recognize King Henry VIII as "Sole protector and only Supreme Head of the Church and clergy in England," adding the restrictive clause, "so far as the law of Christ will allow."

In 1534 both houses of Parliament voted Henry VIII the title of "Only Supreme Head of the Church of England in earth, both in material and ecclesiastical affairs"; no mention was made of the restrictive clause by either branch of Parliament.

Also in 1534, the "Act of Succession" was passed by Parliament. This act guaranteed the security of the throne of England to Ann Boleyn, the concubine of Henry VIII, and their children. Furthermore, this "Act of Succession" declared the marriage of Henry VIII and Catherine of Aragon to be against the law of God and utterly void, and the marriage with Ann Boleyn was ratified. This Act further declared; marriages within the degree of affinity prohibited by the Jewish law were unlawful, and no human power could grant dispensation. A list of the prohibited degrees were ordered read in all the churches, and all persons married within the degrees were ordered to separate, and their children, by law, were bastardized. The enormity of this crime against Christian people acting in good faith staggers the imagination, but there is consolation in the knowledge that while Henry VIII might dominate Parliaments and revoke the laws of God on earth, his influence in heavenly realms was nil.

The "Act of Succession" further stipulated that an oath was to be taken by all the king's subjects over 21 years of age without exception swearing they would observe the whole contents of the Act; both houses of Parliament took the oath supporting the Act before a Commission headed by Archbishop Cranmer on March 30th, 1954.

The Act itself did not prescribe the form of the oath; that depended upon the conditions and temperament of those ordered to subscribe. When the members of religious houses were required to swear, a very severe and explicit oath was presented to them. Not only did it contain an acknowledgement of the king's supremacy, but also a promise to "preach and persuade on every occasion that Henry's marriage with Queen Ann was just and legitimate, and that the succession to the throne belonged to their children."

The mandatory oath was eventually taken by all the religious houses. Some houses, notably the "Carthusians and Order of Observant Friars" refused to swear. Six of the Carthusians died on the block in the view of Thomas More who was looking out from a window in the Tower; several hundred "Observants" were imprisoned and others were expelled from their houses; it is recorded that more than fifty of them died as a result of persecution. The rest of these loyal servants of God were banished to France and Scotland. The apostate Franciscans and Dominicans were given access and control of their houses. In the carrying out of these nefarious plans the moving spirits and ruthless directors were George Brown and Hilsy, (Provincials of the Augustines and Dominicans, respectively). They were assigned to this task of visiting religious houses by Cranmer and were given strict orders to bear down on any who dared reject the "Act of Succession. It is to be regretted that "bearing down" was unnecessary, as all signed as demanded.

In February 1535 the Catholic bishops were obliged formally to renounce their obedience to the Pope of Rome, not a single one refused. Out of approximately 9400 inferior clergy (secular priests and regulars) not more than three hundred remained loyal to the Vicar of Christ. As did the Hierarchy and inferior clergy, so too the various ecclesiastical foundations, colleges, etc., all signed without protest, except Baliol College, Oxford, where the signatories declared that they intended "nothing against the Divine Law, the Orthodox Faith, or the doctrine of the Catholic Church."

Many Catholic historians, principally in England, attempt to find some extenuating circumstance which might mitigate the cowardly conduct of the English Catholic Bishops and inferior clergy in rejecting the authority of the Vicar of Christ; expediency—hope of a return or a reversal of conditions in a few years, have been offered as a defense; all to no effect; the bald unmistakable fact stands out; the Catholic priests and bishops, and clergy failed the Vicar of Christ in his dark hours of trial; they sold their Divine Founder and His Vicar on earth, for the proverbial mess of pottage, and became renegades from the Church of Christ. If the Catholic bishops and priests had defied their King and remained faithful to Christ's Vicar, the Anglican and Protestant churches of today, in all probability would not be in existence.

There are many sincere Anglicans and Episcopalians who sincerely feel their Church to be Catholic in doctrine and tradition, yet they resent any intimation of being Catholic in the sense of Roman Catholicism. It is difficult to fathom this reasoning in the light of history which tells the story simply and succinctly.

The most compelling proof that the Church of England is Protestant is the oath taken by an English Sovereign when consecrated. The Ruler takes a constitutionally mandatory oath. "I do solemnly and sincerely in the presence of God, profess, testify, and declare that I am a faithful Protestant, and that I will according to the true enactments which secure the Protestant succession to the throne of my realm, uphold and maintain the said enactments to the best of my power according to law." Nothing ambiguous about the oath! It definitely bars any Catholic from the throne of England.

The Protestant Sovereign of England is the Supreme Head of the Church of England, making all appointments to the Anglican bench of bishops, which are in turn confirmed and consecrated by the Archbishop of Canterbury, in his capacity as "Primate of all England." He knows beyond question, that he is not only crowning a Protestant as King, but also is consecrating the Spiritual Head of the Protestant Anglican Church of England.

The Church of England therefore is definitely Protestant in foundation, practice, and intention. All claims to the contrary notwithstanding; the recorded stubborn facts, historically proven, destroy the fictionary claims of Apostolic succession and valid ministry in these two Christian churches, (Anglican and Episcopal). Their insistence that they are the sole custodians of the primitive Apostolic Catholic Church and Faith does not stand the acid test of ruthless research.

Briefly then in summation; the Church of England was forced into schism by Henry VIII; it was diverted partly from its Catholic moorings during the reign of the boy-king Edward VI, and completely and irrevocably Protestantized by Queen Elizabeth I, and by her successors upon the throne of England to this day. The recent enthronement of Queen Elizabeth II, witnessed the taking of the same Protestant oath as Queen, and the Supreme Head of the Church of England throughout the world.

The Parliaments of Henry VIII—Edward VI—Queen Elizabeth Ist, ruthlessly assailed the Church of Christ, in their desperate attempts to destroy His Kingdom on earth. The members of the English Parliaments performed the works of Satan, but received their compensation from the Crown.

The Roman Church, the Spouse of Christ, was deeply wounded by the rebellion of England, her fairest daughter; like all devoted mothers she prays for the return of the wayward child to again enjoy the love she is ever ready to pour upon them.

For close to two thousand years the Church of Christ has faced relentless enemies from within and without. Unmindful of the scourges visited upon her Pontiffs as Vicars of Christ, Holy Mother Church goes serenely forward in her quest to "restore all things in Christ" happily aware that the promise of her Divine Founder that "I am with you always even unto the consummation of the world" is a living assurance of the success of her mission.

Holy Mother Church then is the authoritative Voice of Christ: guided by the Holy Ghost, God, Spirit of Truth, she will continue her teaching and salvaging of souls: she exists today—the same yesterday—the same tomorrow—the indestructible, impregnable—eternal——

"THE UNSHATTERED ROCK."

The End.